Practical
Marketing
Research

Practical
Marketing
Research

□□□

Jeffrey L. Pope

A DIVISION OF AMERICAN MANAGEMENT ASSOCIATIONS

Library of Congress Cataloging in Publication Data

Pope, Jeffrey L.
    Practical marketing research.

    Includes index.
    1. Marketing research. I. Title.
    HF5415.2P63   658.8'3   81-66232
    ISBN 0-8144-5651-0   AACR2

First Printing

Contents

Introduction

□□

If your job involves marketing research, then you've probably already figured out one thing: most marketing research books don't help you much to do your job. Most of the research books around are *textbooks,* and they talk mostly about *why* research works or should work. But you already know that research works. That's why you're in this business, right?

What you want to know is *how* to do research. You know research could help make a packaging decision, but you need to know how to conduct a packaging test. You know research could help you screen new product concepts, but you need ideas about how to do new-product screening. How do you research a new product name?

This book didn't start out as a book; it began as a notebook for our staff. Our company, Custom Research Inc., is a marketing research firm that works every day for a large number of clients on a wide range of research problems. We needed a notebook that described what we'd learned from experience about the best way to approach different kinds of studies. As the notebook was being written, we found clients asking for copies of chapters. That told us there was interest in a practical, real-world-oriented research guide, so the notebook was revised to become a full-size book.

The goal of this book is simple: *to provide a reference source for many of the things you need to know to be a competent professional marketing researcher.* To accomplish this goal, the book's content is designed to focus on:

Applications—What's really happening in the research world. Research on actual marketing problems.

Real-World Issues—To be practical and usable for you, principles need to deal with how to get things done in the real world. This book is based on experience from thousands of actual research projects involving hundreds of different companies.

Practitioners—This book is designed for readers with responsibility for the research function within a company, either as part of their job or as their primary responsibility. This is not a student textbook.

Specific Problems—The contents of the book are organized around the kinds of marketing problems the techniques are designed to solve: new product concepts, packaging, advertising, sales testing, and so on.

Most of the examples in this book are taken from the world of consumer goods research, especially food products, health and beauty aids, and household-care items. That's simply because these types of companies do the most marketing research. Market Facts, Inc., a large research firm, recently did a study which concluded that grocery and drug companies spend five times as much on marketing research as durable-goods and service companies of comparable size.

The principles in this book apply, with only minor variations, to most types of businesses. There's an entire chapter on industrial and medical research describing the application of research to those markets. In addition, companies in many other categories are becoming increasingly active in research. These include retail outfits (department stores, specialty shops, restaurant chains), financial institutions (banks, savings and loan institutions, insurance companies), and manufacturers of durables (furniture, appliances, automobiles). In all these markets, the research principles are the same. The approaches are similar; only the details differ among markets.

If you're new to marketing research, this book will help orient you to the field. If you already have some experience, it will broaden your base of knowledge. And if you're a senior researcher, it will give you information on facets of the business you've probably never encountered.

Finally, this book is designed as a handbook. Each chapter stands by itself. It's meant to be used as a reference source for dealing with specific problems.

Most marketing researchers are "puzzle solvers"—people who like to analyze problems and figure things out. The puzzle presented by every study is unique in some way. This book gives you tools to help tackle the research puzzles you encounter every day in the real world.

Part I

The Role of Research in Business

□□

1

A Short History of Marketing Research

□□

"History is more or less bunk," declared Henry Ford. But it can also be very interesting if the history happens to involve *you.*

Little children ask, "Where did I come from, Mommy?" If you're involved with marketing research, you probably have a similar curiosity about how the field developed.

Many other business disciplines, such as sales, production, and finance, have existed in some form for thousands of years. But the history of marketing research is much shorter, because all the real growth in the field has come in this century—most of it within the past 50 years.

EARLY BEGINNINGS

Andrew Jackson	335
John Quincy Adams	169
Henry Clay	19
William H. Crawford	9

That's the result of one of the earliest known examples of research, a "straw poll" taken by the *Harrisburg Pennsylvanian* in the 1824 presidential campaign.

Do you know how the election turned out? If you look it up, you'll find this poll was wrong. None of the three top candidates received a majority of electoral votes, so the election went to the House of Representatives. There Clay threw his support to Adams, who was elected. (Jackson came back and won in 1828, so perhaps this first poll was more predictive than anyone realized at the time.)

The accuracy of polling and other research has increased considerably since the 1800s. But this early example shows that surveys have long seemed a logical way to predict things, whether the matter at hand was an election or the introduction of a new product.

MARKETING APPLICATIONS

But nineteenth-century election polls are just trivia, since research wasn't used as a business tool until many years later.

In the first quarter of this century, formal research departments started to appear around the country. The first groups were found in four types of organizations:

Manufacturers. DuPont, General Electric, and Kellogg were among the first to begin doing research.

Publishers. The Chicago Tribune and Curtis Publishing were early pioneers.

Advertising Agencies. Lord & Thomas Advertising and N.W. Ayer Advertising are generally credited with having the first agency research functions.

Universities. Harvard and Northwestern each established a "Bureau of Business Research" before 1920.

Then during the 1920s and 1930s, research departments became more common in business of all types.

GROWTH FACTORS

Why is research in such widespread use today? Why do most companies of any size have a marketing research function of some type? Growth can be linked to three factors.

1. **Company size.** Businessmen used to conduct their own first-hand research, although few would have called it that. The shoemaker in Colonial America had no need for research. He knew the wants and needs of his customers by dealing directly with them every day. The local druggist and grocer in 1900 had the same first-hand contact with their "markets."

But things have changed today. Companies are bigger—much bigger—and the managements of most multimillion-dollar businesses have little or no direct contact with the end users of their products or services. Marketing research has replaced firsthand experience as the link between businessmen and their customers. It has become the management tool for staying in touch with the wants and needs of the market. So growth in the size of businesses has created the need for marketing research.

2. Computers.   While business size created the need for research, computers created the capability for doing it. Most of the marketing research done today would be impossible without the computer. Even a simple study involving 10 or 15 questions and 300 respondents would be extremely tedious to tabulate accurately by hand. And large-scale studies of several thousand respondents would be virtually impossible to handle even in "total"—forget about the cross-tabs or any multivariate analysis. People who were in the business 30 or 40 years ago tell about rooms full of people working to tally survey results. A task that is now done in minutes or seconds by a computer routinely took hundreds of labor hours.

Computers have been widely available to business only since the mid-1950s and early 1960s, and that's when marketing research began to blossom.

3. Communication and Transportation Technology.   Imagine trying to conduct a typical research study today without telephones, cars, or airplanes. Planning the study would be hard enough; conducting it would be almost impossible. If you really want to shudder, think about producing questionnaires, instructions, and reports in the years "B.X."—before Xerox!

In short, the need for research by large companies that use more sophisticated management techniques has coincided with the technological developments that have made large-scale research feasible. That's what has made marketing research the large and growing industry it is today.

2

The Role of Research in Marketing

Just as education has its three R's, marketing has its four P's (Figure 1). Marketing comprises *all* the functions of a business involved in getting goods and services from the producer to the user. In other words, marketing is getting the right *product* to the right *place* at the right *price*—and letting someone know about it through *promotion*.

These same factors apply to every type of product and service, not just to advertised consumer products. For example, *Time* magazine, in a cover story on the Boeing Company, quoted an executive of Germany's Lufthansa Airlines as saying, "There is no secret at all about Boeing's success. The company just keeps coming up with the right plane, at the right price, at the right time."

The goal of the marketer is to put all these components together in a way that will maximize profits. This is no simple task, since each of the components has several subparts that all need to work together. The total of these parts for a product or service is called its "marketing mix" (Figure 2).

PRODUCTION VS. MARKETING

There are two alternate philosophies that can be used to select the components of the marketing mix: the production concept or the marketing concept.

A company that follows the *production concept* says essentially, "We sell what we can make." In the early days of the industrial revolution, this was the prevalent philosophy of business, and it worked just fine.

Goods were in short supply, and people were anxious to buy almost anything. Henry Ford used to say that people could have any color of car they wanted as long as it was black. And in the early 1900s that view was

8

Figure 1. The four P's of marketing.

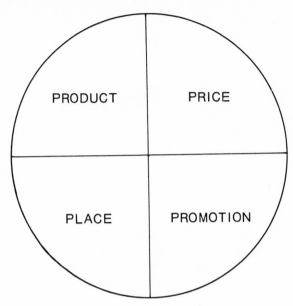

Figure 2. Details of the marketing mix.

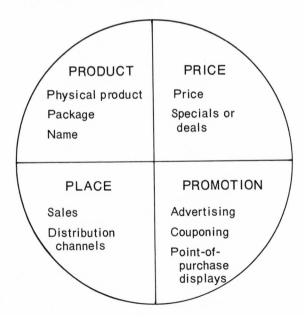

adequate to build one of the world's largest companies. There was little need then for research in companies operating under the production concept.

But as manufacturing techniques improved, producers developed the capacity to supply more of most products than consumers could buy. Today, goods are no longer in short supply; there's an excess of supply over demand. Since the end of World War II, the focus in most companies has shifted from production to marketing.

The *marketing concept* says that a company's total effort—product, place, price, and promotion—should be adapted to the needs and wants of customers, *not* on what the manufacturer can most easily produce.

TRIAL AND ERROR VERSUS RESEARCH

There are two basic ways to discern the market's wants and needs: trial and error, and research.

Figure 3. The marketing process.

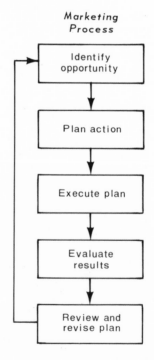

Trial and error involves simply putting a product or service on the market and seeing if it sells. On a small scale for small companies, this may be cheaper and easier than research. The simplest way for the local corner restaurant to see if a new item will sell is to add it to the menu and watch what happens. But for a large chain like Burger King, the "try it and see if it sells" approach is much too costly and risky.

Today, marketing research provides a tool for most large marketers of goods and services to reduce their risk by anticipating the wants and needs of their markets.

THE MARKETING PLANNING PROCESS

Every marketing decision involves some variation of the process depicted in Figure 3. A good practical definition of marketing research would be that it's a tool to help make better decisions at each step in the marketing process. There are a lot of fancy, technical definitions of marketing re-

Figure 4. Marketing process for a new product.

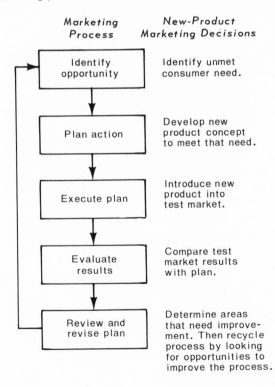

Marketing Process	New-Product Marketing Decisions
Identify opportunity	Identify unmet consumer need.
Plan action	Develop new product concept to meet that need.
Execute plan	Introduce new product into test market.
Evaluate results	Compare test market results with plan.
Review and revise plan	Determine areas that need improvement. Then recycle process by looking for opportunities to improve the process.

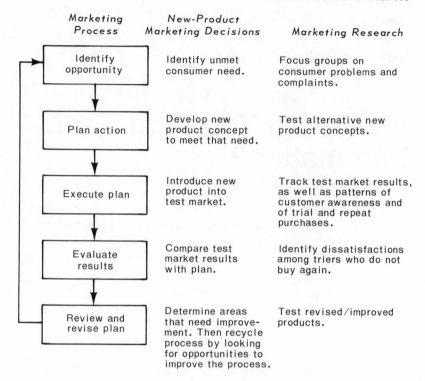

Figure 5. Contributions of marketing research to the marketing process.

search, but they all come down to one thing: *helping make better marketing decisions*.

For example, a typical new-product introduction would involve the steps shown in Figure 4. At each step in the process, research can help give direction to the marketing decisions that have to be made. Figure 5 illustrates this for our new-product-introduction example. Comparable steps would be taken for advertising, packaging, or pricing decisions, or for any other component of the total marketing mix. And research can be done to help reduce the risk at each step in the process.

3

Where Do You Find Information?

First Man: "It's all around me! All around me!"
Second Man: "What?"
First Man: "My belt."
                                                        —Old Vaudeville Joke

It's that way with marketing information, too: it's all around you. This book is about survey research. But survey research is only one type of marketing information. So, before we move on to focus on survey research, it's good to look at where surveys fit into the total research spectrum—and, specifically, where the information comes from.

It's easiest to start with consumer packaged goods (food, household-care products, and health and beauty aids), because the techniques for gathering information on these types of products are the most developed. But many of these techniques are applicable to other products as well.

If you follow a consumer packaged product through its "life" from manufacture to consumption, you'll see that marketing information about it is collected at several points along the way (Figure 6).

Let's take a brief look at those sources of information.

Manufacturer's sales data. Generally, these are the only perfect data around. They're your own data and not a sample. So the one thing you know for sure is how much product you shipped.

Warehouse withdrawals (SAMI) and audit data (Nielsen). You want to know not only how much *you* sold but how that compares to what everyone *else* sold, too. In other words, you want to know your *market share*. SAMI and Nielsen are the two major sources for this information.

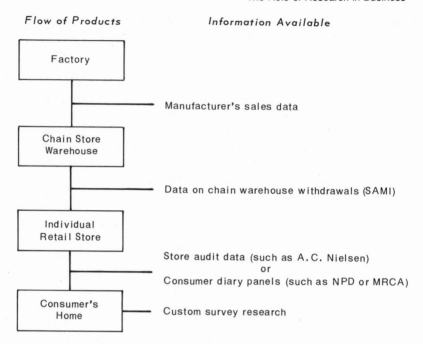

Figure 6. Collecting marketing information for consumer packaged goods.

Consumer diary panels.   These complete records of every purchase (in selected product categories) by a sample of consumers enable you to analyze the consumer "dynamics" of a market. Who are the people who bought the product this month? Are they the same who bought last month (loyal purchasers) or different people (brand switchers)? How many buyers purchased on "special" or "deal"? How many buyers purchased with a coupon? Consumer diary panels provide the most reliable method of collecting this type of information.

Custom survey research.   This is the best (often the *only*) source of information that can't be developed from one of the other sources. Many of us spend most of our time working with survey research. But remember, it's only one of the many available methods of obtaining marketing information. All products or services have similar distribution chains, and it's often possible to tap those chains at points other than just the end user. In markets other than consumer products, however, there often aren't syndicated research services already available, so it may take some creativity to find information sources.

Industrial or commercial markets.   Products sold in these markets often move through distributors, so consider them as sources of names of prospects or customers to research. And don't overlook the opportunity to do research on the distributors themselves. In a way, they're customers of the company, too.

Medical markets.   Although consumers are the real end users of health-care products and services, they rarely make a brand decision. That's usually done by the professional responsible for the individual's care. Fortunately, there are excellent lists available of physicians and dentists, often split by specialty. And detailed information is available on virtually every hospital in the nation—information that's better, in many ways, than what's available on consumer households. So it's usually possible to draw very representative samples of hospitals and physicians for studies in the health-care industry.

Retailers.   Stores and restaurants have two important advantages over other businesses for doing research: their distribution chain is shorter, and they have direct contact with their customers. Surveying retail customers in-store is an efficient and effective way to study them right at the point of purchase.

Financial institutions.   Banks, savings and loan institutions, and insurance companies have the unique advantage of knowing who each of their customers is and exactly what services that customer uses. This makes it possible to target surveys precisely at even the smallest subsegment of customers.

Durable goods.   Automobiles, furniture, and appliances typically are sold through fewer retailers than consumer packaged goods. This makes it feasible to use retailers as sources of information about buyers—or, in other cases, as sources of customers' names. And don't overlook the importance of occasionally studying the retailers directly, too.

Finding exactly the right point at which to collect research information is important to both the cost and the quality of the results. So don't always settle on the first source of information that comes to mind. Some thought and creativity may uncover a better and cheaper way.

4

How to Develop a Research Strategy

□□

People have different needs as they move through the stages of life—childhood, adolescence, adulthood, and old age. So do products. And that's where the concept of a research strategy comes in. It means tailoring the research to the needs of a product at each point in its life cycle.

The concept of product life cycle is well accepted. It usually breaks down a product's development into four stages, as shown in Figure 7. While the concept of *product* life cycle is well accepted, the idea of *research* life cycle isn't as obvious. Nevertheless, it's important to develop a research strategy that adapts the research to the unique needs of the product at each stage.

INTRODUCTION STAGE

This is the "childhood" of a product. The product is just getting started. Things are developing fast. It's a crucial period: like a child, a product's future is strongly influenced by what happens here.

Figure 7. The four stages of a product's life cycle.

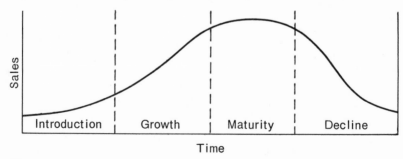

The research strategy should focus on developing and building issues. At this stage, research studies most commonly concentrate on the following areas:

Concept testing. Does the concept have sufficiently broad appeal to be successful? To what market segments does it appeal most? What are the benefits that are most attractive to potential buyers?

Product testing. Is the physical product as good as it can be? How does it compare with the competition?

Concept fulfillment. Does the physical product meet expectations created by the concept? (Good products and good concepts don't necessarily go together. It's always a good idea to check.)

Name testing. This should be done early, since the name actually becomes part of the "concept" once the product hits the market.

Package testing. This is the stage at which the majority of packaging decisions are made and most package testing is done. Once a product is on the market, it's unusual to make a package change. It's better to do the research up front and get it right the first time.

Advertising research. An advertising strategy (as well as actual ads) that executes the concept and is consistent with the name and package must be developed.

Simulated sales testing and test marketing. These are typically the last two steps before a product goes on the market. They're the last checkpoints on the final, complete "bundle" of product, ad, name, and package.

Tracking. From the beginning, it's important to set up a system for tracking the key sales components of customer awareness and trial and repeat purchases. This is often done through periodic waves of telephone interviewing. (Purchase panel data can also be used, although they don't give a measure of customer awareness.) Tracking these components gives a basis for deciding whether sales are building as expected or whether changes need to be made. (For example, if customer awareness is lower than expected and trial purchases are low as a result, the advertising may need to be reevaluated. If repeat purchases are low, product quality may be a problem.)

GROWTH STAGE

This is the "adolescence" of a product. Sales are beginning to take off. And as with a teenager, growth for a product can come too fast and may be painful. The research strategy at this stage should deal with tracking issues. The components of the marketing mix are usually well set by this point. A tracking program (monitoring customer awareness and trial and repeat purchases as components of volume) should be maintained. The objective of this tracking is to look for either of two kinds of "accidents":

1. Unexpected successes. Things are sometimes—not often, but sometimes—more successful than expected. What is planned as a modest new product may turn out to be a runaway success. The tracking research should be designed to spot this quickly, determine why it happened (that's critical), and look for ways to expand, multiply, or accelerate the unexpected success. Believe it or not, many extremely successful products started as ideas that simply found unexpected success when they hit the market.

2. Repairable failures. In the early stages of a product's growth cycle, most of the volume comes from first-time trial purchases. Later, an increasing share comes from repeat purchases. If this *isn't* happening, something is wrong. A supply of first-time buyers can't be maintained forever. So if the sales components of awareness and trial and repeat purchases aren't developing as planned, action needs to be taken to fix the element that's a problem.

It's common for sales to take a slight temporary dip during the growth stage as trial purchases trail off, but before repeat purchases pick up the slack. At this point management's conviction and commitment often get tested, unless the dip has been forecast. If it hasn't been predicted, there's a risk that a good product and a sound marketing plan will be abandoned just before a new sales spurt develops. That's another reason why good planning and good tracking must go together.

Tracking competitive products is the other function of a tracking system during the growth phase. Before its success and market position are established is the time when a product, even a good one, is most vulnerable to competition. The same measures (customer awareness and trial and repeat-purchase levels) should be collected on competitive products to see how much of a threat they pose. In addition, samples of competitive products should be purchased and tested to see how they compare to your own product. Your objective should be to know as much about competitive products' strengths and weaknesses as you know about your own.

MATURITY STAGE

This is "adulthood" for a product. As with a person, there's a risk that things will get stale and go flat. The objective is to successfully manage the "midlife crisis" for a product and find new ways to build interest, excitement, and sales—without abandoning the elements that made the product successful in the first place. Accordingly, the research strategy should focus on *finding opportunities*. Research can help identify ways to bring new interest to a product. Here are some of the ways this can be done:

Product line extensions. New products in a line (new flavors, colors, and sizes) are usually introduced during the maturity stage. They should be tested before introduction to make sure they're up to the quality standards of the existing line. And estimates should be developed to make sure the sales generated by the new items represent some add-on volume and aren't totally the result of "cannibalizing" existing products.

New positioning. Sometimes new volume can be built by changing a product's position and appealing to a broader market or a different set of needs.

New advertising. When a product's sales begin to plateau, companies typically look for new advertising to generate renewed interest. So advertising research is often done, beginning with qualitative research and moving through quantitative copy testing.

Package testing. A new or redesigned package is another way to give a product a "new look" and try to increase sales. Package testing should be done to make sure the new package is really better (in impact, visibility, and connotations) and not just different.

New uses. Category studies may uncover additional uses for a product that can be promoted to stimulate new sales. (The promotion of baking soda as refrigerator deodorizer a few years ago is a classic example of this approach.) This is usually a long shot, and real successes are rare, but it can happen.

DECLINE STAGE

This is the "old age" of a product, when sales begin to drop off. By this point, improved products or technologies have come along, or the public has simply grown tired of the product and has moved on to others. Research strategy should focus on *salvaging* the product—or attempting to salvage it. Realistically, this is not a stage at which much research usually gets done. When sales start to drop off, the first reaction is usually to cut expenses—research expenses included. It's rare for a firm to undertake a large, expensive research study on the slim chance that a "secret" will be uncovered that can turn the product around. When a product starts to decline, management usually tries to slow the drop-off, but rarely expects to actually stop and reverse it.

What are the areas in which research could help? Go down this list and evaluate whether changes in any of the areas would be likely to have a significant impact on the product:

Physical product	Name
Positioning	Package
Market segments	Pricing
Advertising	Distribution

If these are candidates for significant changes, evaluate whether the impact of the change has a good chance of paying back the cost of the research and more. If it does, propose it. If it doesn't (which is more likely), accept that fact and don't propose that more research costs be added to the overhead burden the product already has to support.

In summary, people have different needs and interests at different points in their lives. Similarly, products have changing research support needs as they grow, mature, and decline. One research program can't fit all the needs. Different research strategies must be developed for products to fit them at each stage in the product life cycle.

5

How to Use Research in Marketing Planning

□□

An intelligent plan is the first step to success . . . if you don't know where you are going, how can you expect to get there?
—Basil S. Walsh

The marketing plan is the document that guides all the marketing activities for a company or a product. It sets out objectives, defines how success will be measured, and describes the strategies and tactics that will be used. Although products and markets vary substantially from one industry to the next, the type of information in a marketing plan is very similar across different businesses.

THE PLANNING PROCESS

The fundamental purpose of planning is to give the total marketing program a well-thought-out focus. This keeps the pieces of the program from becoming fragmented and possibly even fighting with one another. For example, the product, the packaging, and the advertising all need to contribute to accomplishing a single goal, such as positioning the item as a convenient, old-fashioned, or "new improved" product. That goal and the reasoning behind it are contained in the marketing plan.

The planning process usually involves four steps: opportunity identification, planning, execution, and evaluation. This process represents a *cycle* that's repeated over and over, usually on a yearly basis. A marketing opportunity is identified, and a plan is developed to take advantage of it. That plan is executed, and the results are evaluated. Often that evaluation identifies a new opportunity, and the process starts over again. At each step along the way in this process, research plays a crucial role.

Opportunity Identification

This first step in the planning process is key, since it determines the direction for everything that follows. It usually requires some creativity or insight to identify an opportunity that may not be obvious. The types of opportunities that could form the basis for a marketing program include:

Introducing a new product.

Developing an improved product.

Adding "flanker products" (additional flavors, colors, sizes, and so on) to a product line.

Repositioning a product.

Targeting a product at different or additional market segments.

Changing packaging.

Using couponing or sampling.

Revising advertising in a significant way.

How are these kinds of opportunities identified? Creative insight can come from almost any source, even ones seemingly unrelated to the product or the market. But opportunity identification most often occurs through three types of research studies:

1. *Group interviews.* But be careful with these: it's easy to turn the comments of one vocal person into a consumer "mandate" for a new product, new package, or revised ad campaign.

2. *Market segmentation studies.* This type of study can help identify homogeneous segments of the market that look like promising targets.

3. *Product positioning research.* These studies describe consumers' perceptions of a product category and the relative positions of brands in it. They're a useful method for identifying "holes"—needs unfilled by other brands—that could represent opportunities for effective advertising or new products.

Planning

At this point, the marketing action needs to be selected and a plan developed for its execution. Whatever the action, it's usually researched first to increase the plan's odds of success. So the research that's done is typically a test of the effectiveness and impact of the marketing variable on which the plan will focus. Here are some examples of such research:

Product testing. Is the new or improved product really better than the current product and competition?

Package testing. Does the new package have more shelf impact than the current package and competition?

Advertising testing. Which new ad claim seems most important to consumers? What is the persuasion power of the new ads? Are they memorable?

Execution

At this step of the planning cycle, research moves into a monitoring and measuring role. The execution step is where line marketing people become busiest as they translate the plan into action. Research's role here is to begin collecting the information that will make evaluation of the plan's results—and improvement of the plan if necessary—easier.

The most common survey research tool here is some type of AAU (advertising, awareness, and usage) study. This usually takes the form of a series of periodic waves of telephone research to measure:

Customer awareness
Trial purchases
Intent to make a trial purchase
Repeat purchases
Intent to make a repeat purchase
Attitudes of buyers toward the product and their reactions to using it
Advertising recall

In addition, of course, some types of syndicated market data (SAMI or Nielsen for consumer packaged goods) are often purchased to provide share data to supplement company sales information.

Evaluation

This is an analytical step and usually doesn't require collecting additional survey data. It involves comparing actual results with the plan to see if the effort succeeded or failed.

But this shouldn't be just a matter of ruling "thumbs up" or "thumbs down." It's important for the researcher to stay in the role of player and not become just a scorekeeper. The researcher should ask: If the plan didn't succeed this time, how can it be made better next time? In this way, the evaluation step feeds right back into the opportunity identification step of the next planning cycle. From every evaluation should come the seeds of identifying the next opportunity.

How can the plan be changed, improved, and modified to be more effective? If all the research can be focused on that question, then research will play a valuable role in the marketing planning process. Otherwise it risks being nice-to-know, but useless, information.

Part II

Choosing the Interviewing Method

□□

6

Using Personal Interviews

□□

Before discussing the subject of personal interviews, I must point out one thing: there's no one interviewing method that's always better. That's why selecting the type of interview to use is often the most important decision you make in designing a survey research project.

You have three basic choices: in-person, telephone, or mail. Once you make that decision, many aspects of the interview are fixed. And a wrong decision risks wasting money and time—or, worst of all, producing misleading results. So it's important to choose the right method.

If one method were always more accurate than the others, the decision would of course be easy. But studies have shown that well-conducted studies of each type *can* produce similarly accurate results. No one type is always better. Instead, the choice between interviewing methods for each project depends on which offers the best combination of two factors: suitability for the study's objectives, and feasibility (cost, timing, execution). Consequently, the decision requires a good understanding of the advantages and disadvantages of each type of interview.

This and the next two chapters provide a summary of the strengths and weaknesses of each method of interviewing: personal interviews, telephone interviews, and mail questionnaires.

WHEN TO USE PERSONAL INTERVIEWS

When you form a mental picture of an "interview," what do you see? If you're like most people, you've been conditioned by years of newspaper and magazine cartoons to think of someone, clipboard in hand, asking questions on a doorstep.

And that used to be the way research was usually done. In the 1930s and 1940s, if you wanted to conduct an interview, you rang the doorbell and asked your questions.

While the classic door-to-door interviewing isn't extinct, it's clearly an endangered specied, for several reasons:

☐ With half or more of all women employed outside the home, it's difficult for interviewers to find respondents at home during the daytime.

☐ This means most door-to-door interviewing has to be done at night or on weekends. It's often difficult to find interviewers who are willing to walk door to door at night through unfamiliar neighborhoods.

☐ Increasing crime rates, especially in large cities, have made many people reluctant to let strangers into their homes, even if those strangers are survey interviewers.

Nevertheless, personal interviews have some important advantages that keep the method alive for certain kinds of research.

ADVANTAGES OF PERSONAL INTERVIEWING

Personal interviewing comes closest to being the "universal" research approach. Theoretically it could be used on almost every study, if cost considerations didn't make that impractical. Here are the major advantages of this approach:

Flexibility and versatility.   This is the key advantage of personal interviewing: you can do almost anything. You have the greatest freedom in questionnaire length and format. A personal interview is often most effective for getting detailed attitude and opinion information. And interviewers can sometimes do a better job of probing and clarifying open-end questions in a face-to-face interview. In short, virtually any type of question can be asked in a personal interview.

Exhibits.   This is the other key benefit of personal interviewing: you can show or give things to respondents. This means you can expose them to advertisements and ask their opinions about them. You can hand respondents test packages to open. Or you can give them samples of test products to take home and use.

So if it's necessary to show some type of exhibit during the interview, a personal contact is usually required.

Observation.   Having an interviewer present provides the option of observing things the respondents do, rather than only asking them questions. For example, you might observe whether the respondent opens a test package correctly or whether the test product spills when the respondent tries to pour it. Another time you may want to measure how long women spend in a supermarket examining bacon packages before making a final selection. These kinds of observation measures are possible only in a personal interview.

Sampling.   In theory, at least, it's possible to draw a very representative sample of the total population using homes (or "dwelling units," as they're called in sampling terminology) as a basis for the sample. In practice, of course, actually executing a door-to-door sample and interviewing everyone in it presents problems that often make it infeasible or not worth the very high cost involved.

Speed.   By dividing the total sample among several markets and conducting the interviews in each city simultaneously, it's possible to complete large studies very quickly. Personal interviewing conducted this way is usually faster than doing a study by mail, although it may not be quicker than by telephone.

DISADVANTAGES OF PERSONAL INTERVIEWING

Offsetting these important advantages are two major drawbacks that limit the applicability of personal interviewing. The first is cost. Personal interviewing, especially door-to-door interviewing, typically costs several times as much per interview as mail or telephone research. So, except where a personal contact is absolutely necessary, budget considerations argue against door-to-door personal interviewing.

The second problem—execution—is more serious. While door-to-door sampling may often be desirable, consider this:

□ Any large, representative national sample will invariably include many sampling points in the inner cities of major metropolitan areas, such as New York, Atlanta, Chicago, Dallas, and Los Angeles.

□ With about half of all adult women employed outside the home, most contacts on any project will have to be made on weekends and at night.

□ To obtain a truly representative sample of these households, several callback attempts will have to be made on respondents who are not at home or are unavailable to be interviewed. This can mean repeated visits to distant neighborhoods in a city to try to complete a single interview.

Would *you* want to be the interviewer on a study like this? Probably not. And if you'd consider taking the job, how much would you charge? Probably a lot. That's why door-to-door studies are so expensive—and it's virtually impossible to hire interviewers to go into certain neighborhoods of some cities at any price. High cost, along with risks to interviewers' safety, are the reasons that large, nationally representative door-to-door studies have almost disappeared.

TRENDS IN PERSONAL INTERVIEWING

Still, for some kinds of research (those involving ads or packages, for example), it's necessary to personally talk with respondents. This has generated a new kind of personal contact: intercept interviews. These involve contacting or "intercepting" respondents in high-traffic locations, such as shopping malls or stores. This is one of the fastest growing and, today, the most common kinds of research.

Intercept Interviews

The concept behind this interviewing method is simple: it's more efficient to let respondents come to the interviewer, in a shopping mall or store, than it is to send the interviewer out to the respondents' homes.

Of course, the drawback to intercept interviewing is that it can't theoretically produce a sample that's as representative of the population as the best door-to-door study. Intercept studies also must usually be limited to 30-minute interviews.

On the other hand, given the problems of actually executing door-to-door studies, those samples aren't usually perfectly representative to begin with. And samples of respondents in intercept studies are often more representative than you might expect.

Many large, regional shopping centers (which typically contain several major department stores) attract a large cross-section of shoppers to sample from. And, similarly, it's possible to find respondents from a wide range of socioeconomic groups by conducting interviews in several supermarkets in different types of neighborhoods.

All in all, the samples developed from intercept studies often reflect the total population closely enough for purposes of marketing decision-making. And the cost per interview of intercept studies is usually only a fraction of going door-to-door. Adequate sample control and dramatically lower costs—that's why intercept studies have largely replaced door-to-door samples for personal interviews.

Prerecruited Central-Location Studies

For some types of projects it may be most efficient to screen respondents ahead of time by telephone, for example, then invite those who qualify to come to a test location at a specific time to be interviewed. This method is often best when:

Incidence (the proportion of qualified respondents) is low. If only 5 percent or 10 percent of all people contacted will qualify to be interviewed, it's usually best to do this screening in advance, then conduct the full-scale interviews all at once.

Interview is long. Many people find it inconvenient to spend 45 minutes or an hour on the spur of the moment to be interviewed. Prerecruiting allows them to make an appointment to be interviewed at a convenient time.

Mail–Telephone Combinations

On projects for which it's still necessary to make some contact in person, it's often possible to reduce costs by using either telephone or mail on portions of the study.

Product tests are an example. A personal interview (intercept or door-to-door) is usually needed at the beginning of an in-home use test to qualify respondents for the study and give them samples of the test product. But instead of conducting the callback interview in person to get an after-use evaluation of the product, it may be more efficient to obtain reactions by telephone, through the mail, or with a combination of telephone and mail.

PROJECTS THAT TYPICALLY USE PERSONAL INTERVIEWING

Personal interviewing is usually used when you have to show or give the respondent something. The most common examples of this are product tests, advertising tests, and package tests.

Other common types of personal interviewing studies are complex attitude and opinion studies, in which the length of the interview or the types of questions asked make mail or telephone questionnaires impractical.

7

Doing Research by Telephone

□□

AT&T used to claim, "Long distance is the next best thing to being there." Not true. In conducting some kinds of marketing research studies, the telephone is actually *better* than being there. In other studies, of course, it may be far less than "next best"; it may be totally unacceptable. But as the use of door-to-door interviewing has declined, telephone research has replaced it for most large, national studies.

ADVANTAGES OF TELEPHONE INTERVIEWING

Sampling.   A key advantage of telephone interviewing is that it makes it relatively easy to draw a large, geographically dispersed sample. And the use of random digit dialing makes it possible to reach even newly moved households and homes with unlisted numbers. (See the section in this chapter on "Trends in Telephone Interviewing" for a description of random digit dialing.)

Callbacks.   A drawback of door-to-door interviewing is the need for an interviewer to travel across town to make a second attempt to reach a respondent—perhaps only to find he or she isn't available. With telephone interviewing, callbacks can be made much more easily, which makes it relatively simple to follow good callback sampling procedures.

Supervision.   When interviewing is done from a central telephone facility, it's possible for a supervisor to monitor a portion of each interviewer's work to make certain the questionnaire is being administered properly. This close supervision is impractical for most personal interviews.

Questionnaire flexibility.   Compared with mail questionnaires, telephone research can use more complex questionnaires (skip patterns, probes, refer-backs, and terminations), because an interviewer is involved to control the questioning.

32

Access to hard-to-reach people.   In any study using personal interviewing, it is difficult to reach consumers in small towns or rural areas. There are few professional interviewing services available in these places. With telephone interviewing, however, these consumers are just as easy to reach as respondents in large cities.

Speed.   When a central interviewing facility is used, it's possible to assign enough interviewers to a study to complete hundreds of interviews each day. This makes it possible to complete even large, national studies in a short time.

Pretesting.   You can pretest a telephone questionnaire in the morning and begin full-scale interviewing on a nationwide basis that afternoon. Obviously that isn't practical with personal interviewing or mail studies.

Cost.   Telephone research usually costs only a fraction of the cost of studies involving personal interviews, especially door-to-door contacts. It's still usually more expensive, however, than mail research.

DISADVANTAGES OF TELEPHONE INTERVIEWING

At the same time, telephone research has some characteristics that limit the kinds of studies for which it can be used.

Length of interview.   The ideal length for a telephone interview is between 10 and 15 minutes, with 30 minutes being about the maximum that's feasible. If it isn't possible to obtain the information needed for a study in this length of time, then telephone research isn't a good alternative.

No exhibits.   It's impossible, of course, to show a respondent anything during a telephone interview. This can be a major limitation on certain studies. It makes it totally impractical to conduct certain types of research (advertising-copy testing and package testing, for example) by telephone. Sometimes this obstacle can be overcome by mailing the respondent an exhibit, then calling to conduct the interview. Even if you're creative, however, this remains an inherent problem with telephone research.

Question limitations.   It's difficult to administer lengthy scales by telephone, which in many cases limits your ability to sensitively measure the issue at hand. Also, the repeated use of similar scales in a questionnaire becomes tiresome to the respondent more quickly on the telephone than in person. Card sorts are another type of task that can't be administered in a telephone interview.

TRENDS IN TELEPHONE INTERVIEWING

WATS interviewing centers.   Years ago, when telephone interviewing was starting, interviewers usually conducted the work out of their homes. Today, however, most telephone interviewing is done from large, central

WATS interviewing centers, where dozens of interviewers work at the same time calling people all over the United States. These central facilities offer much better supervision and sampling control than the old-fashioned "kitchen" approach. Moreover, the economies of scale possible with WATS telephone service usually make this type of interviewing surprisingly competitive in cost with telephone research done from interviewers' homes.

Random digit dialing. Although sampling from telephone books is adequate for many telephone studies, there are always a number of households (probably at least 20 percent) not listed in even the most current telephone directory. Some families have moved into the area since the directory was compiled, while others have chosen to have unlisted numbers. Random digit dialing is a technique that can be used, if the study objectives require it, to reach some households that aren't in the directory.

Random digit dialing is based on this concept: every possible telephone number in America can be sampled by randomly generating ten digit numbers (a three-digit area code plus a seven-digit telephone number). In reality, of course, many of these randomly generated numbers do not have telephones assigned to them. So to make random digit dialing more efficient, it's common to generate only the last four digits of the number—using selected area codes and exchanges that are known to be assigned to residential numbers.

Another variation of this is known as "plus one" sampling, where one is added to the last digit of a number in the directory. (For example, 934-3456 becomes 934-3457 with this method.) This is a way to add some "randomness" to the sample and reach some households not in the directory, without going to completely random digit dialing.

Random digit dialing is more costly than sampling from telephone books, but if offers a way to reach consumers who might not be included in a sample drawn only from telephone books. Are the people who aren't listed likely to differ significantly from those in the directory in their attitudes or usage regarding the product being studied? That's the question you have to ask yourself to determine whether random digit dialing makes sense for a study. Because of the improved sample coverage it can provide, random digit dialing is gaining acceptance for use on studies where the best possible sample is desirable—and worth the higher cost.

Cathode-ray tubes. In many central WATS telephone interviewing centers, paper questionnaires are being replaced by cathode-ray tubes (CRTs). These look like small television screens with typewriter keyboards and are wired directly to a computer. The CRT displays questions for the interviewer to read over the telephone to the respondent. The interviewer then types the respondent's answer directly into the computer on the CRT keyboard. The elimination of paper questionnaires—which also cuts out editing, keypunching, and data cleaning—and direct interaction between the interviewer and the computer result in faster turnaround, greater accuracy, closer control, and often lower cost. As a result, CRTs are growing in use for telephone research.

PROJECTS THAT TYPICALLY USE
TELEPHONE INTERVIEWING

Telephone research is an efficient way to collect facts and opinions from a broad national sample of people. For this reason, it has largely replaced door-to-door interviews for many attitude and usage studies—particularly "tracking studies," which are repeated periodically to monitor customer awareness, attitudes, and usage in a product category.

In addition, telephone research may be an efficient way to conduct callback interviews with people who have previously been contacted in person—participants in product tests, for example. Telephone interviews can be used after a test period to obtain respondents' opinions of the product they have been testing.

Finally, telephone research is often used to contact respondents drawn from a specific list (coupon redeemers, for example). When there are a limited number of potential respondents and they are geographically dispersed, telephone interviewing is often the only practical way to reach them. For this reason, telephone research is growing in use on executive, industrial, and medical studies.

8

Pros and Cons of Mail Questionnaires

□□□

When Government makes a mistake, it is a
big one, like the Post Office or Viet Nam.
—Ben Heineman, president of Northwest Industries

Sending out a questionnaire in the mail often seems like an attractive alternative. It's relatively easy to do and usually quite inexpensive compared with telephone or personal interviewing. While mail research has some major limitations that make it unreliable for many types of studies, its benefits can be significant.

ADVANTAGES OF MAIL RESEARCH

Cost.   Using address labels and a cover letter addressed "Dear Respondent" is an inexpensive way to distribute a large number of questionnaires. This is the main appeal of mail research.

Efficiency of large samples.   Not only is mail research inexpensive to begin with, but it gets relatively even more efficient as sample sizes grow. For example, the cost difference between mailing out 2,000 and 1,000 questionnaires may be only the costs of the postage and of a little printing.

Access to hard-to-reach respondents.   You can reach geographically dispersed respondents or hard-to-reach people (farmers, for example) at the same cost as geographically concentrated, easy-to-reach people. In this respect mail is similar to telephone research.

No interviewer bias.   Since there is no interviewer present, there can be no interviewer bias. Unfortunately this can also be a problem, since it means there's no interviewer to probe or clarify incomplete answers.

36

Exhibits. While it's impossible to include large exhibits in a mailing, it's quite feasible to incorporate drawings or photos into a mail questionnaire. It's also possible to include such things as fabric swatches in a mailing. This can be an important advantage, in certain types of studies, over telephone interviewing.

DISADVANTAGES OF MAIL RESEARCH

For most projects, the limitations of mail research far outnumber the advantages, which accounts for mail studies being rarer than either personal or telephone research. For most types of studies, these limitations make using a mail questionnaire inappropriate.

Low rate of return. On a typical mail study sent to a "cold" list of randomly selected respondents, no more than 5 percent or 10 percent of the questionnaires will be returned. This can sometimes be increased—occasionally increased dramatically—but it's always a potential problem with mail studies.

Nonreturner bias. This is a major weakness of mail questionnaires: not only do a small share of people respond, but respondents who return complete questionnaires are often not typical of the total sample.

For example, on a mail survey about a new product, consumers who return questionnaires are likely to be those who either like the product intensely or have a complaint about it they want to voice. It's common for older, retired people to have a higher return rate than younger, busier consumers—yet it's often the younger consumers you are most interested in studying.

In short, the typically low rate of return, along with serious questions about the representativeness of the respondents who do reply, make mail questionnaires unreliable for many purposes.*

Poor control. You can't control who fills out the questionnaire—or even control for sure who gets it. Many mailing lists of names aren't up to date. And someone other than the person to whom you've sent the questionnaire may complete and return it.

Question limitations. Since there is no interviewer present to administer a mail questionnaire, each question must be carefully structured—there's no way to clarify a question the respondent doesn't understand. Perhaps more important, there's no opportunity for probing or following up on incomplete or unclear answers.

*A bit of research trivia: In 1896, Professor Harlow Gale, of the University of Minnesota, sent a mail questionnaire to 200 Twin Cities advertisers to survey their opinions of what made advertising successful. Unfortunately, his efforts were hampered when he achieved only a 10 percent return rate—a problem that still plagues mail studies.

Format. Since a mail questionnaire is always self-administered, it must be very simple and straightforward. If there are too many complex questions or difficult skips, many potential respondents will simply get frustrated and throw the questionnaire away. Newspapers are said to assume only a sixth-grade education among readers, which is probably a good guideline for mail questionnaires, too.

Speed. With mail surveys, it usually takes several weeks for returns to come in—longer, of course, when follow-up mailings are made.

Pretesting. It takes just as long to pretest a mail questionnaire as to conduct the full-scale project, so a pilot study often isn't feasible.

Names. For consumer studies, it's best to have a specific name to address the questionnaire to. And having an individual's name is even more important on industrial, executive, or medical studies. Addressing a questionnaire to "Engineer" at a large company or "Floor Nurse" at a hospital isn't adequate. Unfortunately, a list of such names, especially on industrial or medical studies, may be nearly impossible to obtain.

TRENDS IN MAIL QUESTIONNAIRES

Mail questionnaires are suitable only for certain kinds of tests, with medical and industrial markets being among the most frequent users.

Since low response rate is a primary weakness of mail questionnaires (along with the non-returner bias resulting from low response), many of the efforts to improve mail questionnaires center on increasing return rates. Doing that makes mail research a more acceptable alternative for some kinds of studies.

The first step in any mail study is to make sure you're doing the best possible job of designing the "package" you send to respondents. Guidelines for doing this include:

1. Make the "package" the respondent receives look good.

   □ Use first-class postage.
   □ Mail an incentive with the questionnaire, if an incentive is used. (Incentives can be very important in mail questionnaires.)
   □ Personalize the cover letter; address it to the respondent by name.
   □ Make the entire package look professional. Don't skimp on paper or printing quality. Avoid the look of a bulk mailing.

2. Make the questionnaire look easy to answer and return.

   □ Enclose a postage-paid envelope.
   □ Keep the questionnaire uncluttered-looking.
   □ Try to keep length to four pages or less.

☐ Consider putting the questionnaire on both sides of a folded 17''
× 11'' page, which tends to look less imposing than a four-
page, single-sided questionnaire.

3. And, of course, make sure you use a mail questionnaire only on a
study where the limitations of mail don't make it inappropriate.

Consider doing something unusual, creative, or dramatic to increase the
return rate on your mail questionnaire. If it's important to reach a small
number of specific respondents, as is typically the case in industrial or
medical studies, this is often particularly useful.

For example, one company used a combination of mail and telephone
techniques on a study among upper-management executives. A small
lockbox containing survey materials was sent to each respondent. A letter
was attached, informing the person that he would be called in a few days,
given the combination for the lockbox, and interviewed on the basis of the
contents of the box. The lockbox, of course, was a strong attention-getting
device. Who could throw it away unopened? The box added enough interest to the questionnaire that a large proportion of the respondents agreed
to take part in the study when they were contacted by telephone.

With all the junk mail most people receive each day, it takes something
special to make a mail questionnaire stand out and motivate the respondent
to return it.

PROJECTS THAT TYPICALLY USE
MAIL QUESTIONNAIRES

Mail questionnaires are most often used for executive, industrial, or
medical studies, where respondents share a relatively high interest in the
products being studied. In these studies, there is often only a small, geographically dispersed sample to draw from, so the extra effort and expense
of special incentives or unusual approaches (such as the lockbox) can be
justified.

It is rare, however, for a mail survey to be used on general studies of
consumer products and services. The response rate on these projects is
usually too low to produce reliable results.

MAIL PANELS AND PURCHASE PANELS

Because of the cost appeal of mail research, two approaches have been
developed to retain the economies of mail studies, yet overcome the low-
response problem. Both use respondents who have previously agreed to
take part in mail studies, usually in return for a token gift as an incentive.

Mail panels periodically send custom-designed questionnaires to their panel members, while consumers who are on *purchase panels* agree to keep a "diary" of all their purchases in several product categories each month.

The question most frequently asked about these two methods is whether diary panel members are representative of the population. ("Who would agree to keep track of everything they buy at the grocery store?") Nevertheless, the record shows that these panels generally provide a good way of developing straightforward information on large samples of consumers at relatively low cost.

The major mail panel firms are Home Testing Institute (HTI), National Family Opinion (NFO), and Market Facts. The leading purchase panel suppliers are NPD Research Inc. and Market Research Corporation of America (MRCA).

Part III

Step by Step Through a Research Project

□□

Part III

Step by Step
Through a
Research Project

9

The Steps in a
Survey Research Study

□□

How do you get from the beginning to the end of a project without forgetting any important steps along the way?

Well, it helps to have an overview of the process, which can then serve as a checklist to make sure everything gets done—or at least omitted on purpose and for good reason.

A project's flow could be viewed a number of different ways. The basic steps needed to get a typical project done are shown in Figure 8. While

Figure 8. Fifteen steps in a research project.

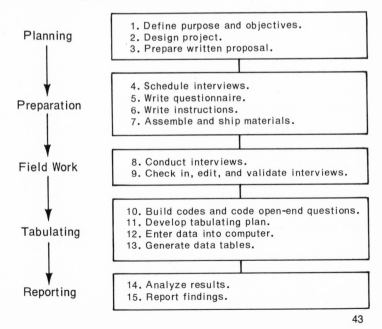

Planning
1. Define purpose and objectives.
2. Design project.
3. Prepare written proposal.

Preparation
4. Schedule interviews.
5. Write questionnaire.
6. Write instructions.
7. Assemble and ship materials.

Field Work
8. Conduct interviews.
9. Check in, edit, and validate interviews.

Tabulating
10. Build codes and code open-end questions.
11. Develop tabulating plan.
12. Enter data into computer.
13. Generate data tables.

Reporting
14. Analyze results.
15. Report findings.

43

there are many other steps and activities along the way, these 15 steps are the major ones. Some things can be done simultaneously (such as scheduling interviews and writing the questionnaire), while others need to happen in sequence (writing the questionnaire and writing the instructions, for example).

In addition to these steps, test materials (ads, product samples, packages, and so on) need to be ordered and ready on time.

PROJECT MANAGEMENT

Each project needs one person (usually with a title such as "project director") to be responsible for coordinating and managing the study from beginning to end. This person must be:

Able to handle a lot of things at one time
Organized
Detail-oriented
Able to find ways to keep things moving, get things done
Deadline-conscious

If you're running a project yourself, make sure someone's designated to act in this role. If you're working with an outside research supplier, be sure to meet, then stay in touch with, the project director. The project director is like the quarterback of the team and will play a key role in getting the project done properly and on time.

THE STEPS

Many companies have flowcharts or checklists of the detailed steps in a research project to act as reminders of the tasks to be done and to keep the study on track. Many of these steps are the subjects of whole chapters in this book. However, here's a capsule description of each phase:

1. *Define purpose and objectives.* "If you don't know where you're going, any road will get you there." Everything that follows in the project (and since this is the first step, that's *everything*) will go smoother if you take time at the very start to clearly determine why the project is being done, what the study should be designed to measure, and what decision will be taken on the basis of it.

2. *Design the project.* You then need to develop a plan for a study which will meet that purpose and objectives. This is the place to put in "head time" on a project to make sure the design really fits the problem and isn't just the closest thing you can think of quickly.

3. *Prepare written proposal.* Are you sure *everyone* involved with the project understands what's to be done? Movie mogul Samuel Goldwyn said, "Verbal contracts aren't worth the paper they're written on." Verbal descriptions of research designs can have comparable value. They're just too easy for people to misinterpret. The written proposal pins things down and provides the means to make sure everyone agrees and understands.

4. *Schedule interviews.* Do this as far ahead as possible, since it becomes a deadline around which most of the other steps must be planned.

5. *Write questionnaire.* You now have the difficult task of translating your objectives into specific, clear, unambiguous questions. (That's why there are two chapters on this subject.)

6. *Write instructions.* Don't forget to give the interviewers and supervisors detailed instructions on how to conduct the study in exactly the way you want it done. Don't assume anything.

7. *Assemble and ship materials.* If possible, avoid leaving this until five o'clock on the afternoon before the interviewing is set to begin 2,000 miles away the next morning. Be skeptical of the miracles promised in ads for freight companies and the U.S. Postal Service.

8. *Conduct interviews.* This is what the whole study is set up to accomplish. It seems so simple, but there are seven steps before it and an equal number to follow.

9. *Check in, edit, and validate interviews.* These three little steps can save a lot of problems later.

Check in: simply count the number of completed interviews received.

Edit: check within the questionnaires for internal consistency. (For example, people who never heard of a brand shouldn't have been asked when they last bought it. But on a big study you can almost bet the questionnaires will show that happened a few times.)

Validate: spot-check to make sure the people whose names are on the questionnaires were actually interviewed and asked the questions properly.

10. *Build codes and code open-end questions.* Answers to all the "why?" questions, as well as to any other questions calling for discussion-type answers, need to be translated into numerical responses that the computer can tabulate. This can be tricky (which is why there's a chapter on coding, too).

11. *Develop tabulating plan.* Now's the time to begin thinking about how you want the computer to deliver your results. What format do you want? What subgroups of people do you want to look at in detail? Plan the tabulating plan by going back to the purpose and the objectives of the study and looking for ways to lay out the results to meet those objectives.

12. *Enter data into computer.* This puts the data where you can use them, work with them, and then . . .

13. *Generate data tables.* Here you get the results of the study back from the computer in the form specified by your tabulation plan.

14. *Analyze results.* Now you spend more "head time" trying to translate all the numbers into answers to the key questions of the study.

15. *Report findings.* Finally, the payoff! Now you bring the results of the project to bear on the problems and decisions that started it all. This is the part that's really fun. It's what research is really all about—but (unfortunately) it constitutes only a small part of the total process.

10

Background, Purpose, and Objectives Checklists

□□□

Understanding the *background,* the *purpose,* and the *objectives* of a study is critical. The initial design of the project is determined by this information, and the report of the results is usually organized around answering the questions posed under these headings.

The three topics are related, but they differ in important ways. Each can be most easily defined by a question:

Background: How has this problem come to exist?
Purpose: What decision will be made on the basis of the research?
Objectives: What information must the research provide to help make that decision?

An example can help clarify the distinction between a study's "purpose" and its "objective." The *purpose* of a product test could be to "help decide which of two new products, A or B, should be introduced." The *objective* of the same study might be to "determine which product, A or B, is preferred by consumers"—but that preference alone might not determine which product is introduced. Differences in cost, profitability, production capacity, requirements for new equipment, or many other factors could also play an important role in the decision.

So while it is important to keep the decision to be made (the "purpose") in mind, it's also important to clearly define the specific information that is expected from the study (the "objectives").

If you're dealing with research problems within a company for which you've worked for a while, much of the "background" of a problem will be understood. You don't need to review it for every project.

But if you're working in a new company, on an unfamiliar product, or with a new outside research supplier, you should go over the background issues in detail. And the "purpose" and "objectives" checklists bear review on every study.

Project Background Checklist

1. Briefly, what is the company's history? What is the company's "personality"—go-go, conservative, or what?
2. What are its major product lines? What's the relative importance of each product line?
3. What is the product's sales history? Is it growing, stable, or declining?
4. What are the competitive products? What are the market shares? What new products have entered the market?
5. In one sentence: What is the problem? Then expand on that one sentence: Who? What? When? Where? Why? How?
6. Is this a big problem or a little problem?
7. What previous research has been done on this subject? What did it show?

Project Purpose Checklist

1. What decision will be made or what action will be taken as a result of the research?
2. What are the implications of this action? Is it a "big deal" or a "little deal"?
3. What are the alternatives available?
4. What are the risks in the decision or action?
5. What are the potential payoffs of the decision?
6. When will the decision be made? Are there externally enforced deadlines on the decision?

Project Objectives Checklist

1. What *specific* information should the project provide?
2. If more than one type of information will be developed from the study, what is most important? What are the priorities for the information?
3. What results are expected? Is there agreement among those involved with the project? If not, why not?
4. Have decision rules been established for evaluating the results? If so, what are they? If not, why not?

Discussing these questions should provide enough understanding to help you begin designing the study.

11

How to Estimate Research Costs

□□

Never ask of money spent
Where the spender thinks it went.
Nobody was ever meant
To remember or invent
What he did with every cent.
                    —*Robert Frost, "The Hardship of Accounting"*

Wouldn't that be nice, if cost were no object and we could do all the research we pleased? Well, welcome back to reality. Cost is always an object in research; it sometimes seems like *the* object.

While it's true that good design and careful execution shouldn't be ruled by cost, neither can realistic budget constraints be ignored. It's a fact of research life.

Here is a step-by-step description of how research costs are estimated by research companies and a list of the factors that most directly influence costs. (The next chapter describes specific ways to *cut* costs.)

PRINCIPLES OF COST ESTIMATING

Most research firms estimate costs for projects using some variation of this basic formula:

$$\text{Total costs} = \frac{\text{labor hours required}}{\text{to conduct study}} \times \frac{\text{dollar billing}}{\text{rate per hour}} + \text{expenses}$$

It's really that simple. Even though the specific methods used by different research companies can become very complex, the principles involved are

49

quite simple. Let's look at all the pieces of a cost estimate and how they are assembled to develop a final budget figure.

Labor

A large part of the cost of any survey research project is "labor"—the charges for the time people spend conducting the study. On most projects there are two kinds of labor involved:

Interviewing and data entry. This is directly related to the size and complexity of the study—number of people interviewed, number of questions to be coded and keypunched, and so on.

Administration. This includes the time required to design, direct, and supervise the study.

Interviewing.   The key factor in determining the cost of the interviewing is time. How many interviewing hours will it take to conduct the interviews or how many interviews can an interviewer complete in one hour's time? So many factors affect this completion rate that it would be impossible to list them all, but these are the major ones:

Qualifications and incidence. How many people does the interviewer have to screen before a qualified respondent can be found?

Length of questionnaire. How long does it take to administer the questionnaire to a qualified respondent?

Type of interviewing method. What type of interviewing is to be used— telephone, door-to-door, intercept, central location, and so on?

Other factors, such as time of day of the interviews, quotas, and the need for specially trained interviewers, can also affect the cost of the interviewing.

The actual interviewing done by research companies is usually conducted in several cities and is subcontracted to independent interviewing services in each city. Each location has supervisors and other office staff, who are responsible for training and supervising the interviewers. So in addition to the number of interviewing hours, there are also costs for supervision of the project. These supervision costs are charged directly on an hourly basis or by adding a percentage to the cost of interviewing. In addition, mileage, location rental, respondent fees, and charges for equipment are part of the total interviewing costs.

Data entry.   After the interviewing is completed, the information on the questionnaires must be entered into a computer for tabulating. If there are unstructured answers from open-end questions, these answers have to be coded into an answer structure. All closed-end or structured answers can be entered directly into the computer by keypunch or from a keyboard or CRT terminal.

Some of the major factors affecting the cost of coding and data entry are:

Number of questionnaires to be tabulated
Number of answered questions on each questionnaire
Number of open-end and closed-end questions on each questionnaire
Complexity of questionnaire format

Administration.   The final (and in most cases smallest) part of the total labor cost is time spent in setting up the project, typing and assembling the questionnaires, and supervising tabulation of the results.

Even though most of this time is spent by the higher professional levels within the company, the total number of hours is small in comparison to the time spent on interviewing and data entry.

Some of the factors influencing the project direction and tabulation supervision are:

□ Amount of time spent on the design of the project and questionnaire.
□ Size and complexity of the project. The test design and number of interviewing locations are examples of things which affect the time needed to coordinate a project.
□ Changes in design, or implementation problems.
□ Amount of tabulating required.
□ Complexity of analysis and report.

Once the total number of hours of each type of labor is determined, the hourly rate charged for each type of job is multiplied by the number of hours to calculate the total cost of labor. (See the cost estimating form included as Figure 9 in this chapter.)

Expenses

The other part of the project cost is expenses. Most projects, regardless of type, have the following expenses:

Printing   Computer time
Long-distance telephone tolls   Travel expenses
Postage and shipping

Other expenses which vary by type of project are:

Location rental   Product costs
Equipment rental   Product storage and delivery costs
Incentives for respondents   Field supplies

The labor costs and expenses are usually computed and recorded on a cost estimating form such as the one in Figure 9.

Figure 9. Cost estimating form for a marketing research project.

CRI

COST ESTIMATING FORM	Project Title
	Project Number
	☐☐☐ – ☐☐☐

CLIENT NAME_____ Date_____

PROJECT DIRECTOR_____ Number of Respondents_____

TAB SUPERVISOR_____ Number of Cities_____

TYPE OF PROJECT_____ Completion Ratio_____

DESCRIPTION: Design (   )   Field (   )   Project Direction (   )   Tab (   )   Report (   )

Explanation of Project:

FIELD: (By City)	Cost	TELEPHONE FACILITY:	Hours		Cost
_____	_____	(230) Interviewing.	_____	=	_____
_____	_____	(228) Training.	_____	=	_____
_____	_____	(234) Supervisor.	_____	=	_____
		(235) Monitoring.	_____	=	_____
		(236) Editing	_____	=	_____
TOTAL FIELD COSTS . . . . . _____		(232) Calling for Numbers . .	_____	=	_____
LABOR:		(233) Assistant Manager . . .	_____	=	_____
	Hours Cost	(227) Manager Telephone . . .	_____	=	_____
(210) Project Director. . _____ = _____		(270) Telephone Charges . . .	_____	=	_____
(213) Project Assistant . _____ = _____		(275) CRT Costs	_____	=	_____
(215) Project Manager . . _____ = _____					
(211) Travel Time . . . . _____ = _____					
(216) Reporting . . . . . _____ = _____		TOTAL TELEPHONE FACILITY COSTS	_____	=	_____
(222) Quality Control . . _____ = _____		TABULATING:			
(224) Typing. . . . . . . _____ = _____		(223) Senior Tab Supervisor .	_____	=	_____
(226) Assembling. . . . . _____ = _____		(218) Tab Supervisor.	_____	=	_____
( ) Other . . . . _____ = _____		(219) Computer Specialist . .	_____	=	_____
		(225) Computer Assistant. . .	_____	=	_____
		(217) Tab Assistant	_____	=	_____
TOTAL LABOR COSTS . . . . _____		(220) Study Processing. . . .	_____	=	_____
OTHER EXPENSES:		(221) Coding.	_____	=	_____
(278) Printing/Xerox/Reducing . . . _____		(272) Data Entry	_____	=	_____
(266) Shipping/Postage. . . . . . _____		(276) Computer.	_____	=	_____
(268) Telephone . . . . _____					
(252) Travel Expenses . . . . . . _____					
( ) Other Expenses. . . . . . . _____		TOTAL TABULATING COSTS. . . . . _____			
( ) Other Expenses. . . . . . . _____					
		TOTAL TO BE BILLED. . . . . _____			

TOTAL OTHER EXPENSE COSTS . . . . . _____   accounting – white copy
                                                    project file – yellow copy

Contingency Allowance

Because it is difficult to estimate costs precisely, many research companies include a contingency of plus or minus 10 percent. This means: "If the project is conducted the way we've assumed, we believe the actual costs will be within 10 percent of what we've estimated." If costs are more than 10 percent higher, the research company makes less profit. If costs are less than 90 percent of the estimate, it makes a higher profit.

This ±10 percent contingency range is meant to cover normal estimating uncertainty with the original specifications. It is *not* intended to provide for changes in the specifications. If the specs are changed, the base estimate should change, too.

EVALUATING COST ESTIMATES

It's not unusual for clients to get competitive bids from different suppliers. That's the American way. But clients need to keep several things in mind when comparing cost estimates from different research firms:

1. *Keep your eye on the "bottom line"—it's the key.* The total estimates are the only things that can be compared directly. Some firms use hourly billing rates that incorporate profit; others add a profit margin to the total. Looking at the pieces will make comparison confusing. The bottom line is the key to comparing estimates.

2. *Large differences in competitive cost estimates may reflect different assumptions by the suppliers.* If you get four bids on the same project, chances are that the difference between the high and the low bidder will be no more than 10 or 15 percent. If one is too high or low, check to make sure that the firm is basing its estimate on the same assumptions and specifications as the rest.

3. *Beware of lowballs.* As in all businesses, research firms sometimes submit lowballs to get business, keep business, or bolster sagging volume. As a client, go into this type of situation with your eyes open and protect yourself if you take a lowball bid. The risk of the lowball bid is that the supplier will try to make the bid by cutting corners, so be especially careful that quality control procedures are followed on these types of projects. As a research user, relying on lowball research bidders is a risky way to make money for your company.

4. *The supplier and the client are partners regarding costs.* It's fair to say that most research firms don't plan to get rich on a single project, and most clients recognize that their suppliers have to make a reasonable profit to stay in business. The best arrangement between client and supplier is based on trust and recognition of the shared goal of producing professional, action-oriented research.

12

Twelve Ways to Cut Research Costs

□□□

I wrote this chapter a few years ago as an article that described ways to keep research costs under control. Strangely, although reaction was generally good, the piece generated some negative repsonse. The tone of the critics was usually, "Good research should never be sacrificed for cost considerations!" That's true, of course, but it's also true that cost is a fact of life that can't be ignored. To claim researchers are–or should be–above such crass issues as budgets is simply naive. Our job is to help management make better business decisions by providing useful information efficiently. We shouldn't sacrifice quality for costs, but neither should we "overbuild" projects to cost more than they need to. This chapter is simply an attempt to point out ways to get the job done at the most reasonable cost possible. Six years after it was written, I still happen to think the points are valid, maybe more so than ever.

Most companies' marketing research budgets are being squeezed by managements that suspect there's some fat in there that could come out. They're generally right. The budgets for most research projects could be cut and still accomplish their objectives.

Costs for many types of research have at least doubled over the past ten years. That wasn't a big problem when times were good and budgets were fat, but the current economic situation seems to have sharpened marketing directors' memories. They suddenly recall that today's $10,000 project cost $5,000 when they were assistant product managers.

For a variety of reasons, we can never get back to yesterday's cost level, but clients usually can do better at cutting costs than they're doing. Since

Reprinted with permission from *Marketing News*, June 6, 1975. Published by the American Marketing Association.

our company makes a living selling research, I feel a little like the chicken telling the fox where the holes are in the barnyard fence. But openness about costs always has been part of our philosophy. If a client asked me, "How can I cut my research costs?" here's what I'd tell him:

1. Use more telephone interviewing.   On a typical large-scale national study, telephone interviewing costs as little as one-fifth of what personal sampling costs. Moreover, it's getting nearly impossible to execute a truly representative national sample through personal interviewing. There are getting to be a lot of neighborhoods in this country where interviewers simply won't go at night (would you?), and with more than 50 percent of all women now employed, night or weekend interviewing is imperative. So telephoning not only is a cheaper interviewing method, it's also sometimes a better one.

Sure there are some kinds of information you can't collect over the telephone—detailed attitude data are an example. But unless this information is so vital to the study that it's worth multiplying the cost of the project several times, you're better off dropping it and going the telephone route.

2. Change the cities where you do research.   Too often the cities for a sample are selected by naming the first three or four that come to mind. The most predictable candidates using this method: New York, Chicago, Los Angeles, and Atlanta. Unfortunately, all cities are not created equal in research costs. On a recent study we found the costs per interview in New York were more than twice those in Pittsburgh and Denver, among others. These differences exist for a number of reasons, some more understandable than others. But regardless of their legitimacy, the differences are real.

Sometimes you're locked into the cities where you have to work (when you're researching products in test market, for example). But if you've got flexibility in the selection of markets, don't necessarily use the first ones that you think of.

3. Avoid door-to-door interviewing.   There's something intuitively appealing about doing research by knocking on people's doors and asking them questions. This also happens to be the most costly way ever invented to do research.

Sometimes you can't follow point 1 and use telephone interviewing. In a product test, for example, you usually have to get face to face with consumers at some point to give them the product to try. But, if possible, stay away from their doors. It costs you a lot to talk with them there by the time you pay an interviewer to drive out and walk up and down the street ringing doorbells.

As an alternative, recruiting people in shopping centers and giving them tests products to take home can cut in half the costs of door-to-door product tests. When the right controls are used on shopping center procedures, it's hard to see the advantages of door-to-door product tests that justify paying twice as much for them.

4. Do more multiproduct studies.   For some clients this is about as simple as suggesting that all the countries in the Middle East get together on a peace agreement. As a supplier, I'm scared by the thought of trying to coordinate this type of project; but if a company can put one of these projects together internally (on products within a division, for example), there's a lot of money to be saved.

5. Eliminate open-end questions.   It may not be possible to cut out all open-end questions, but it's almost always practical to eliminate some of them from a study. An open-end question costs three to five times as much to ask, code, and tabulate as a structured question. Some clients continue to ask the same "why-do-you-like-it?" questions on the same products project after project, long after they've learned all that consumers have to say on the subject.

Related money wasters are such redundant open-end questions as "What would you like to see changed about it?" and "Why haven't you bought it?" A good rule is: if you can use a single set of codes for more than one question—as you almost invariably can for the two questions just mentioned—then you've really got just one question, not two. Useless open-end questions are one of the biggest sources of wasted money in marketing research.

6. Cut questionnaires to the bare essentials.   A lot of research dollars are spent on fishing expeditions—hoping consumers will say something profound that no one has even suspected before. These long-shot questions are almost always suggested at research planning meetings by the phrase, "As long as we're there, let's ask them . . ." Just about every study has at least a few of these that could be cut with no appreciable effect on the results. The instinct to include these questions is the same one that has built Las Vegas and made state lotteries lucrative. And the odds of being successful are about the same, too.

7. Be careful about sample sizes.   This is a tough area to evaluate, because there's no such thing as the "right" sample size. It's largely a matter of judgment. But sampling statistics being what they are, doubling the sample size (and the interviewing costs) doesn't come close to cutting your confidence intervals in half. Are great big sample sizes worth it? Often not. The point is to avoid oversampling "just to be safe." It costs money, and it's usually not all that safe, anyway. Instead, consider an alternative.

8. Do sequential research.   By this I mean, consider doing a small-scale study first to see if it produces any surprises. Go ahead with a full-blown study only if it does.

For example, if you're doing a periodic product test to check quality against competition and all tests in the past have shown you're about equal, start with a modest-size project to see if anything has changed. Chances are good that nothing has, and you can save yourself the cost of a big test. A lot of money is wasted on big studies verifying with great statistical certainty what firms already suspect or know for sure.

9. Tabulate only the information you really need.   There's something in most researchers that tells them information isn't available unless it's on paper somewhere. So they tabulate everything they can think of from a study, just to have it on file. As a result, they end up with stacks of expensive computer printouts that they can't find time to read through, let alone understand.

We need to realize that most research data are retained for a long time. Our company, for example, saves data tapes for at least seven years— longer if the client wants. Long after the study is completed, you can go back and tabulate any piece of information you need.

The most efficient approach to tabulating a study is to determine what information you need to understand the subject, then tabulate only that. Leave the rest on the tape, and go back to it only if you find you need it. This takes some hard thinking, which is why it rarely gets done. Unfortunately, computers have made us all a little sloppy about this kind of planning, because they spit out tabulations so easily. But they don't do it free!

10. Ask: "Is this technique really necessary?"   Tough times are good times to take a hard look at the need to experiment with expensive quantitative techniques of analysis. Is this really the time to try out a factor analysis, cluster analysis, or multidimensional scaling, just to see what it might show? If you've got good reason to believe it will help you, go ahead. These techniques can save money in the long run. But is this the time to play hunches? Maybe not.

11. Leave your suppliers alone.   Obviously, a certain amount of coordination and planning is necessary on any research project. But at some point, demanding too much coordination (even if you think of it as "client service") turns into hand-holding; and somewhere, somehow you're going to have to pay for that. The best approach is to find a supplier you can trust, give him clear instructions about what you want done, then leave him alone to do his work. Since you're paying a research company primarily to do research, you'll save by keeping meetings, reviews, and revisions to a minimum.

12. Challenge your research suppliers to save you money.   (Lord forgive me for saying this.) Now, understand I *don't* mean you should hassle

your suppliers about costs. It's funny how some clients are raising prices to their customers and asking us not just to hold, but actually lower, our prices to them. (There seems to be more of that lately, but that's another story.) What I do mean is, stop after outlining a project to suppliers and ask them, ''Now what could be done to cut the cost of this project?'' I think you'll be surprised at the good ideas they have.

As I said, most good research companies make their living selling research, but they also take pride in doing it efficiently. It's curious, but I sometimes feel we're more anxious to save money for clients than they are. I'm not sure why that is, but I think it has something to do with leaving your backside partially exposed, which nobody is ever anxious to do. So challenge your suppliers to cut your research costs, and if you're serious about it, I'll bet they usually can.

These aren't perfect solutions. You always have to give up something to save money. But in most cases, what you're saving is much more than what you're losing. Unfortunately, few research users are close enough to the day-to-day mechanics of the business to know the kinds of savings that are possible. But the times may be right to start digging in and finding the soft spots.

13

How to Write a Questionnaire

□□

Vigorous writing is concise. A sentence should contain no unnecessary words, a paragraph no unnecessary sentences, for the same reason that a drawing should have no unnecessary lines and a machine no unnecessary parts.

—*William Strunk, Jr.*
The Elements of Style

Does the exact wording of a question really matter that much? Yes, it matters a great deal, probably more than you imagine. Studies have shown that exactly how a question is worded and asked can even reverse the results. For example, the *New York Times*–CBS News Poll asked this question: "Do you think there should be an amendment to the Constitution prohibiting abortions, or shouldn't there be such an amendment?" The responses were:

Favor amendment	29%
Uncertain	9
Oppose amendment	62

Later in the survey, the same people were asked a slightly reworded question, which produced a very different result: "Do you believe there should be an amendment to the Constitution protecting the life of the unborn child, or shouldn't there be such an amendment?"

Favor amendment	50%
Uncertain	11
Oppose amendment	39

The two wordings produced opposite indications of the direction of public

59

opinion. So using the right question and the proper wording clearly does make a difference—often a crucial difference.

A questionnaire must do two basic things: (1) translate the objectives of the research project into specific questions the respondent can answer, and (2) motivate the respondent to cooperate and give his information correctly. All the rules, guidelines, and tips about writing questionnaires are nothing more than ways to accomplish those two purposes.

STEPS IN WRITING A QUESTIONNAIRE

Each researcher develops his own approach to writing a questionnaire. Whatever the technique, however, it usually includes the following six steps:

1. Consult your statement of the study objectives and develop from it a list of "information to be obtained." This can take the form of specific questions, phrases, or key words (such as "likes" or "dislikes" of product). This list will form the basis for developing your questions. This step is critical. Don't bypass it. A questionnaire cannot be written until you understand precisely what information you need to get.

2. Consider the method of data collection—mail, telephone, or personal interviews. This obviously affects the ways in which questions are asked, their order, and how the questionnaire should be formatted.

3. Draft the questionnaire.

4. Get someone else—preferably someone who is *not* directly involved with the study—to read through your questionnaire draft and critique it.

5. Pretest the questionnaire.

6. Make the necessary revisions and proceed with the study.

Another useful learning device is to "de-brief" the interviewers at the conclusion of the study. While it's too late to do anything about this study, interviewers' comments on what worked and what didn't work well during the study can be helpful for improving the next project.

CHECKPOINTS

Once the questionnaire is drafted and you read it over, there are some points to double-check:

□ *Does the questionnaire answer your objective for the study?*

□ *Are all the questions necessary?* Extra questions add to expense and increase the demands made on the respondent.

□ *Will the respondent be able to answer the questions?* This means, is he likely to have the information you are asking for? Can he remember it? Questions that ask respondents to tell you things they can't remember accurately usually lead to bad information, because respondents will try to give you the information even if they have to guess.

☐ *Will the respondent be willing to answer the questions?* Sensitive, private issues can be a problem in this respect—although people are often more willing to discuss these kinds of issues than you would expect. Questions that are too much work or require the respondent to expend extra effort to collect the information he needs for an answer can bring the interview to an abrupt halt.

☐ *Does it flow?* Does it sound more like a natural conversation than just a series of unrelated questions? Is it internally consistent and logical? In other words, does it make sense?

☐ *Is it reasonable in length?* The only way to really test this is to read it through *aloud* and have someone answer it. Just reading it over to yourself is not a good indicator of length.

☐ *Can an interviewer or a respondent fill it out?* Can someone who knows less about the study than you do complete the questionnaire? A pretest can help determine this, but often you can avoid problems simply by being honest with yourself about this.

☐ *Is the sequence of questions right?* Be sure you have arranged questions so that one will not influence the response on another.

☐ *Have you included transitions and introductions?* If the questionnaire is going to seem conversational, you need to build bridges between questions and sections in the questionnaire.

SECTIONS OF A QUESTIONNAIRE

There are three basic sections to most questionnaires.

1. Qualifying questions.   These are the questions which need to be asked in order to determine if you are talking with the proper type of person for this study. Examples would be:

☐ What brands of soft drinks have you purchased within the past week?
☐ Do you own a dog?
☐ Do you, or does any member of your immediate family, work for a fruit product manufacturer, marketing research company, or advertising agency? (This is called a "security screen.")

The answers to these questions determine whether the respondent is qualified for participation in the study. The questions immediately following the qualifying questions are critical. These questions must:

☐ Capture attention and create an interest in what you are researching. You need to get the respondent involved right away.

☐ Build rapport between the interviewer and the respondent. The more comfortable they feel with each other, the smoother the interview will go and the more complete the information will likely be.

☐ Make it seem easy for the respondent to answer the questions. This is usually done by including some general, simple, nonthreatening questions early in the interview to help the respondent to get "warmed up" and feel it is easy to answer the questions.

    2. Basic questions about the category being studied. This category includes all the questions, both open-end and closed-end, which constitute the body of the questionnaire. This is usually the largest section.

    3. Classification or demographic questions. This includes information about the respondent's age, sex, and income, as well as his or her name, address, and telephone number. Classification questions tend to be the least interesting to the respondent and are likely to be the most sensitive, so they are usually placed last.

GUIDELINES ON QUESTIONNAIRE WRITING

    As mentioned before, questionnaire writing is an individual thing, and each person does it a little differently. But here are some tips on putting together questionnaires. They are so basic that they apply to almost anyone in virtually any study.

    1. Because one question may influence another, always proceed from the general to the specific. Consequently, open-end questions are put at the beginning of the questionnaire. It is best to ask a "likes" and a "dislikes" question before you bias or educate the respondent with a list of 20 product attributes. Always remember that every question can influence every other question that follows.

    2. Arrange questions in a logical order so that the flow is similar to the way the respondent would think about a subject. Make sure there are proper transitions and introductions. For example, if you are going from a general category such as cake mix to questions concerning brand last used by the purchaser, you might say: "I'd like you to think about the cake mix you used last time you baked a cake. You mentioned you used Betty Crocker Cake Mix. In the next few questions, I'd like you to think only about the Betty Crocker mix you used last time."

    3. Be sure the respondent won't have to work too hard to get the information you're asking for. If an executive has to dig for sales volume information on a line of individual products, you are unlikely to get an accurate answer. If respondents are asked how many times they've ever waxed their car or made popcorn, they will probably guess at the answer.

We frequently make assumptions that our respondents know—or care—as much as we do about the subject we're researching. Many of the products we research are low-involvement products for the people who buy them. That is, people usually are not involved with cereal, floor wax, or pizza. So make sure you are not asking consumers to tell you more than they can about the category.

4. Do you need several questions instead of one? Some questions ask for more than one decision by a respondent, making interpretation difficult. If one question can be broken into several more specific questions, that's usually the best way to do it.

5. Be careful that respondents don't neglect to state their most important reasons simply because they seem so obvious. This is particularly important with questions about price. If you ask, ''Why do you buy Private Label Dog Food instead of Alpo?'' many respondents may neglect to explain they do so because it's cheaper. That seems so obvious to them they assume you are looking for other reasons.

6. Respect the respondent's privacy. We believe we have a right to ask people questions, but they also have the right to refuse to answer them. Researchers have no inherent ''right'' to make people talk to them, so don't coerce or pressure people who don't want to take part in a study, whatever their reasons.

7. How do you handle sensitive issues—questions which respondents may be reluctant to answer? First, recognize that people will often provide more information than you might expect, if the interview tone is straightforward and businesslike. Tampons and other feminine sanitary products, for example, are routinely researched and tested. So sensitivity is likely to be less of a problem than you think. But let us assume you are studying subjects you think people might be reluctant to discuss openly. Here are some ways to minimize the problem:

□ Ask the question within a group of less difficult questions. Then, if the interview is going along smoothly, respondents may be more willing to give an answer.

□ Use a general introduction indicating that the behavior asked about is not unusual—that many people have the problem or use the product.

□ Depersonalize the question or make it projective. Use phrases like ''other people'' or ''some people'' to make the responses easier.

□ Use exhibit cards with letters or numbers which correspond to the answers. This can be useful, since the respondent only has to mention the code letter or number, which seems to help maintain a certain sense of privacy.

8. After you've finished writing the questionnaire, read it out loud so you can be sure you've included all the instructions for the interviewers. This will help you uncover any cumbersome or unclear wording. Let others read the questionnaire, too. They can bring a fresh perspective and spot things you can't. Finally, be personally involved with pretests and monitoring whenever possible. You're sure to learn something.

14

How to Pick the
Right Kind of Question

□□□

Remember the parlor game (also a radio and TV show) called "Twenty Questions"? In this game, one team picked the name of a person, place, or thing, and another team had to guess the first team's choice by asking only questions that could be answered yes or no. More often than not the guessing team won—sometimes in many fewer than 20 questions.

In some ways, an interview is like a game of "Twenty Questions." As the researcher, you're trying to learn something from the respondent through a series of questions. And just as in the parlor game, the exact wording and sequence of the questions can be crucial to your being successful.

That's really what questionnaire writing is all about: putting the right questions together in the right order. Of course, you're not limited to 20 questions or yes/no answers. But if it's possible to guess almost anything with only 20 simple questions, it seems likely that many marketing research questionnaires are longer and more complicated than they need to be. Or maybe we're usually trying to find out too many things at once.

Questions are the tools of the survey researcher. And like any craftsman, a researcher ought to use his tools for the job they were designed to do. The tip-off to a questionnaire done by an inexperienced person is usually that the questions don't exactly fit. They aren't quite the right questions for obtaining the information that's being sought. That's where a knowledge of all the types of questions available comes in handy. The more choices you have, the better your chances of selecting the best question.

TYPES OF QUESTIONS

There are really only two types of questions: open-end and closed-end. You can let the respondent answer in his or her own words (open-end), or you can let the respondent select an answer from your words (closed-end).

It's a little more complicated than that, of course, because there are many variations on those two basic types. This chapter describes the kinds of questions most often used in survey research studies for business. If these questions were arranged into natural groupings, the categories would look like this:

I. *Open-end questions*
   A. Basic open-ends
   B. Follow-up questions
      1. Probing
      2. Clarifying

II. *Closed-end questions*
   A. Multiple-response questions
      1. Dichotomous
      2. Multiple response

   B. Scales
      1. Unipolar
      2. Bipolar
      3. Hedonic
      4. Buying intent
      5. Agree/disagree

   C. Ordering questions
      1. Preference
      2. Ranking

   D. Miscellaneous
      1. Semantic differential
      2. Constant sum

The following pages provide an overview of these types of questions.

Open-End Questions

EXAMPLES:

□ "What did you like most about the product?"
□ "Why do you say that?"

USES:

□ Collects information with a minimum of direction to the respondent.
□ Useful where the range of possible responses is very broad and can't be elicited with a closed-end question.
□ Gets the respondent's own words.

THINGS TO REMEMBER:

☐ Very expensive to ask, code, tabulate, and analyze. Should usually be used sparingly, only where it serves a specific purpose.
☐ Be sure the questions include written instructions to the interviewer to "probe" and "clarify" the responses.
☐ Interviewers must record responses absolutely verbatim.
☐ Results depend heavily on quality of interviewing and coding.

Probing Questions

EXAMPLES:

☐ "What else?"
☐ "What other things?"
☐ "What else did you like about the product?"

USES:

☐ A standard technique for getting a full, complete response to an open-end question. ("Clarifying" questions are another type of question used for the same purpose.)
☐ Should be used routinely by interviewers as a follow-up on open-end questions until the respondent has nothing more to add.

THINGS TO REMEMBER:

☐ Must be completely non-leading.
☐ *Never* ask about subjects not already volunteered by the respondent. For example, don't probe with: "What did you think about the texture?" if the respondent has not mentioned texture.

Clarifying Questions

EXAMPLES:

☐ "In what way was it too oily?"
☐ "What exactly do you mean when you say the bottle was difficult to handle?"
☐ "Can you explain what you mean by that?"

USES:

☐ This is a standard technique for getting a clearer explanation of a response to an open-end question. ("Probing" is another type of questioning used for the same purpose.)
☐ Should be used routinely by interviewers as a follow-up to any vague or general term used by the respondent.

THINGS TO REMEMBER:

□ Must be completely non-leading.
□ *Never* suggest a response or direction to the respondent when clarifying:

>CORRECT: "What didn't you like about the color?"
>INCORRECT: "Was the color too dark?"

□ Interviewers often aren't sure what words need to be clarified. It's helpful to provide a list, as part of the instructions for any open-end questions, of key words to be clarified.

Dichotomous Closed-End Questions

EXAMPLES:

□ "Do you do most of the grocery shopping in your household?"
>YES ( )
>NO   ( )
□ "Have you ever eaten Cheerios brand cereal?"
>YES ( )
>NO   ( )

USES:

□ One of the most basic types of questions.
□ Many types of information naturally split into two categories.
□ Easy to ask, answer (usually), and tabulate.

THINGS TO REMEMBER:

□ Be sure the question *really* has only two answers. Often "don't know" and/or "both" are legitimate responses, too.
□ If there are more than two possible responses, consider including them in the question, if it will make it easier for the respondent to answer. At the least, list the other answers on the questionnaire for the interviewer to use in recording, and include a "do not read" instruction next to those responses.

Multiple-Response/Closed-End Questions

EXAMPLES:

□ "Which of the following brands of cake mix have you purchased within the past 12 months?"
>BETTY CROCKER ( )
>DUNCAN HINES   ( )
>PILLSBURY   ( )

☐ "Was the product better than you expected, not as good as you expected, or about the same as you expected?"

BETTER THAN EXPECTED	( )
NOT AS GOOD AS EXPECTED	( )
ABOUT THE SAME AS EXPECTED	( )

USES:

☐ Should generally be used instead of an open-end question wherever all the responses can be determined beforehand.

☐ Easier and less expensive than open-end questions to ask and tabulate.

☐ Assures that all respondents will answer on the same dimension. More directed than open-end questions.

THINGS TO REMEMBER:

☐ Be sure it is really a closed-end question. You must be able to anticipate and list all possible responses.

☐ *Never* prelist categories of answers to an open-end question and ask interviewers to "code" responses into the correct categories. Interviewers are trained to record verbatim answers, not to code.

☐ Can be followed with an open-end question (such as "why") to obtain more detailed information.

Unipolar Scales

EXAMPLES:

☐ Which statement best describes the *color* of the french fry? Was the *color* of the french fry:

EXCELLENT	( )
VERY GOOD	( )
GOOD	( )
FAIR	( )
POOR	( )
VERY POOR	( )
EXTREMELY POOR	( )

☐ How interesting did you find this advertisement? Was it:

EXTREMELY INTERESTING	( )
VERY INTERESTING	( )
QUITE INTERESTING	( )
SOMEWHAT INTERESTING	( )
SLIGHTLY INTERESTING	( )
NOT AT ALL INTERESTING	( )

Uses:

☐ Best for measuring product attributes where there is no opposite end point that's equally desirable or undesirable. (Where there are equal end points, use a bipolar scale.)

☐ All well-constructed scales share the quality of being adaptable to statistical tables. Numerical values can be assigned to each point and statistical routines run (means, standard deviations, analysis of variance, and so on). This is not possible, of course, with non-scale data, such as open-end questions.

Things to Remember:

☐ Try to include another product as a benchmark or reference point for interpreting results.

☐ Can be more difficult to interpret than a bipolar scale. In the example above, is "quite interesting" good or bad? It's difficult to tell without using another product for comparison.

Bipolar Scales

Examples:

☐ Which of the following statements best describes the *color* of the bacon? Was the *color* of the bacon:

MUCH TOO DARK	( )
SOMEWHAT TOO DARK	( )
JUST ABOUT RIGHT	( )
SOMEWHAT TOO LIGHT	( )
MUCH TOO LIGHT	( )

☐ Which of the following statements best describes the *spice level* of the salami? Was the *spice level* of the salami:

MUCH TOO SPICY	( )
SOMEWHAT TOO SPICY	( )
SLIGHTLY TOO SPICY	( )
JUST ABOUT RIGHT	( )
SLIGHTLY TOO BLAND	( )
SOMEWHAT TOO BLAND	( )
MUCH TOO BLAND	( )

Uses:

☐ Usually the best way to evaluate attributes in product tests, because it gives some general direction for improvement.

☐ Easy and efficient to ask, answer, and tabulate.

THINGS TO REMEMBER:

- □ Often need a benchmark competitive product for comparison with test products.
- □ Usually better for comparing alternative products than for providing absolute measures.

EXAMPLE:

- □ Considering everything about this product, which statement best describes how much you like or dislike this product *overall?*

LIKE IT EXTREMELY	( )
LIKE IT STRONGLY	( )
LIKE IT VERY WELL	( )
LIKE IT FAIRLY WELL	( )
LIKE IT MODERATELY	( )
LIKE IT MILDLY	( )
NEITHER LIKE NOR DISLIKE IT	( )
DISLIKE IT MODERATELY	( )
DISLIKE IT INTENSELY	( )

USE:

- □ Good way to measure overall "liking" for a product—especially its physical attributes.
- □ Six positive points usually provide sensitivity to differences, even among similar products.

THINGS TO REMEMBER:

- □ Does not necessarily reflect buying intent. For example, a premium product may have a high hedonic score but, because of its price, generate lower buying intent.
- □ On a food product, hedonic and overall-taste scales usually mirror each other.

Buying-Intent Scales

EXAMPLE:

- □ Which of these statements best describes how interested you would be in buying this product?

I DEFINITELY WOULD BUY IT	( )
I PROBABLY WOULD BUY IT	( )

I MIGHT OR MIGHT NOT BUY IT   ( )
I PROBABLY WOULD *NOT* BUY IT   ( )
I DEFINITELY WOULD *NOT* BUY IT   ( )

USES:

□ Since sales are usually the end measure of a product's success, this type of question comes closest to evaluating sales potential in a survey setting.

THINGS TO REMEMBER:

□ Respondents need to be given enough information (price, color, size, and so on) about a product to form an intelligent opinion about buying.
□ Does not perfectly reflect sales. Responses must be discounted somewhat: not all respondents who say "definitely buy" will actually buy.

Agree/Disagree Scales

EXAMPLE:

□ For each statement, please indicate whether you:

AGREE STRONGLY   ( )
AGREE SOMEWHAT   ( )
AGREE SLIGHTLY   ( )
NEITHER AGREE NOR DISAGREE   ( )
DISAGREE SLIGHTLY   ( )
DISAGREE SOMEWHAT   ( )
DISAGREE STRONGLY   ( )

USE:

□ A common way to measure attitudes: get degree of agreement or disagreement with a series of statements.

THINGS TO REMEMBER:

□ Interpretation can be difficult. For example, disagreement with a negative statement doesn't necessarily mean agreement with the opposite positive statement.
□ Listed responses may not accurately reflect respondents' answers.
□ Statement wording is very critical.

Preference Questions

EXAMPLES:

□ "Overall, which of the two products you used do you prefer, Product 72 or Product 74—or do you like them both equally?"

□ "Which flavor do you prefer, mint or regular—or do you like them both equally?"

□ "Which of these colors do you like best for a paper towel in your kitchen?"

USES:

□ A logical way to collect information in most product tests.

□ Tends to direct respondent toward choosing one as better, regardless of magnitude of difference. Small, but perceptible, product differences can result in lopsided preferences.

THINGS TO REMEMBER:

□ It's usually best to offer a "no preference" choice, since there's nearly always a group that can't differentiate or doesn't care.

□ Preference data can be very volatile, since small perceived differences can result in large swings in preference.

□ If there are more than two items to choose among, ranking may be more useful information than preference.

Ranking Questions

EXAMPLE:

□ "Please rank these characteristics from most important to least important to you, with 1 being the most important and 7 being the least important."

USES:

□ An easy way to collect information on any group of items (brands, characteristics, and so on).

□ Relatively simple to ask and tabulate.

THINGS TO REMEMBER:

□ Does not reflect intervals between items ranked. (First may be far superior to second; second and third may be nearly equal to one another.)

□ Assumes respondent is aware and knowledgeable enough to rank all the items.

□ Can become tedious for the respondent, especially if done repeatedly and/or on a large number of items.

□ To prevent misunderstanding, tell respondents whether "1" represents their first choice or last.

Semantic-Differential Questions

EXAMPLES:

☐ Please place an X in the box that best represents your opinion of the First National Bank:

Friendly [| | | | | |] Unfriendly

Old-Fashioned [| | | | | |] Modern

USE:

☐ Used mostly for collecting attitude information, especially "image profiles" of products, brands, or companies.

THINGS TO REMEMBER:

☐ Contain few verbal "clues": points between ends are not labeled or numbered. This is theoretically desirable, but it can be unclear or confusing to some respondents if not clearly explained.

☐ Some scales have no clearly "preferred" end point, so analysis can be difficult. In the example above, which is better for a bank, being "old-fashioned" or being "modern"?

☐ Precise wording of end points is critical. They should be opposites.

Constant-Sum Questions

EXAMPLE:

☐ "Please divide these eleven chips among these six brands of cake mix, according to your preference for the brands."

USES:

☐ Provides a quantified measure of "preference" among several brands.

☐ A useful way to quantify attitude shift on a "before/after" basis, such as in advertising testing.

THINGS TO REMEMBER:

☐ It can be difficult to clearly describe the task to respondents.

☐ Be careful to specify whether you want respondents to allocate on basis of preference, expected next X purchases, or some other basis.

☐ Tabulation and analysis can be complex.

TIPS ON QUESTIONNAIRE WRITING

1. Avoid harsh, extreme end points on scales. Most people are reluctant to select harshly worded scale points, especially end points. This means the number of points on your scale is effectively reduced.

2. Use exhibit cards. Especially on closed-end questions with more than four or five alternatives, it becomes difficult for respondents to retain all the answers in their heads. Listing the answers so that the respondent can look at them makes the interview more comfortable and improves the quality of the information obtained.

3. Rotate the order in which multiple responses are read to respondents if there's no logical order. In a long list of items—brands, for example—there tends to be a bias toward the first and last items. So rotate the point at which the interviewer starts reading the list to eliminate such a bias.

4. Be aware of question order. Each question influences all the ones that follow. For example, you should generally ask about:

☐ Appearance before taste. It's difficult to evaluate the appearance after you've already eaten all the test product!

☐ Overall evaluations before specific attributes.

☐ Buying intent before specific attributes.

☐ Open-end "like" and "dislike" questions before scale questions or questions about product attributes.

5. Keep self-administered questionnaires absolutely as simple as possible. Try to avoid complicated question patterns, especially skips. It's also wise to assume respondents will read through the whole questionnaire before completing any of it. This makes unaided awareness questions, followed by an aided brand list, virtually impossible to ask on a self-administered questionnaire. In some cases, it may be possible to control jumping ahead by separating the questions into two completely different questionnaires.

QUESTIONNAIRE FORMAT GUIDELINES

The wording of questions in a questionnaire is the most important concern, but it's also important to lay out the questions in such a way that the interviewer can easily understand and handle them. Here are some tips on questionnaire format:

1. Include all parts of a question on one page whenever possible.

2. Don't split an answer list, with part on one page and part on another. The same applies to open-end questions. Don't put the question on one page and the space for the answer on the next.

3. Type all interviewer instructions on the questionnaire in capital letters. Anything *not* in capital letters should be read to the respondent. Always put a "READ LIST" or "DO *NOT* READ LIST" on every closed-end question.

4. If a "skip" instruction involves skipping to a different page, have the questionnaire laid out so that the interviewer begins at the top of the new page. If it's a skip that will be used a lot, it helps to print the key page on a different color. That way your instruction can say: "Skip to Q.10 *ON BLUE PAGE.*"

5. Another way to make the interviewer's job easier is to put a box around answers that will be referred to later in the questionnaire. For example, if you have a question that will be answered only by people who got a free sample, set up the sample question like this:

Did you receive a free sample of Gobbledy Gook in the mail?

YES $\boxed{1}$

NO   2

Then later on, when your instructions say: "REFER TO Q.3. IF RE-SPONDENT ANSWERED YES, CONTINUE. IF NOT, SKIP TO Q.19," the interviewer can quickly see where he or she is supposed to look.

6. Don't be afraid to use double-spacing or at least a space and a half when setting up questionnaires. By squeezing questions together you increase the chance of confusing the interviewer, and that creates errors.

7. Keep the materials an interviewer has to handle in a personal interview to a minimum. For instance, use exhibit cards only when needed. You usually don't need an exhibit card for short scales with only four or five choices. The interviewer can easily read the choices to the respondent. Exceptions to this are the buying-intent scale (it's usually a critical part of the study, and you want *no* chance of misunderstanding) and income questions.

8. Always have a space for the interviewer's name, the date of the interview, and the main city and state on the front of the questionnaire. If you're interviewing at more than one location in a city, have a way to identify which location the questionnaire came from.

9. Have a study title and date on each questionnaire. Make the title as specific as possible to avoid confusion with other similar projects. Also include the *type* of study: telephone, mall intercept, door-to-door, and so on. Here's an example:

PERSONAL PRODUCTS
TELEPHONE TRACKING STUDY
APRIL 1981

10. Be sure the project number appears on every separate document for the study (questionnaires, contact sheets, instructions, and so forth). This provides a clear reference point if materials get separated.

11. Use different-colored questionnaires to identify different parts of a study. This will make the instructions easy to follow, as in this example:

A. IF RESPONDENT HAS USED HI-C DRINK, GO TO <u>PINK</u> QUESTIONNAIRE.

B. IF RESPONDENT HAS HEARD OF, BUT <u>NOT</u> USED HI-C, GO
   TO <u>YELLOW</u> QUESTIONNAIRE.
C. IF RESPONDENT HAS NOT HEARD OF HI-C, GO TO <u>WHITE</u>
   DEMOGRAPHIC SECTION.

15

Pretesting:
Researching the Research

□□

After the questionnaire has been drafted and reviewed by someone other than the person who devised it, it is always a good idea to pretest it.

A pretest is a small sample of interviews (usually ten to twenty) conducted as a final check before you go ahead with a large-scale study. It's a way to double-check on possible problems and make corrections before you proceed with a study.

WHAT IS BEING TESTED?

A pretest is used primarily to evaluate the questionnaire and determine:

Does the questionnaire flow naturally and conversationally?
Are the questions clear and easy to understand?
Can the questionnaire format be followed by the interviewers?
Do respondents seem to understand what they're being asked? Can they answer the questions easily?

But in addition to testing the questionnaire, a pretest can also be used to:

Test the study methodology. If a large number of exhibits are being used, for example, a pretest may help iron out the best procedure for handling them smoothly.

Check on the sampling procedure. Can interviewers follow the sampling instructions? Is the procedure efficient? Does it have "holes" in it that become apparent in the field?

Establish a completion ratio for a telephone study. This can help verify the costs and timing before the full-scale study is begun. Since this is a key factor in estimating costs of a telephone study, a pretest can be especially useful for this purpose.

Measure an expected return rate for a mail study. Then you can decide if your planned sample size is too big, too small, or about right.

WAYS TO PRETEST

The most straightforward way to pretest, of course, is to simply conduct a few interviews and evaluate them. This is a standard pretest, and it's often done. But sometimes another approach works better. Here are two of these approaches:

Using the first day's work as a pretest.   This is commonly done in telephone studies. Plan to interview for a day, then pause a day to evaluate and make any changes before going ahead with the rest of the study. Centralized telephone studies allow this kind of flexibility. And assuming everything works well on the first day, those results can be counted toward the final quota and used in the total sample for the study. This approach allows you to get a running start on the project.

Using one city as a pretest.   If a study involves a large, elaborate setup of displays, for example, it may not be practical to arrange all this for only ten or twenty interviews. A compromise that still retains some of the value of a pretest is to conduct the interviews in one city first (assuming it's a multicity study), then evaluate that before going ahead with the interviewing in other cities. This gives you a chance to check how things are working while there's still time to make changes before the bulk of the interviewing is done. This is not as good as a standard, separate pretest, but often it's the only alternative that's feasible.

RULES OF THUMB

Guidelines for conducting a good pretest include:

□ Interview people as similar as possible to the actual respondents to be included in the study. Contacting experts or special authorities in the field doesn't tell you how the questionnaire will work with more typical respondents.

□ Use typical interviewers to conduct the pretest. Don't use only your best, most experienced interviewers for a pretest, or your results will not indicate how the larger-scale study is likely to go.

□ The researcher should be actively involved in the pretest. This may involve monitoring some pretest interviews or de-briefing the interviewers after the pretest and getting their reactions to the questionnaire. By the way, interviewers are an excellent source of feedback on how well a questionnaire is working. Don't miss a chance to get their reactions. The more involved the researcher is in the pretest, the more useful it is likely to be.

16

Guidelines for Interviewing

□□

Being an interviewer is, and always has been, a demanding job. But if you think people are difficult to interview today, consider this: in the 1920 Soviet census—taken only three years after the 1917 revolution—dozens of enumerators were beaten up, and 33 were murdered. That's hostility!

Fortunately, things are a little more friendly these days, but interviewing still demands skill. As in many fields, experience is the best way to develop interviewing skills. Nevertheless, there are some guidelines for interviewing that will help make you become a better inverviewer faster.

GENERAL ATTITUDE

Rapport is an important part of the interviewing relationship. To help establish rapport, and interviewer should be:

Friendly.   Be friendly and assertive enough to talk to people and get them to talk to you, but not so pushy that you frighten people. Don't become too chatty so that the interview gets too lengthy or wanders off the subject matter. Try to be the kind of person respondents will feel they can trust.

Patient and flexible.   Since you're interviewing respondents in their homes or places of business, you'll have to adjust yourself to the environment. You must wait patiently if the respondent has other interruptions, such as caring for a crying child, or whatever. Don't become angry or offended and ruin any good relationship you might have established.

Unbiased.   Always remember that a respondent's answers will be influenced by his or her perceptions of you. Respondents should feel relaxed, not that they must answer to please you. Sighing, changing your tone of voice, and other sounds you make can bias a respondent's answer.

Sometimes a new interviewer, in his or her enthusiasm to encourage and win a respondent, will make affirmative exclamations: "You're so right," "I certainly agree with you," and so on. Although the intention is to show interest, more often it results in biasing the respondent. If you concur with one attitude, the respondent later may be reluctant to express another. Remember that you are here to acquire information, not to color it.

ASKING QUESTIONS

Read all questions verbatim, clearly, and slowly so that the respondent is able to understand every word. Questions are carefully thought out, and particular wording is chosen for good reason, so read questions as written. This also ensures that each respondent is asked exactly the same questions.

Never interpret. If a respondent does not understand a question, *never* interpret, unless specifically instructed to do so. Reread the question, but don't try to interpret or explain it. If the respondent is still unable to answer, make a note of the circumstances in the margin and go on to the next question.

When doing in-person interviews, don't let respondents read the questionnaire over your shoulder. There may be parts of the questionnaire that he or she should not see, because they may bias other answers.

Be sure to follow all procedures and instructions. Much thought goes into the procedure for conducting an interview, and it is very important that each interview is conducted in the same way by all interviewers.

At the end of an interview, before you hang up on or leave the respondent, quickly look over the questionnaire to be sure all questions are answered and the answers are clear, meaningful, and recorded legibly. Be sure to thank the respondent for his or her cooperation at the end of the interview.

OPEN-END QUESTIONS

Open-end, subjective questions such as "Why do you think so?" or "Why do you say that?" give the respondents a chance to express themselves freely. Often answers given in a respondent's own words are not clear at first. For example, a respondent may say that the "appearance was nice." This really doesn't tell *what* he likes about the appearance.

In order to understand the full meaning of these answers, the interviewer must use some specific techniques:

1. Record the answers in the exact words used by the respondent to indicate accurately the respondent's feelings. Never summarize or paraphrase what is said. Record the answer in the respondent's own words. Include any slang or other expressions which reveal a respondent's true feelings. Record everything the respondent says verbatim.

2. Probing and clarifying. There are two basic techniques used in recording answers to subjective questions which assure that these answers are clear and meaningful. One technique is called "probing"; the other is called "clarifying."

Probing is the procedure used to get further information and obtain a complete response. It involves asking the respondents for information in addition to that already given.

Clarifying, as the name suggests, is a procedure used to get a clearer or more specific meaning of a respondent's answer that has been given. Respondents often speak in ambiguous terms. It is your responsibility to clarify the ambiguous statement and find out more precisely what the respondent meant. For example, if the respondent says, "It smells nice," the interviewer must find out what about the smell was nice.

3. Do not ask leading questions when clarifying and probing. The important thing is to clarify and probe without putting words in the respondent's mouth or inserting your ideas. Probing and clarifying questions must never suggest answers to the respondent. You are to ask only non-leading questions. Here are some examples of non-leading probing questions:

What else?
Is there anything else?
What else (repeat appropriate phrase from question)?

You must never lead the respondent by asking about subjects that he did not voluntarily mention. For example, never ask, 'What did you think about the color?'' if the respondent does not mention color. Some examples of non-leading clarifying questions are:

Can you explain what you mean by that?
Why do you say that?
What are your reasons for saying that?
In what way was it (repeat respondent's exact words)?

Never suggest how the respondent may feel. For example, if the respondent says the product has a poor appearance, never say, "Was the color too bright?"

17

Validation: Was the Research Done Right?

□□□

After the interviewing is completed comes an important quality control step: validation.

Validation involves recontacting a portion of the respondents and conducting a brief follow-up interview to confirm that the original interview was, in fact, conducted and was handled properly. Usually 10 percent of each interviewer's completed questionnaires are validated.

This step is designed to assure the quality of the data and evaluate the performance of the interviewers. The validation of each study should answer two basic questions:

1. Was the interview actually conducted?
2. Did the interviewer follow the correct procedures?

It is usually difficult to re-ask specific questions from the study. The time that has elapsed since the study may change some answers, and people's responses to attitude questions can vary from day to day. For these reasons, validation usually covers general areas, such as:

Method of contact—to be sure a personal interview wasn't actually handled on the telephone, for example.

Questions asked—to verify that no important questions were skipped, such as qualifying or demographic questions.

Respondent's familiarity with interviewer—to determine that the interviewer did not contact friends or acquaintances. A basic rule for interviewers on every study is never to interview anyone they know. It destroys objectivity.

General reactions to the interview—to check on the general quality of the contact.

SAMPLE VALIDATION QUESTIONS

The validation form for a study should be based on the objectives of the study. It should check on the most critical questions and qualifications—things that would seriously damage the results if not handled properly.

Ideally, a validation form should include both direct and follow-up questions. The follow-up questions are designed to help clarify a respondent's answer which does not agree with the expected or "correct" answer.

Here are some typical general validation questions and the follow-up questions that might be used:

Could you please describe the study and how you were interviewed? This is usually the first question asked during a validation interview. It should yield information about how, when, and where the interview was conducted.

If there were any irregularities in procedures, they are often uncovered here. The respondent may say, "This nice lady telephoned me and asked if I'd like to try some free samples of a new product." If the test was supposed to be a personally administered concept and product test, this shows there is obviously a problem. But the respondent may not give all the information you need, so some follow-up questions need to be included:

Where did the interview take place?

For a concept test: *Do you remember seeing any descriptions of products or advertisements for products?*

For a product test: *How did you obtain the product? Did you both prepare and taste the product?*

Did you know the interviewer? Interviewers are instructed not to interview their neighbors, relatives, or people they have interviewed in the last six months. If the respondent answer "yes" to this question, the validator should follow up to clarify with a question such as:

Have you been interviewed by the interviewer before?
How many times have you been interviewed by the interviewer?
How long ago were you interviewed by the interviewer?

These follow-up questions can be misleading unless you remember: if there is a placement questionnaire and later a callback questionnaire, it is possible that the respondent will say he or she has been interviewed by the same interviewer before. There are other types of tests where situations similar to this one are possible. Warn the validators of these possible situations.

Did you see any cards from which you selected answers? If there were exhibit cards used in the study, it is important that the respondent saw cards to select answers from and was not merely read the questions by the interviewer. It takes more time for the interviewer to shuffle these cards, but more consistent replies are gathered when each respondent selects an answer from a prepared list of choices.

Were you asked to give your total family income? This is an important validation question to ask, because sometimes interviewers shy away from asking demographic questions. It also fits nicely into the validation after a question asking the respondents if they saw cards from which they selected answers, since income categories are usually listed on cards.

In addition, income is usually one of the last questions asked on the questionnaire, and it is good to take a sample of questions from different parts of the questionnaire to make sure the interviewer went through the entire questionnaire with the respondent.

Do you have any suggestions that might be helpful in a similar study in the future? It's important for the respondents to feel that their opinions regarding the interview are important. This question serves the purpose of letting them know this. If the respondent was irritated by some procedure of the test, it is important that you know about it, and this is one way to find that out. This is usually the last question asked in the validation.

Qualifying questions are also validated. On most studies it is critical that only certain types of people have been included in the sample. Qualifications could include age ranges in which the respondent must fall and frequency of use of product types. In some cases, it's important to make sure that only homemakers or grocery shoppers were interviewed. Ask the respondent if he or she remembers the interviewer asking this question, or ask the respondent, "Is this the answer you gave the interviewer?"

REPORTING VALIDATION RESULTS

After the validation is completed, a validation report should be filled out to summarize the quality of work done by the interviewing service or research company. A typical validation report form is shown in Figure 10.

WHAT IF VALIDATION UNCOVERS PROBLEMS?

If the validation indicates that the interviewing was not conducted properly, the interviewing service or research company should immediately be notified and asked to explain the problem.

Often, apparent problems in validation are nothing more than communication problems between the validator and the respondent. These can be clarified once the validator understands exactly what was done in the field.

However, if any interviewer's work is called into question, the normal procedure is to validate additional questionnaires, up to 100 percent of an interviewer's questionnaires. In most cases, to be safe, if there is question

Figure 10. Sample validation report form.

Validation Report to _____

City _____

Test # _____

Date of Validation _____

Interviewer _____

Respondent had serious communication problems				
Respondent not homemaker				
Respondent knew interviewer				
Interviewer used incorrect means of contact				
Interviewer did not complete interview correctly				
Interviewer did not come to home correct number of times				
Respondent did not fill out forms				
Respondent not shown cards/exhibits/ posters				
Respondent did not receive product				
Respondent not shown demographic cards				
Income not asked				
Education not asked				
Respondent not qualified				
Respondent did not prepare product				
Respondent did not taste product				
Respondent had help in preparing product				
Falsification				
Comments about interviewer				
All correct				

about any of an interviewer's work, all of that interviewer's questionnaires will be excluded from the study.

Cheating or improperly done work is very rare in research—much rarer than people outside the business would expect. Systematic validation is one procedure that helps *prevent* these problems from occurring. If interviewers know their work will be validated, most will follow interviewing procedures carefully and conscientiously.

18

Coding: The First Step in Analysis

□□□

GIGO—"garbage in, garbage out"—is an axiom of the computer field. It means that the results which come out of the computer won't be any better than the information that goes in.

In research, what goes into "the system" is the individual answers of all the respondents in a study. What comes out is a set of nicely categorized and organized tables, ready to be analyzed and to be used to develop conclusions and recommendations.

The process of translating the actual individual responses into categories is called "coding." Coding determines whether the results are useful information—or simply garbage.

WHAT IS CODING?

Open-end questions are discussion-type questions that elicit such a wide range of responses that the possible answers are too varied and numerous to be prelisted on the questionnaire. An example of an open-end question is: "Why do you like pizzeria pizza better than frozen pizza?"

For these questions, a space is left on the questionnaire for the interviewer to record the answer *verbatim;* later the responses are categorized or "coded." Never attempt to have interviewers do on-the-spot coding of answers to open-end questions. Interviewers are not trained for this task and shouldn't try to make snap judgments about categorizing responses. And unless the answers are recorded verbatim, the respondents' actual answers are lost forever, and it's impossible to check the quality and accuracy of the coding.

The purpose of coding is to reduce all the varied responses to a question to a few types of answers that can be tabulated and then analyzed. On the sample question ("Why do you like pizzeria pizza better than frozen pizza?"), it would be important to know how many people mention crust, compared with the number who mention cheese. And of those who mention crust, what's the importance of crust thickness compared with crust texture? And of those who mention crust thickness, do more prefer thin crust or thick?

From this it should be obvious that coding open-end questions to provide different levels of detail—crust vs. cheese, thickness vs. texture, thick vs. thin—is very demanding. Reducing all the responses to a few important categories without losing the "feel" of the results in meaningless generalities is tricky business. Coding and code development are a very demanding step in the flow of a survey research project.

DEVELOPING CODES

The first step in coding is to determine the kinds of responses that have been given to a question. This is normally done by taking a sample from the completed questionnaires—25 percent is "typical"—and listing the answers and their frequency.

Next, the comments listed are organized into logical groupings. These groupings are determined by the frequency of the responses, as well as by the objectives of the test. For example, in a product test of two products with different spice levels, detailed codes would typically be developed to pick up spiciness comments.

Finally, these categories, or "codes," are assigned numbers corresponding to computer column numbers so the questionnaires can be tabulated after they're coded.

For example, in a product test on furniture polish, one of the variables tested might be gloss. All the comments relating to shine would be put into one grouping with a code for each detail mentioned about the shine.

The code might look like this:

Shine—Column 68

Furniture shined as soon as product applied	1
Shine lasted a long time	2
Shine was like glass/mirror	3
Shine was easy to get	4
Shine looked real	5
Shine wasn't greasy	6
Other miscellaneous shine comments	7

TIPS ON CODING

1. Code ideas, not words. This is critical. Coding is not simply coding the words people say but rather understanding the *meaning* of what is said.

2. Check prior studies for codes already developed. Don't reinvent the wheel. Most companies ask similar questions about their products or services from study to study. Using the same codes not only is easier but also makes the projects easier to compare.

3. Be sure to cover critical issues—even if no one mentions them. If a product test involved a change in the sweetness level of two cereals, for example, you'd want to be sure to include a sweetness code—maybe even several more detailed codes within a sweetness category—regardless of whether the prelisting of responses from the sample of questionnaires showed any mention of sweetness. Sometimes it's important to know for sure that not one person in a study gave a certain response. You can do this only if you include a code based on the study's objectives. Then you can say with certainty that no one mentioned it, because there was a code set up to catch any responses that occurred.

4. Review objectives of the study with those doing the coding before they start to work on a project. They should thoroughly understand what the study is about and what they should look for.

5. Read each respondent's answer completely before coding anything. That's the only way to be sure to get all ideas correctly and in the right context.

AN EXAMPLE

How the coding process works, as well as how demanding it can be, is best illustrated with a brief example taken from an actual test of a shampoo product (see Figure 11).

On this study there are two separate codes—columns 10–13 are for coding the "likes" and columns 14–17 are for coding the "dislikes." The column headings relate to different attributes of shampoo. If you were coding, you'd first look for the correct category heading, then look for the correct comment under that column and code that number in that column. There can be more than one number in a column, and not all columns will always have numbers in them.

For example, if, in the "likes" questions, a respondent said, "The shampoo was gentle and mild," you would look at column 10, since this is the "gentleness" column, and find the comment "gentle/mild/not harsh." You would then write an 11 next to the comment. If someone said, "I would rather have a shampoo with a creme rinse," you would look in column 16 for comparison to other shampoos and write in a 74 ("prefer one with a creme rinse") beside that response.

Figure 11(a). Sample codes for coding "likes" questions.

TEST NO. _____ Shampoo _____

QUESTION: Likes

COL. 10 Gentleness	COL. 11 Results on hair
11 Gentle/mild/not harsh	21 Good for hair/helps hair
12 Wouldn't strip hair of natural oils	22 Leaves hair manageable/no tangles/ no need for creme rinse
13 Doesn't cause/helps flyaway hair	23 Gives hair body
14 Wouldn't dry out hair	24 Mends split ends
15 Wouldn't make skin/scalp break out	25 Leaves hair not flyaway
16 Organic/natural	26 Leaves hair silky/smooth
17	27 Leaves hair soft
18	28 Leaves hair shiny
19	29 Hair looks/feels good/clean
10	20
1 −	2 −
1+ Other gentleness	2+ Other results on hair

Question:

COL. 12 Cleaning	COL. 13 Miscellaneous
31 Leaves no oil/keeps hair dry	41 Cheaper/economical/good price
32 It cleans well	42 Smells good/nice/clean
33 Lifts out oil/dirt/artificial conditioners	43. Hairdresser recommended
34 Don't have to scrub as much	44 Comes in different formulas
35 No need to wash as often/ keeps hair cleaner longer	45 Concentrated/use only a small amount
36 Doesn't leave a residue on scalp	46 Good for whole family (unspecific)
37 Good lather	47
38 Good for oily hair	48
39	49
30	40
3 −	4 − Other miscellaneous
3+ Other cleaning	4+ Don't know/nothing

Figure 11(b). Sample codes for coding "dislikes" questions.

TEST NO. _____Shampoo_____

QUESTION: Dislikes

COL. 14	Harshness	COL. 15	Cleaning
51 Too strong		61 Doesn't clean well	
52 Strips hair/takes too much oil out		62 Leaves a residue on scalp	
53 Dries hair out		63 Poor lather	
54 Skin reacts badly to it		64 Not good for oily hair	
55		65	
56		66	
57		67	
58		68	
59		69	
50		60	
5–		6–	
5+ Other harshness		6+ Other cleaning	

Question:

COL. 16 Comparison to others	COL. 17	Miscellaneous
71 Prefer herbal/organic shampoo	81 Don't like the name	
72 Prefer medicated/dandruff shampoo	82 Too expensive	
73 Same as other shampoos – doesn't work any differently	83 Not economical for long hair	
74 Prefer one with a creme rinse	84 Use what hairdresser recommends	
75 Prefer another brand (unspecified)	85	
76	86	
77	87	
78	88	
79	89	
70	80	
7–	8– Other miscellaneous	
7+ Other comparison to others	8+ Don't know what/disliked/nothing	

The three sample questionnaires from this study [Figures 12 *(a)–(c)*] illustrate how different responses to these two questions would be coded.

Figure 12(a). Sample questionnaire #1.

```
1.  What, if anything, did you particularly like about
    this shampoo?
                                                        2¹
        My hairdresser recommends it, so               42
    it must be good for your hair.    It               43
    smells good too.



2.  What, if anything, did you particularly dislike about
    this shampoo?
        It's too expensive.  It doesn't have
    a creme rinse, so you still have to buy that        74
    too.  It really doesn't work any better             73
    than other shampoos for the amount of               82
    money you pay for it.
```

Figure 12(b). Sample questionnaire #2.

```
1.  What, if anything, did you particularly like about
    this shampoo?
        there are different kinds for different         14
    types of hair.  I use the one for dry              27, 28
    hair.  It doesn't dry out my hair.                 44, 45
    It leaves it soft and shiny.
        It works so well + only have to
    use a little bit for each shampoo.                 (else)

2.  What, if anything, did you particularly dislike about
    this shampoo?
        Nothing.  I liked it.                            8+
```

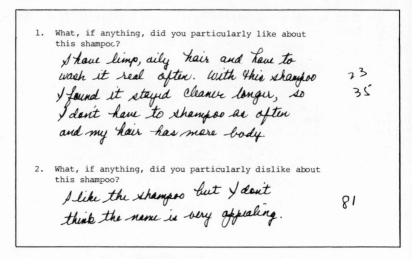

1. What, if anything, did you particularly like about
   this shampoo?

   I have limp, oily hair and have to wash it real often. With this shampoo I found it stayed cleaner longer, so I don't have to shampoo as often and my hair has more body.

   2 3
   3 5

2. What, if anything, did you particularly dislike about
   this shampoo?

   I like the shampoo but I don't think the name is very appealing.

   8 1

Figure 12(c). Sample questionnaire #3.

CHECK CODING

As the coding is being done, each coder's work should be periodically checked. When the coding is completed, the study is ready to be "check coded." Essentially, check coding is done by actually *recoding* 10 percent of each coder's work. The check coder's coding is then compared to the coder's coding to make sure the same judgments were made.

After the check coding is completed, the information on the questionnaires is ready to be entered into the computer for editing and tabulating.

19

How to Develop a Tabulation Plan

□□

Computers are fast, reliable, stupid, and rigid.
—Richard J. Harris
A Primer of Multivariate Statistics

Everyone would agree that the development of computers has helped create the marketing research field as we know it. It's difficult to imagine tabulating most of the studies done today, even simple ones, by hand.

At the same time, computers have the potential drawback that they can be *too* efficient. The author of the quotation at the top of this page continues: "An aspect of computers' 'behavior' which deserves more emphasis than is popularly accorded is their high reliability, that is, their ability to (indeed, their inability not to) perform any set of instructions programmed into the computer hundreds of thousands of times without once departing from those specifications in the slightest detail."

In other words, if you're not careful, the computer can easily bury you in paper. That's the purpose of a tabulation plan: to help you get all the paper (tables) you need, but nothing more.

PURPOSE OF A TABULATION PLAN

A tabulation plan should be designed to accomplish three purposes:

1. Provide data for the total sample.
2. Determine, through cross-tabulation, what differences exist among demographic or attitudinal subgroups within the sample.
3. Select any other complex types of analysis (statistical tests or multivariate techniques) that are needed to help interpret the results.

95

The specifications for tabulating the data from the study to accomplish these purposes are contained in the tabulation plan.

The tabulation plan for each study should focus on answering the question that is the key overall issue for that study. For example, different projects might attempt to answer any of these major questions:

> Are any of the proposed new products better than the current product?
> What are the levels of customer awareness and trial and repeat purchases in the test market?
> Which of the new product concepts have broadest appeal?
> Which package is most visible on the shelf?

Begin with this primary question, taken from the project proposal, and design the tabulation plan to answer it. All the tables run for the project should contribute to clarifying that key issue.

EDITING AND ERROR REPORTS

The first step after coding the questionnaires is to do editing and error reporting. This is a "quality control" step to make sure that no questionnaire has missing information. *Editing* means checking the questionnaires for completeness and accuracy. It can be done manually, by looking through every questionnaire, or it can be done by computer. It is generally more accurate and efficient to have the computer do this checking.

Edits are simply checks of logic conditions, usually described as "if," "and," "or," and "not" conditions. For example, suppose question 6 on a questionnaire were the following:

6. Have you purchased a new car within the past six months?

        YES ( )   CONTINUE
        NO   ( )   SKIP TO Q.8

An edit would be done of question 7 to determine that all the people who said "yes" to question 6, but only those who said "yes," answered question 7. If any who said "no" to question 6 mistakenly answered question 7 (instead of skipping to question 8), their answers to question 7 would be deleted as part of the editing process.

Most comprehensive computer tabulating programs can do this checking. Obviously, most questionnaires require so many edits that it would be very tedious to do them by hand. Instead, a set of editing instructions is fed into the computer with the questionnaire data. The computer checks every question on every questionnaire against the logic conditions and prints an *error report* of the questionnaires with errors. The error report is used to correct errors according to a set of guidelines set up for each question.

A final check should be run after all the corrections to make sure the data are "clean" (free of logic errors). If they are, you're ready to actually tabulate the results.

BANNERS AND STUBS

Figure 13 is an example of what a typical computer-generated table looks like. The banner is the series of column headings which run horizontally across the top of the table. In this case, the banner shows income, age, and household size. The terms "banner," "break," and "cross-tab" are used interchangeably.

The stubs are the responses to the question being tabulated and usually run vertically down the left side of the table. In this example, the stubs show the convenience-rating scale points of "excellent," "very good," and so on.

TYPICAL BREAKS

In the example, one- and two-person households rated the product as more convenient than larger households (47 percent vs. 19 percent excel-

Figure 13. Computer-generated results table.

TABLE 101
5 POINT RATING - CONVENIENCE

| | | *----INCOME----* | | *---AGE GROUP--* | | *---NUMBER IN--* | |
| | | | | | | *-----HOUSE----* | |
	TOTAL SAMPLE	LESS THAN $15000	$15000 OR MORE	34 OR YOUNGER	35 OR OLDER	ONE/ TWO	THREE OR MORE
TOTAL	424	139	285	133	291	267	157
NO ANSWER	-	-	-	-	-	-	-
ANY RESPONSE	424 100.0	139 100.0	285 100.0	133 100.0	291 100.0	267 100.0	157 100.0
EXCELLENT/VERY GOOD (NET)	242 57.1	77 55.4	165 57.9	76 57.1	166 57.0	163 61.0	79 50.3
EXCELLENT — 5	156 36.8	44 31.7	112 39.3	44 33.1	112 38.5	126 47.2	30 19.1
VERY GOOD — 4	86 20.3	33 23.7	53 18.6	32 24.1	54 18.6	37 13.9	49 31.2
GOOD — 3	33 7.8	19 13.7	14 4.9	13 9.8	20 6.9	18 6.7	15 9.6
FAIR — 2	87 20.5	25 18.0	62 21.8	21 15.8	66 22.7	45 16.9	42 26.8
POOR — 1	62 14.6	18 12.9	44 15.4	23 17.3	39 13.4	41 15.4	21 13.4
MEAN	3.44	3.43	3.45	3.40	3.46	3.61	3.16
STD DEVIATION	1.51	1.42	1.55	1.51	1.51	1.57	1.37

lent). This is important, because the product tested was a new portion-control package targeted at smaller households. But there weren't any significant differences between the ratings on the two income breaks or the two age breaks. *The primary purpose of cross-tabs is to provide a check of whether there are differences in responses among subgroups within the sample.* If there are, then additional tables can be run and a more detailed analysis made.

Some of the most typical breaks for cross-tab purposes are:

Demographics—by age, sex, income, education, household size, presence of children in the household, and employment of the female outside the home.

Geography—by city or region.

Usage—by awareness or usage of a brand or product category.

These standard breaks are common to all types of studies. On product or concept tests, it's often helpful to run two additional types of breaks:

Purchase intent—to determine how and why those who express interest are different.

Order of product use—to check whether the order of use affected product evaluations. When everything is rotated properly, this bias should be eliminated or, at the least, should affect all products equally. But it's always a good idea to check.

PERCENTAGING AND BASES

The tabulation plan must specify how the data are to be percentaged. The plan's specifications should be consistent with the way the project will be analyzed. The alternative is for the person preparing the report to spend hours of tedious repercentaging with a hand calculator.

Percentaging can be done vertically, horizontally, or both. Vertical percentaging is the most common and normally the most helpful to the analysis. It quickly shows whether there are different responses to each question among the cross-tab groups.

Bases need to be specified for each question, too. Most questions are based (percentaged) on only the number of respondents who were asked the question. That usually makes the most sense for the analysis.

Should "don't know" responses and "no answers" (respondents who erroneously fail to answer a question) be included in the bases for percentaging? "Don't knows" should usually be included, since "don't know" represents as legitimate a response to most questions as "yes" or "no."

Knowing what proportion of people "don't know" will usually add to your understanding of the results. That's not true of "no answers." These most often represent interviewing errors—a question was accidentally skipped. The number of these people is shown on the table, but it adds nothing to the analysis of the study results to include them in the base. So "no answers" should usually be excluded from the base used for percentaging.

Some questions need special bases. For example, evaluation of a "why" question following a preference question should be based only on the number of respondents preferring each product. And evaluation of a "how often" question following a product purchase question should be based only on the number of people buying each product.

Net counts can add considerably to the analysis of open-end questions. A "net" is simply the number of people making one or more comments in a broad response category. For example, a respondent might say he thought a product was "easy to hold and easy to use." That person would be counted for both of those detailed comments in the following example, but would be included only once in the net count of "convenience" comments:

Convenience (net)	31%
Easy to hold	25
Easy to use	17
More convenient size	14
Other convenience comments	5

In other words, "nets" count people rather than the total number of comments. In this example, 31 percent of the respondents made some reference to convenience, although it's clear many made more than one comment about convenience.

The final check on the tabulation plan is to examine the sample size in each of the proposed banner points or breaks. If only a handful of respondents turn out to fall into one of the categories included in the banner, the break will be useless for analysis. This is checked through a report called an "80-column dump" or "marginals." This is simply a listing of the distribution of answers to every question on the questionnaire.

Finally, before the tables are run, all simple statistical functions to be run on some or all tables should be specified. These include:

Mean
Median
Standard deviation
Standard error
Analysis of variance (ANOVA)
T-test
Chi square test

Planning these ahead of time will avoid going back and running extra tables later. It's usually less costly if they're run at the same time as the rest of the data.

A bit of philosophy and a word of warning: there is nearly always a temptation in working up a tabulation plan to want to run "everything by everything"—to cross-tab every question by the responses to nearly every other question. The computer makes this feasible, and it often seems like a good precaution "just in case." *This is nearly always the wrong approach.* It wastes money, of course; but more important, it buries you under a pile of tables that becomes an obstacle to thorough analysis. It's usually impossible to get an overview and understanding of the results when you're slogging through hundreds of computer tables.

As an alternative, try this approach:

1. Run the questionnaire with one banner first, to get the total and a few basic cross-tab breaks. Even better yet, do your first analysis from the totals shown on the marginals. Chances are that you can get most of what you need from that, even before you run the first table.

2. If you think other breaks might be useful, select one or two questions for which you'd expect the breaks to make the greatest difference, and run them first as a sort of pretest. If you see no differences on those questions, you can probably save yourself the trouble and expense of running and analyzing the whole study by those breaks. On the other hand, if you do see differences on those questions, go ahead and run more tables, since you now know the extra tables are likely to be useful to your analysis.

20

Writing Research Reports That Get Read

The results of marketing research are often intangible. A decision (maybe a very important one) usually gets made, but afterward there's often little physical evidence of all the time, money, and effort that went into the project. That's why reports are so important: they're often the only documentation of a study. So it's important that they be done well.

Of course, every company and each person writes a little differently. There's no one right style for a report. But you need *some* style, some viewpoint to give your writing consistency. This chapter discusses some ideas to help you write better research reports.

GUIDELINES

In the research business, the written report of the findings of a project is extremely important. It has immediate use in making decisions, and it also serves as a historical record. The purpose of these guidelines is to help you improve your reports and to make the job easier. Use these ideas as a checklist—adopt the ones that work for you and discard the rest. These are the major ideas about preparing reports:

1. A report should interpret and explain the study's results, not just summarize them. Don't be afraid to draw conclusions from the findings. That's what the user of the research expects from you.

2. Think of your audience for the report as product managers, not researchers. This will help avoid making it overly detailed and technical.

3. Think of the report as having three sections:

□ Report digest—a complete description of the study and its findings in two or three pages.

□ Detailed findings—which discuss the results at a level of detail that can be understood by a product manager.

□ Tabulations—although not usually physically a part of the report, think of this as the place the researcher can go for details, if he wants them.

4. Use underlined "sentence conclusions" to summarize findings. But make sure they are conclusions, not just restatements of facts obvious to the reader.

5. Break up the report format with different kinds of exhibits. A report full of nothing but tables looks dull and doesn't invite readership.

6. Group related subjects in the report, regardless of where they appeared in the questionnaire.

7. Preparing a report involves three steps:

□ Understanding—the results and what they mean.

□ Organizing—the findings by subject and giving them a flow that leads naturally to your conclusions.

□ Writing—the copy to explain and clarify the results.

PHILOSOPHY BEHIND REPORT WRITING

It's important to think about the purpose of a report and your role in writing it. Here are some guidelines.

A report should interpret and explain the study's results, not just summarize them. Too many reports just summarize in words what is clear from looking at data from the project: "Overall, 73 percent of the homemakers in the test prefer product A." That doesn't help much in understanding the results. You should go a step further and draw a conclusion about what the results mean: "Most consumers prefer product A." You conducted some research among a sample of people. They prefer product A, so you assume most people in the population do, too.

Don't be afraid to draw conclusions. Researchers often tend to be overly concerned about reaching conclusions. It's true we shouldn't draw conclusions on subjects we know little about, but we usually carry this too far. Remember:

□ If you're writing the report, you probably know more about the project than anyone else. That puts you in the best position to know what the results mean.

□ The user of the research is expecting you to use your judgment, not just restate the facts.

Your judgment is probably better than you think, and you're being paid for your interpretation. So don't be too modest about your ability to give your analysis of what the results mean.

☐ A report should be complete enough to stand by itself. It shouldn't require the tabulations or the proposal to clarify what you did or what you learned. For many of the people who read the report, it will be their only exposure to the project—or they will have forgotten whatever they heard before. So it should be a complete story all by itself.

☐ Think of your audience as product managers, not researchers. In planning studies, we deal most often with other marketing researchers, but projects are ultimately conducted for managers, who will use the results to make decisions. Direct the tone and content of your report to them. If we write to other researchers, we tend to be overly technical and use too much research jargon.

☐ Go back to the proposal to help organize your thinking about the report. By the time you get to the end of a project, you may be too immersed in the details of the field work or tabulating to remember precisely why the project was done in the first place. Read the proposal over to get the project back in perspective.

☐ Focus the report on the basic "purpose" of the project. All the findings and interpretations should be organized to deal with that purpose. If the purpose, as stated in the proposal, was to determine whether the revised version would replace the current product, all the findings should focus on that issue. Other results should be put either in a separate section of the report or in the appendix. The purpose of the report—*not* the order of the questionnaire—should determine the organization and focus of the report.

☐ Make sure you understand the results before you write about them. By the time you finish reviewing the data—and before you start writing your interpretation of the results—you should have a grasp of the findings. You should understand in an overall sense what the results mean and be able to verbally describe them to someone in a few simple sentences. If you don't understand the results, you'll tend to just restate facts when you start to write. If you have a grasp of the results, you'll do a better job of explaining and interpreting instead of restating.

☐ Think of the report as having three sections: the report digest, the detailed findings, and the tabulations. This viewpoint will help you decide what to include in each section.

Report digest. Think of this as something the president of the client company can read in five minutes and understand why the project was conducted, what was done, and what was learned from the study. Your tendency will almost certainly be to make this section too long.

Detailed findings. View this section as being written for the product manager or the person directly responsible for the product being studied. Include the things he'd want to know and the amount of detail he'd want, and use a tone he can understand. Remember, he has only a general knowledge of marketing research and even less of statistics.

Tabulations. The tabs from the project, which usually are bound separately, are for the researcher. If he wants lots of detail, he can find it here. While the tabs aren't physically part of the report, viewing them as the part of the report intended for the researcher helps you realize that every little bit of detail doesn't need to be in the written report to be available for the client researcher to look up.

The relationship of report sections to your target readers is summarized in Figure 14.

REPORT MECHANICS

Here are some guidelines on how the report should look and how it should be organized.

The appearance of a report is very important. If it looks interesting, people will want to read it. If it looks dull, they won't. If it looks well organized, they'll assume your thinking is organized. A disorganized, rambling report will often be assumed to reflect sloppy thinking. Finally, a neat, attractive-looking report says that you are a professional. No one likes to deal with slobs.

Make sure the title on the report is complete and descriptive. Something like ''Cheerios Research'' isn't very good, since General Mills has a warehouse of research that would come under this title. Generally, make the title a description of the subject investigated, such as ''Cheerios Nutritional Advertising.'' Use simple terminology; avoid jargon or technical words. Do not include the research technique (taste test or in-home test, for example) in the title unless it helps clarify a subject on which many types of research have been conducted.

Figure 14. Relationships between report sections and intended readers.

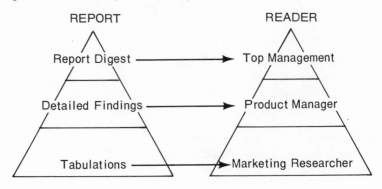

Keep the report digest brief—usually it should have no more than two or three pages. It's a "digest," so it should be complete but not detailed. The absence of detail in the report digest is the key to making it readable.

The report digest usually contains three sections:

1. Background and purpose. This should be only a paragraph or two long—usually only about half a page. It should contain brief statements of the external and internal conditions leading to the need for the project and the project's purpose (that is, the decisions to be made on the basis of the findings).

2. Research procedure. This section typically includes a description of data collection methods (in very general terms) and a sentence referring the reader to the appendix or tabulations for details. This should usually be no longer than a half page. There is a tendency to make this section too long and go into more detail than most of the readers will care about. If you had an elaborate sample and you're obliged to tell about it, put it in the appendix and only mention in the digest where the details can be found.

3. Major conclusions. This section usually consists of a couple of pages (rarely more) that summarize the principal conclusions, interpret the results in terms of the study's purpose, and make recommendations or suggest action, if that's appropriate.

Remember: write the report digest so the company president can read it in five minutes and understand all he needs to know about the study. Read it over from this perspective when you've finished writing it to see if the amount of detail seems appropriate. When in doubt, leave things out of the digest.

Consider printing the report digest on colored paper to help set it apart from the rest of the report.

Use "sentence conclusions" (such as this sentence) to summarize findings. These should be interpretive conclusions about the information reported in the text and/or illustrated in the exhibits. Such a sentence may summarize findings from several exhibits. Underline these points to make them stand out.

"Sentence conclusions" should not be simply restatements of facts obvious to the reader. Say to yourself, "What can I conclude from this fact?" Then write the answer as the sentence conclusion. Interpret and explain; don't just restate the exhibit in sentence form.

Break up the report format with different kinds of exhibits. A report full of nothing but numerical tables looks dull. Try to use bar charts, pie charts, graphs, and other types of exhibits that will provide a change of pace from tables.

In thinking about your report's format, remember there are three kinds of people who will be reading it:

□ "Number" people—who are best communicated with by numbers.
□ "Word" people—who best understand ideas expressed in words rather than in numbers.
□ "Picture" people—who need pictures (charts or graphs) to help them understand the findings.

A finding reported as in Figure 15 communicates with each of these types of readers, since it describes the finding in numbers, words, and pictures. Some readers will understand the pie chart, others will like the numbers, and others will best understand the sentence conclusion.

Group related subjects in the report, regardless of where they appeared in the questionnaire. Don't be tied to the questionnaire order in the report. That order was developed to produce a flow that would make the questions easy for the interviewer to ask. The reader of your report usually is not interested in your questionnaire sequence. He wants to relate associated pieces of information in order to come to a conclusion about a subject so that he can make a decision. If possible, go back to the proposal for the

Figure 15. Report exhibit geared to number, word, and picture people.

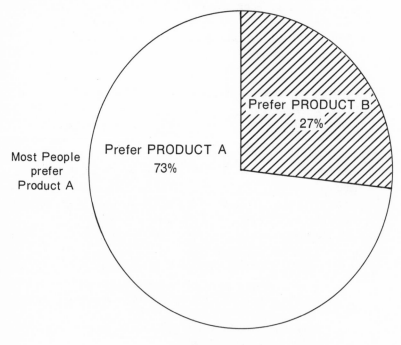

(No. of respondents: 302)

project to get an outline of the major issues or subjects dealt with in the study.

Try to simplify exhibits rather than pack in every fact you can think of. In particular, avoid throwing in technical details about how the results were obtained. Usually they don't add to the findings (they may even confuse them). Your readers assume that you conducted the study in a proper and professional way, so you don't need to keep trying to prove it with little tidbits or technical detail.

To illustrate with an example, Figure 16 contains all the information that generally needs to be in an exhibit.

Some comments:

☐ Use the word "exhibit" in preference to "table." It's broader, and your exhibits shouldn't all be tables.

☐ Give each exhibit a simple title that describes its content.

☐ Generally show only percentages—don't also show the number of people giving each response. If anyone really cares (which is unlikely), he can figure out the number giving a response from the base. If the base is very small, then show the number only, not the percentages. There is almost never a need to show both.

Figure 16. Typical report exhibit of test product preference.

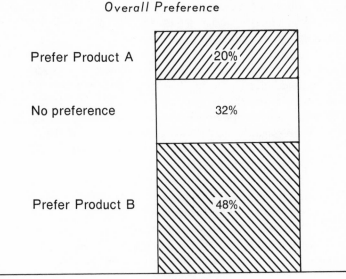

(No. of respondents: 239)

☐ Indicate the base at the bottom of the exhibit, not the top. It's a minor point of reference, not a finding, so put it down out of the way. ("Number of respondents" is a little more descriptive than "base," but that's not a big issue.)

Put copy and the exhibits that illustrate it on the same page, if at all possible. The reader usually has to be able to see the exhibit to fully understand the copy. Use the facing page, if necessary, to get copy near an unusually large exhibit. As a last resort go to the previous page. For an exhibit to be effective in illustrating a finding, the copy and the exhibit need to be physically located together.

STEPS IN WRITING A REPORT

It's easier to describe a report format than to prescribe how to write what's to be put in that format. Nevertheless, these are some suggestions on how to go about organizing and writing a report.

Preparing a report involves three steps: understanding, organizing, and writing. Notice that the process *ends,* rather than begins, with the writing step. You first have to develop an understanding of the results. You need to have an overall grasp of the findings and what they mean.

One way to do this is to go through the data, pulling out the key findings and making up pencil tables of them. This accomplishes two things: (1) it serves as a device to help you understand what's in the tabulations, and (2) it gives you the tables to serve as raw material for the report. Once you finish going through the tabulations in this way, you'll usually have a pretty good understanding of what's there.

Next, organize what you've got into a more logical sequence: (1) group related subjects together, and (2) put the subjects in an order that flows naturally in developing the conclusions that are important.

At this point you should have a good idea of what the report will say, even though you haven't written a word yet. Now start writing. Begin with the sentence conclusions, then add copy to explain or clarify the conclusions. Remember: these are "conclusions," not just restatements of facts.

Write the "report digest" last. You can't write "major conclusions" until you know what the conclusions are. You'll find it easier to be concise in the digest if you've worked through all the details first. At that point it's much easier to tell what's "major" and what's not.

Learn to dictate. As you spend more of your time writing reports, this can become a big timesaver. Go through the "understanding" and "organizing" steps described above, then dictate the copy to go with the exhibits.

Dictation not only saves time, it also helps you be more conversational in your writing, which we all need. There is something about writing a report that makes us tend to sound very serious, official—and usually dull.

At the least, try to learn to dictate rough copy for reports. It's a great way to get some ideas down on paper, so you can edit and revise them—which is usually easier than composing them in the first place. Dictation is easier than you think. The main obstacle is feeling self-conscious, but that's quickly overcome. If you can talk, you can dictate.

Develop your own routine for writing reports. This is probably the most personal thing we do, and no two people will do it just alike. Work on an approach to putting together reports that's comfortable for you, then stick with that routine. But have some kind of routine.

Use an appendix. The appendix is the greatest thing ever invented for report writing. It provides a place to put all those things that don't have a home anywhere else.

Here's a rule of thumb: *use the appendix for things that you want to save as part of the project's history but that have no direct impact on the findings.* Here are some examples of materials that typically belong in the appendix:

Data used to make projections or estimates
Lists of competitors and their products or prices
Product descriptions and illustrations
Packages or promotional materials
Ad samples or storyboards
Explanations of complex research procedures or techniques
Tables on respondent characteristics (age, income, and so on)
Project exhibits

These kinds of materials add value and credibility to the report, but they only obscure a straightforward statement of the findings. So put them in the appendix.

Part IV

Solving Specific Marketing Problems

□□

21

Product Testing

Every good cook is an expert on product testing: tasting the soup, adding a little more salt, tasting again, and so on until it's just right. That process—test, revise, and test again—is the same one that multibillion-dollar corporations use to develop and improve their products.

Product testing is one of the most basic and most widely used types of marketing research. It deals with the very basic question, "How does this product compare with that one?" The best way to answer that question is to let the customers who will use the product in the marketplace give their opinions. Furthermore, the application of product testing is clear, since the results usually lead directly to a management decision.

Testing is particularly important in the area of frequently purchased consumer products (food, health and beauty aids, household products, and so on), where improvements in physical products can quickly change market shares in a product category. But product testing also is gaining use for industrial products, office supplies, and even medical products. In the hospital market, for example, it is important to know if your tape product is an improvement under actual use conditions before you try to market it.

THE ROLE OF PRODUCT TESTING

Product testing is usually done to answer such questions as:

Which product is better?
How much better is it—just a little or a lot?
Why is one product better than the other?

Testing is most often done in the early stages of a product's development, either before the introduction of a new product or to get direction for the development of an improved product. Typically several product tests

113

are done over a period of time while a product is being revised or redesigned, then the product is moved into test market after product testing indicates it has been optimized.

How is performance in a product test measured? Usually in one of three ways:

1. Testing against a standard, either a current product or a competitive product. This is the comparison most often made for an improved product or a product being developed for introduction into a market with a clear leader.

2. Horseracing alternatives. When several alternatives are being developed by a company, it is common to test the alternatives against one another to see which has the greatest consumer acceptance.

3. Testing versus a historical standard. Occasionally testing is done against the performance, on a set of standard scales, of a product which has been successful on the market, but which may not be directly involved in the test. This is an unusual type of standard, however, since the costs required to interview the large samples needed for comparability, together with the execution problems of conducting exactly comparable tests over time, make this testing often impractical.

TYPES OF QUESTIONS

Three types of questions, each of which has a specific role, are most often used in product testing:

Closed-end questions and scales.   These are the most common questions in product testing, because they give the clearest direction for product revisions and are less dependent on the other products which happen to be included in the test. An example would be, "How do you feel about the seasoning level in this product? Would you say it is:

> MUCH TOO SPICY?
> SLIGHTLY TOO SPICY?
> JUST ABOUT RIGHT?
> SLIGHTLY TOO BLAND?
> MUCH TOO BLAND?''

This type of bipolar scale is especially helpful for giving direction to product development. It not only tells whether the seasoning is "right" or not, but also indicates the direction that should be taken (more or less spice) to make it better.

Preference questions.   These questions, which probe either overall preferences or preferences with respect to specific attributes, are used to obtain direct comparisons between products. While this is a simple, easy-to-understand method, its weakness is that it gives no indication of the magnitude of difference between two products. If A is preferred over B, for example, was A great and B awful, was A just the lesser of two evils, or were both good, with A being just relatively better? Preference measures depend heavily on the products being tested, so they are difficult to compare from one test to another.

Open-end questions.   Open-end questions are useful for getting at the "why" behind closed-end or preference questions. "Why do you say that?" can be a useful follow-up to a preference question. Since open-end questions can be difficult to code and interpret precisely, however, their use in product testing is generally limited to providing reasons behind responses to scalar questions.

EXPERT PANELS

Companies sometimes use expert panels, most often personnel from R&D laboratories, to determine whether there is a perceived difference among products. Unless the experts can detect a significant difference between the test samples, the product should not be evaluated by consumers.

However, because their expertise makes them very unrepresentative of the population, experts should be used only to determine whether differences exist. They should *not* be used to evaluate which of two products is better or even whether either of the products is acceptable to consumers.

PRESCREENED CENTRAL-LOCATION AND IN-HOME TESTS

These are the two interviewing methods that can be used for product testing. Each has strengths and weaknesses that make it acceptable in some cases and inappropriate in others.

Prescreened central-location studies.   All things being equal, this is the most efficient kind of testing, since the respondents come to the interviewers, instead of interviewers going to the respondents. Consumers are recruited for this type of test by telephone and invited to the research location, such as a church or community building, where they take part in a test, usually by eating samples of two or three products and answering questions about each one. The efficiency of administering this type of test makes it a very low-cost alternative. The drawback to this approach is that the products are prepared not by the consumers but rather by home economists or trained kitchen personnel. In addition, this testing usually only provides evaluation by homemakers and does not include the opinions of their family members. For these reasons, it is appropriate primarily as an early-screening device, when several alternatives that present similar preparation problems are being considered. For products that involve any preparation or in-home use problems—cake mix and furniture polish are examples—some type of in-home test should be done before a final decision is made.

In-home tests. With this method, consumers are given one or more products for actual use in their homes. This testing is most often used where the product must be either handled or actually used by the consumers or where reactions of all family members to the product are important. Products are usually placed "blind," that is, in blank packages showing only the *type* of product contained. The packages are coded with a letter or number so that they can be identified by the interviewer and the respondent can use them in the right order if more than one product is being tested. But manufacturer and brand name are not shown on the package.

Cutting in-home test costs. In-home testing has the advantage of being the most realistic type of testing, since consumers use products in nearly the same way they would if they bought the products in the marketplace. Because of the complexity of making placements and callback interviews in-home, however, it is also the most expensive form of product testing. To help control the cost of in-home tests where this method is the only one practical, consider these alternatives:

Use intercept interviews, instead of door-to-door contacts, for screening consumers and placing the product. Interviewing consumers in shopping malls, for example, then giving them the product to take home and use, accomplishes the placement for an in-home test without the inefficient, high-cost step of sending interviewers door to door.

Use the telephone for making callbacks, instead of conducting in-home interviews. Test participants can be given a questionnaire or "diary" on which to record their reactions to the product as they use it. Then interviewers can telephone after the usage period to obtain the information from the questionnaire and ask any additional questions. Since personal callbacks can be difficult to arrange and usually involve considerable traveling time by interviewers, this step often saves substantial time and money.

Within the central-location or in-home testing format, there are several ways products can be evaluated, ranging from monadic testing to multiple product test designs.

Monadic Testing

This type of testing simply involves giving consumers one product to use and evaluate, with no other product—except their memory of similar products they have used—for comparison. More than one product can be evaluated in a monadic test, of course, by having different samples of respondents test products simultaneously. Comparative results also can be obtained by having consumers compare the test product with their usual brand, as best they remember it.

The real world is monadic, so this is the most realistic kind of test. In real life, consumers usually try a new product, evaluate it against their recollection of the product they now use, then decide whether they will buy the new product the next time.

But since different consumers test each product, possible differences in respondents must be minimized through large sample sizes. As a result, monadic testing is very costly. A large share of the interviewing costs on any product test is in recruiting respondents, so it is inefficient to use a respondent to test only one product.

Overall, monadic testing is the ''safest'' way to test, but it is too costly to be used regularly by most companies.

Paired Comparisons

Paired-comparison tests are common, since most often a new product is being evaluated against either a company's current product or a competitor's product.

Paired comparisons can be conducted either side-by-side, where consumers are given more than one product to use at the same time, or sequentially, where consumers are given first one product, then another.

Direct, side-by-side comparisons are not widely used, since they may highlight differences that wouldn't be noticed in the marketplace. In reality, of course, consumers almost never use products side-by-side.

The *sequential* product test blends many of the advantages of the paired-comparison test and the monadic test. Respondents are usually given one product, as in a monadic test, then interviewed about reactions to it. Then they are given another product and interviewed about their reactions to it. Finally, test participants usually are asked about their comparative reactions to the two products—which they liked best and why. Sequential product testing is economical, since it yields both single-product and paired-comparison information from the same group of respondents. This method also minimizes sample differences, since all respondents use both products, and there is no problem of matching two parallel testing groups.

At the same time, even sequential monadic testing has some drawbacks. Products may be used in more rapid succession than they would be normally, which may bring out differences that wouldn't be important in the marketplace.

If several products are involved, the paired-comparison procedure gets unwieldy if all the products are tested in pairs versus all others. Finally, there can be an order effect, if very good products are tested against very poor ones. The second product can seem unusually good or bad, compared with the product used first. Or there can be "wear-out"—if highly spiced products are tested, for example—which makes testing more than one product difficult.

Despite these problems, however, sequential product testing usually offers the best combination of clear design and low cost, which is why it is the most widely used form of product testing.

Repeat Pairs

This is a testing technique that helps get at the "true preference" between two products. It helps avoid the dilemma of the 50/50 preference, where you wonder whether the market is truly segmented into two groups or whether consumers are just expressing random choices between the test products.

The test measures two things: Can consumers truly differentiate between the two products? To the extent they can distinguish between the products, which is preferred? The technique is based on the assumption that consumers should be able to pick the same product twice from a pair if they have a "true preference" for one of the products. If, however, the preferences they express are merely random choices rather than true ones, many are likely to make inconsistent choices—that is, pick one product the first time and the other product from the second pair.

Repeat-pairs testing can be conducted by using either in-home or central-location procedures, although central-location techniques work best. The procedure is simple. Two side-by-side paired-comparison tests are carried out, one following the other, on the same sample of respondents. First, they are given two code-labeled products and asked which they prefer. Then they are given another pair of differently coded products—which are actually the same two products again—and asked which they prefer. In both cases, they are required to express a preference.

If consumers in fact have no "true preference" between the products—that is, if all choices are merely random—the results will reflect this. On a purely random basis, one-fourth of the respondents would pick one product twice in a row by chance, an equal proportion would pick the other one twice by chance, and half the respondents would choose one product from the first pair and another from the second. In this respect, the distribution of random choices is the same as the odds of flipping a coin heads or tails twice in a row.

The "true preference" for each brand is measured by the extent to which the proportion of consumers expressing consistent preferences is greater than the 25 percent that would be expected to randomly choose each product twice in a row.

This technique is particularly appropriate for testing cost-improved products, where the goal often is to demonstrate that consumers *cannot* differentiate between the current and the lower-cost formulation. In this situation, being able to separate the "guessers" from the respondents with true preferences between the two products is important.

Because four products must be included in the test, the repeat-pairs technique can get unwieldy for in-home testing. It can also cause problems if products "wear out" fast. It is doubtful that the technique would work on pickles or spicy pizza, for example. Also, the procedure does not handle large numbers of products efficiently, since they must always be tested in pairs.

Nevertheless, where products are very similar and the extent of true "no preference" evaluations is important, repeat-pairs testing is the only technique that can produce reliable results.

BIB DESIGNS

Testing even a few products in pairs can quickly become unwieldy. Among as few as six products, for example, even if order is ignored, there are still 15 different pairs which would have to be tested against each other. BIB designs make this testing feasible and efficient.

"BIB" stands for "balanced incomplete block." In this type of design, a large number of products can be tested together, two or three at a time. The order of use, as well as the products that are tested together, are rotated in a balanced way. However, every product is *not* tested in every possible position against every other product, which is why the design is an "incomplete block." Nevertheless, this method represents a sound design, and analysis of variance can be used to produce results that are statistically very efficient. More important, the technique can incorporate almost any number of products into a test, including such esoteric designs as a "three out of nineteen" study.

Figure 17 is an example of an actual BIB plan for testing 13 products, four at a time. God forbid you should ever need to really test that many products, but it illustrates how this approach can handle complex designs. This is referred to as a "4/13" test plan, which reads, "4 out of 13."

Unfortunately, this type of BIB design does not generate very many direct comparisons on each pair of products, so it is difficult to analyze specific products directly on a "paired comparison" basis. Also, it can be difficult to control and execute a central-location test if a very large number of products are involved. Because of all the possible product rotations, execution problems are even more difficult with in-home tests, in which testing more than three or four products in the same study is usually not feasible.

Figure 17. Standard 4/13 test plan.

RESPONDENT NUMBER	1st	2nd	3rd	4th	RESPONDENT NUMBER	1st	2nd	3rd	4th
1	1	2	4	10	29	8	9	11	4
2	2	10	1	4	30	9	4	8	11
3	4	1	10	2	31	11	8	4	9
4	10	4	2	1	32	4	11	9	8
5	2	3	5	11	33	9	10	12	5
6	3	11	2	5	34	10	5	9	12
7	5	2	11	3	35	12	9	5	10
8	11	5	3	2	36	5	12	10	9
9	3	4	6	12	37	10	11	13	6
10	4	12	3	6	38	11	6	10	13
11	6	3	12	4	39	13	10	6	11
12	12	6	4	3	40	6	13	11	10
13	4	5	7	13	41	11	12	1	7
14	5	13	4	7	42	12	7	11	1
15	7	4	13	5	43	1	11	7	12
16	13	7	5	4	44	7	1	12	11
17	5	6	8	1	45	12	13	2	8
18	6	1	5	8	46	13	8	12	2
19	8	5	1	6	47	2	12	8	13
20	1	8	6	5	48	8	2	13	12
21	6	7	9	2	49	13	1	3	9
22	7	2	6	9	50	1	9	13	3
23	9	6	2	7	51	3	13	9	1
24	2	9	7	6	52	9	3	1	13
25	7	8	10	3					
26	8	3	7	10					
27	10	7	3	8					
28	3	10	8	7					

The BIB design is very common and useful for central-location testing. Test plans for virtually any number of test products are available from reference books.

"Disappointment Score"

This is a method of analysis that can be incorporated into product tests to give an indication of product acceptability and likely repeat rate. ("Repeat rate" is simply the proportions of triers who purchase the product more than once.)

The disappointment score is really a very simple concept: the fewer the people "disappointed" with a new product when they try it, the higher the repeat rate is likely to be. This is a way to quantify that concept.

The approach involves these steps:

1. Qualifying people for participation in a home-use test on the basis of "definitely buy" or "probably buy" interest in the product concept. The base of testers, then, becomes people who are interested in the concept.

2. Giving respondents samples of the product to try in a normal product test.

3. Questioning users after the test period about their interest in buying the product again, now that they've tried it. The proportion who say they now would *not* "definitely buy" or "probably buy"—in other words, who have either neutral or negative buying interest—represents the "disappointment score." For example, if 70 percent said after trying they'd definitely or probably buy, the disappointment score would be 30 percent. If 55 percent say they'd buy, the disappointment score is 45 percent.

The disappointment score relates to measured repeat rate. A rule of thumb is that most new consumer products should have a disappointment score no higher than 30 percent to be successful. That's the level at which predicted repeat seems to fall below 50 percent.

That level—a 50 percent repeat rate—represents a good guideline for successful new products. In a study of 120 new products, NPD Research Inc. reported that the mean true repeat rates for these products, classified by how successfully they performed on the market, were:

	Mean True Repeat Rate
"Successful" new products	64%
"Marginal" new products	47
New-product "failures"	39

In other words, a consumer product with a repeat rate lower than 50 percent is likely to be only "marginal," at best.

The disappointment score isn't so much a technique as a way of looking at data routinely produced by other techniques, primarily a conventional use test. But it seems to put the research results in a context that makes sense, and comes closer to translating the research findings into a real-world marketing measure.

GUIDELINES FOR PRODUCT TESTING

Finally, here are some tips for conducting reliable product tests.

1. *Control for position and contrast bias.* BIB designs (balanced incomplete blocks) provide an efficient way of rotating products to control for position and contrast.

2. *All sensations are potentially biasing on others.* Structure the questionnaire to reduce this problem as much as possible. For example, ask appearance questions before respondents use or taste the product.

3. *People don't always agree on what specific attributes mean.* What's "tangy" to one person may be "sour" to another. Therefore, "descriptive testing" should be done first with trained R&D panels.

4. *There are no reliable "absolute" measures in product testing.* So all products must be evaluated either against other products or against norms from previous testing history.

5. *Discriminant testing with R&D panels can help cut down the number of products to be tested with consumers.* If products aren't perceived as different by trained panels, there's little use testing them among consumers.

6. *Consumers tend to shy away from the extremes on a scale.* Therefore, it is important to use scales with enough points to get discrimination.

7. *Be sure to control the stimuli.* Don't create biases by differences in serving sizes of food products, serving containers, or coding of samples.

8. *When testing more than one product, make sure the date codes on all products are similar.* Shelf life affects almost all types of products, not just food products.

22

New-Product Research

□□□

Remember Hunt's Flavored Ketchups? Corn Crackos Cereal? Heinz Happy Soup? You don't? That's not surprising; neither do most people. They're examples of the seemingly endless parade of new products introduced each year that fail.

It's a simple fact of business life that most new products fail. Of 5,000 new-product introductions studied by the advertising agency Dancer Fitzgerald Sample, fewer than 100—only about 2 percent—achieved adequate sales volume to qualify as even minimal successes. And if the large number of embryonic ideas that never make it past the concept stage are considered, the failure rate is surely even higher than 98 percent.

Why do new products fail? An article in *Advertising Age* several years ago which discussed reasons for the failure of 75 consumer products that had been withdrawn from the market found this pattern:

Vague consumer difference	36%
Poor product positioning	32%
No point of difference	20%
Bad timing	16%
Product performance	12%
Wrong market for company	8%

All these reasons for failure (with the possible exception of "bad timing" and "wrong market for company") can often be avoided through marketing research in the new-product-development process.

In most companies the process of developing and introducing new products goes through these steps:

1. Opportunity identification
2. Concept screening
3. Product development
4. Simulated sales testing
5. Test marketing
6. National introduction

Not every product, of course, goes through all these steps. For example, if the R&D lab of a company develops a new product with a clear technological superiority, that product may move immediately to the product development stage. Or a new product which is simply a proliferation of an existing product line may go directly into national introduction. But regardless of the step at which they begin, most products go through the remaining steps in the process.

This chapter describes the types of research most commonly done at each of these steps. In addition, whole chapters of this book have been devoted to some of the techniques used in new-product research.

STEP 1: OPPORTUNITY IDENTIFICATION

The first step in the new-product process typically includes a secondary data search and qualitative research. The purpose of the secondary data search is to pull together all the background information available on the market being considered to help determine the size of the new business opportunity and the chances for success. The secondary data may include:

Market size estimates
Market size trends
Market shares
Profiles of leading companies
Trade practices
Advertising expenditures by competitors
Technology developments in the category
Consumer use patterns

This information may come from a variety of secondary sources, including industry magazines, trade associations, government publications, and securities brokers. In other cases, syndicated data may be purchased from suppliers such as A.C. Nielsen Co. or SAMI.

The earliest survey research done in the development of new products often is group interviews. The purpose of qualitative research at this stage is to develop hypotheses about consumer needs not being adequately met by current products. This is done by conducting group interviews about a product category, focusing on wants, needs, problems, complaints, and wishes.

The result of these group interviews usually is a series of speculations about "holes" in the market that might offer opportunities for new products. These opportunities often have to be inferred by the researchers and marketers observing the groups. It is futile to expect consumers to invent for you products they'd like to have that no manufacturer has ever thought of. Rather, group interviews serve as a stimulus to give direction for beginning product ideas.

The focus at this stage should be on generating as many ideas as possible, not on evaluating ideas. Since the odds of success for a new product idea are so slim, the purpose at the beginning is to come up with as many ideas as possible, which increases the chances that there may be one good idea in the batch.

STEP 2: CONCEPT SCREENING

After a large number of product ideas have been generated, the next step is to weed out the ideas with little potential and identify the most promising concepts. While the basic technique used to screen new product ideas is quantitative testing, another round of group interviews is often conducted as a preliminary step.

The primary purpose of group interviews at this stage is to check the clarity of the concept statement: do people understand what the product is and what it is supposed to do? At the same time, a few concept ideas may drop out at this point. Some research purists will claim that no product idea should be screened out on the basis of only group interviews. Yet if all the respondents in two or three groups see a major flaw in a concept which eliminates all interest in buying it, it is difficult to maintain much enthusiasm for pursuing the concept further.

It is a fact that most new product ideas stimulate little or no consumer interest. But that's okay, as long as this is discovered early in the concept stage, when ideas are relatively inexpensive to screen, rather than later at the test market stage, when products are extremely expensive to screen. The purpose of concept screening is to answer two questions: (1) Which of these ideas are best? and (2) Are any of them any good? Concept screening essentially "horseraces" the concepts in a test against one another to identify the best ones, then compares concept test performance of the best ideas against historical data on successful products tested similarly to gauge their absolute potential.

Key questions asked in a concept test usually probe the following factors:

Buying intent—is the most critical measure in a concept test and is usually the basis for ranking ideas.

Reasons for interest or lack of interest—answers to questions in this area determine the key appeals of good ideas and identify areas of needed improvement for weak concepts.

Expected frequency of use or purchase—spots products that would be purchased too infrequently to generate sufficient volume to be successful.

Uniqueness—screens out generic or "me-too" products.

Price/value—determines whether price (either too high or too low) is affecting acceptance of the concept.

STEP 3: PRODUCT DEVELOPMENT

Now that you have a concept or idea that seems to generate consumer interest, the next step in the new-product process is to turn that concept into a physical product that can be marketed.

The product development cycle for a new product usually takes longer than any other step. It takes time to formulate or design a product, then produce prototype samples for testing. Since this cycle usually is repeated several times while the product is improved, the product development phase can last years before a product is ready to be marketed.

At this stage the "product" takes on many dimensions besides the physical product itself. This is the last step before actual sales testing (either simulated sales testing or test marketing), so all the marketing elements that the product will incorporate need to be fine-tuned. The research techniques used at this stage are discussed in detail elsewhere in this book. The dimensions of the total "product" that need to be developed include:

Product testing
Package research
Name, slogan, and logo research
Product positioning research
Advertising research

STEP 4: SIMULATED SALES TESTING

Because of the high cost of test marketing, companies are increasingly using simulated sales testing as a final checkpoint before taking products to test market. From this stage on, however, only products that appear to have a good chance of success are pursued. In addition, many concepts that generate strong consumer interest fail to reach the market because no physical product can be found that meets expectations created by the concept.

Simulated sales testing is the first point at which the complete marketing mix for a product is pulled together and tested in finished form. This includes product, name, packaging, and advertising—all of which have probably been researched individually in step 3. The purpose of simulated sales testing is to produce an estimate of volume sales or market share.

STEP 5: TEST MARKETING

Only a small share of products that begin at the concept stage ever get to test market. Because cost of a market test typically begins at $250,000 or higher, depending on the number of marketing variables tested, only products which have given strong indications of being successful are moved to this stage. Test marketing is a last check before rolling the product into national distribution. It is not a way to test things, such as product performance, that could and should be tested earlier and less expensively.

The primary type of survey research done during test marketing is AAU (advertising, awareness, and usage) studies. AAU studies are conducted periodically—every six, eight, or twelve weeks—in test markets to obtain an idea of:

How many consumers have been made aware of the product.

How many have tried the product or intend to try it.

How many triers have made a repeat purchase of the product or intend to repeat.

Users' experience with the product.

Why non-triers aren't buying.

AAU studies serve two purposes. First, they give diagnostic information for analyzing the test market. If the product is doing poorly, is it because of low trial rate, small number of repeat purchases, or both? If repeat is poor, why? This information gives direction for revising the product, advertising, or strategy before national rollout. Or it may lead to a decision to discontinue test marketing and drop the product if the problems can't be fixed.

The second purpose of AAU research in test marketing is to give a benchmark measure for a later national rollout. By conducting similar studies on a national basis as distribution is expanded, it's possible to see whether patterns of trial and repeat—and the resulting sales volume—are following the pattern that made the product successful in the test market. If not, corrective action can be taken.

In addition to these survey measures, some type of store audit data are needed in test marketing to measure store movement and provide a basis for projecting volume.

STEP 6: NATIONAL INTRODUCTION

By this point, if research has done its job, the product should be on its way to success.

One variable that often can't be tested until rollout is distribution: can the sales force persuade retailers to stock the product? Although most companies have internal methods of monitoring this, it nevertheless is often useful to conduct "distribution checks" as a product is rolled out. This type of study is done by taking a representative sample of stores and observing what products in the category (including the new product) are stocked and how many package facings each brand has. This can be an important measure—obviously consumers can't buy the product if it isn't available in the stores in which they shop.

Finally, AAU studies are often repeated on a national basis for new products to compare consumer purchase patterns during the national rollout with test market performance. This will show whether the product is on track for achieving its forecasted volume.

In summary, these are the types of research most often done at each step in the new-product process:

New-Product Step	*Types of Research*
1. Opportunity identification	Secondary data search
	Group interviews
2. Concept screening	Group interviews
	Quantitative screening
3. Product development	Product testing
	Package research
	Name testing
	Product positioning research
	Advertising research
4. Simulated sales testing	Simulated sales testing
5. Test marketing	AAU studies
6. National introduction	Distribution checks
	AAU studies

23

Screening
New Product Concepts

□□

"Anything that won't sell, I don't want to invent."
—Thomas Edison

That idea of Thomas Edison's is shared by most companies today. It's the principle behind concept testing—trying to evaluate the potential for a new product before it is fully developed.

Unfortunately, creating new ideas and turning them into successful new products is a difficult, high-risk process. More than 1,200 new grocery and drug products are introduced each year. They represent the best of the ideas generated by consumer product companies. Yet most of those 1,200 products fail and are gone from the shelves within a year or two. That's where concept testing comes in: its purpose is to help find the one idea in a thousand that could become a successful new product.

This chapter contains an overview of the principles and purpose of concept testing, followed by a detailed discussion of the most commonly used concept-testing questions. Finally, actual concept-testing case histories are described to illustrate how results are used to screen and select new product ideas.

PRINCIPLES BEHIND CONCEPT TESTING

We all know that people usually are attracted by the *idea* behind a product before they become interested in the physical product. They want a more convenient dessert, more beautiful hair, or cleaner floors—products are merely "vehicles" for delivering those benefits.

Because the *idea* is the most critical element in a product, consumers can react to the new product idea without seeing the physical product—they can react before the physical product even exists. If the idea of the product stimulates little interest among potential customers, it's unlikely the physical product will do much better. On the other hand, if the idea does have appeal, the product has potential if it can deliver the benefits promised by the concept.

Today concept testing is widely used and accepted, particularly by marketers of packaged consumer products (food, household-care items, and health and beauty aids). In addition, concept testing is gaining acceptance among marketers of nonconsumable products such as housewares, sporting goods, and clothing. The techniques of concept screening are being adapted even to industrial and medical products.

PURPOSE OF CONCEPT TESTING

When concept testing is done at the very early stages of the new-product-development process, it can have several important benefits:

□ It can identify "winners" and "losers" at an early stage of development, while the concepts are no more than beginning ideas.

□ This allows a company to set priorities and focus its development efforts on the concepts that have the highest chances of becoming successful.

□ If screening is done at an early stage, concepts can be evaluated before significant resources are committed to their development. In this way, marketing research can play an important role in helping companies make optimum use of their R&D laboratories, marketing budgets, and management time.

□ Finally, developing a low-risk screening system encourages the generation of concept ideas. Since any new product effort is dependent on the input of many new ideas, this stimulation can be very healthy for the development of new products.

Concept testing has been proven to work well for screening most kinds of products. The exception is products that are radically innovative and would require people to significantly alter their behavior. For example, it probably would have been difficult to adequately measure, before introduction, the true potential impact of television, cake mix, or instant coffee. These dramatic new products diffused slowly through the population, and people are poor predictors of their long-term behavior with regard to products that require substantial commitment and behavior change. Fortunately for the marketing researcher, these dramatic, innovative new products are extremely rare. The kinds of ideas which most companies spend most of their time screening are very testable with concept-screening techniques.

Since a primary purpose of concept testing is to sort beginning product ideas into "winners" and "losers," it's important to test early, before substantial money is spent on development. If concept testing is used only as

a "disaster check" before large-scale quantitative research or test marketing, a great portion of the potential savings from concept screening has
already been lost. In addition, there is a higher emotional commitment to
ideas that are further along in their development than to beginning ideas. It is
easier to kill a weak concept while it's still at the idea stage than when it's
about to go into test market.

TYPICAL RESULTS

Here's a real-life illustration of why screening many concepts early in the
new-product-development process is critical. To put it simply, most new
product ideas are bad ideas. They generate very little interest from consumers. Fortunately, that's easy to tell from the first test of a concept, which is
why concept testing works.

Figure 18 shows the range of buying-intent scores on a typical batch of
120 new food product ideas we recently tested. As can be seen from the
figure, only 12 percent of the food concepts tested stimulated one-fourth or
more of the consumers interviewed to say they'd "definitely buy" the
product described. As a rule of thumb, a food product should receive a
"definitely buy" score of at least 20 percent to 25 percent at the concept
stage. These all too typical results show that a large proportion of all
concepts tested don't even generate enough initial interest to justify taking
them to the next step of development.

PRESENTATION OF CONCEPTS

Fortunately, product descriptions used in testing need not be elaborate and
expensive. In fact, simpler concept boards seem to work better in the long
run. A fancy ad may inflate reactions to the product idea in the test. And if
elaborate concept boards are used (including color photography, for example), production of the concept boards can become so expensive that it's
impractical to test large numbers of new product ideas.

Only two elements are critical for inclusion in the concept statement:

1. Copy describing the product, how it works, and its benefits. The copy
should not be full of puffery, exaggeration, and hard sell, but neither should
it be too bland. A good guideline for preparing the copy is to try to write it as
a newspaper reporter would—make it interesting and informative, but stick
to the facts.

Good, clear, interesting concept copy is very difficult to write. I've found
that out the hard way. Several years ago, after I took up cross-country skiing,
I first had a Scandinavian drink, "fruit soup," a hot beverage which is
actually a mulled mixture of fruit and wine. It's hard to describe, and that
was the problem. I wrote concept copy for this product that I was sure all of
America would jump at. It generated a buying-intent score of 8 percent—the

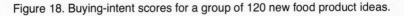

Figure 18. Buying-intent scores for a group of 120 new food product ideas.

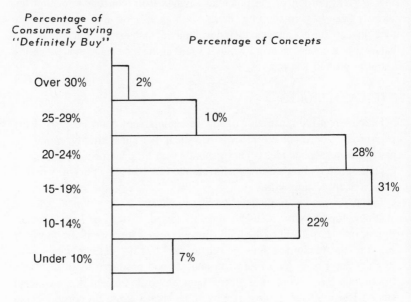

lowest I had seen before or have seen since! So much for my career as an amateur concept copy writer.

2. Some type of illustration, if only a simple line drawing. This seems to help consumers in the test grasp the concept more quickly, and it makes the copy seem more interesting. For most products, drawings seem to be quite adequate. Photographs can be very expensive and do not seem necessary for most categories. The exception may be certain food products for which appearance, or "eye appeal," is expected to be a major factor in the product's success. Most concept boards are 8½" by 11" in size and look something like Figure 19.

Is it necessary to include price in the concept? Probably not, unless the price of the product will be much higher or lower than consumers would expect to pay for other products of the same type. If price is different from what consumers would expect, of course, it becomes an element of the concept that could increase or decrease appeal, and therefore should be mentioned. If price isn't given, it's usually referred to by a phrase such as: "assuming this product were available at a price you considered reasonable."

Should the name of the manufacturer be included? Yes, where the name of the manufacturer adds real value to the concept. Examples would be a glass dish from Corning, a medical product from Johnson & Johnson, or a new household-care item from Johnson Wax. In other cases, where the name of the manufacturer probably will not be included in promotion for the new

Figure 19. Typical concept board.

MOST cereal.

A COMBINATION NO OTHER CEREAL OFFERS.

This is a high-fiber multivitamin and iron supplement cereal
that teams up good nutrition with the honest flavor of wheat.

There's wheat germ for protein. Plus bran for the fiber many
doctors say is important to good health. Plus vitamins and
iron for good nutrition.

A 1 oz. serving of Most cereal gives you 100% of the U.S.
Recommended Daily Allowance of vitamins A, C, D, E, B_6, B_{12},
thiamin, niacin, riboflavin, folic acid, and iron.

product, including the manufacturer's name in the concept probably isn't necessary.

INTERVIEWING PROCEDURE

Of course, the field work for concept screening studies can be done in a number of different ways. However, since the purpose of concept screening is to efficiently evaluate a number of new product ideas, the following general procedure usually seems to work best for consumer products:

1. Conduct the interviews using an "intercept" procedure in shopping malls, food stores, or other high-traffic locations. If the interview itself is relatively brief, this is the most efficient method of contact.

2. Divide the interviewing among several cities. This provides geographic representation where variations in concept reactions would be expected in different parts of the country. Spreading the field work over several markets also generally increases field efficiency.

3. Show each respondent no more than four concepts—perhaps five or six if the questioning about each is *very* short. This is important. Experience indicates that when consumers are given more concepts to evaluate, "wearout" sets in and the quality of information deteriorates.

4. Rotate the order of concept presentation, of course, so that each concept appears an equal number of times in each position during the interview.

5. Avoid showing the same consumers extremely similar concepts. It's usually better to mix up the types of concepts so that test respondents are exposed to a variety of product ideas.

QUESTIONS TO ASK

Without doubt, the most critical question in any concept test is the one that measures buying intent. What you really want to know is: how many people will buy this product?

The most widely used question for evaluating buying interest is this one:

"Which of these statements best describes how you feel about buying this product?"

> I definitely would buy it.
> I probably would buy it.
> I might or might not buy it.
> I probably would not buy it.
> I definitely would not buy it.

All the other questions that may be asked about a new product idea are for diagnostic purposes—to help explain why a concept has strong or weak appeal. These additional questions include:

1. A follow-up, open-end question about why the respondent is or is not interested in buying the new product. Typical wording: "Why do you say that?" Alternatively, focus the answers more by asking a two-part question:

(a) "What's your main reason for saying that?"
(b) "What other reasons do you have for saying that?"

This helps uncover the importance of different concept appeals and benefits.

2. Questions about the expected frequency of purchase—to help screen out novelty or low-frequency products. Typical wording: "Which statement best describes how often you think you would buy this product?"

Once a week or more often
Once every two or three weeks
Once a month
Once every two or three months
Once every four or six months
Once or twice a year
Less often than once a year
Never

Consumers are notoriously inaccurate in estimating how often they will use a product or even how often they currently buy products they already use. But the frequency question can help screen out novelty or what might be called "birthday cake ideas"—products that are interesting to consumers, but which they wouldn't buy often enough to make the product successful.

3. Questions pertaining to the uniqueness of the concept—to help identify "me-too" or generic ideas. Typical wording: "How different do you think this product is from other products now on the market?"

Extremely different
Somewhat different
Slightly different
Not at all different

4. Questions relating to price/value reactions—if price is included in the description and is felt to be potentially either a positive or negative factor. Typical wording: "Which statement best describes how you feel about the value of this product?"

Very good value
Fairly good value
Average value
Somewhat poor value
Very poor value

5. Questions aimed at identifying other products the new product would

replace—to help identify the expected degree of cut-in or cannibalization on the company's existing products. Typical wording: "People often substitute new products for products they currently use. A new product may partly or totally replace something the family has been using. Do you feel that *this* product might partly or totally replace a product you are now using? If yes, what product would it be?"

6. Questions about whether the product solves a problem that isn't being satisfied by products now on the market—to better understand the product's appeal and uniqueness. Typical wording: "Do you feel this product might solve a problem or need you or other members of your family now have that isn't being satisfied by products now on the market?"

7. Questions to check whether there is anything confusing or difficult to understand about the concept—to check on the clarity of the product description. Typical wording: "Was there anything in the description of this product that was confusing or difficult for you to understand?"

Yes. (If so: "What?")
No.

8. Questions aimed at determining whether the item is seen as more suitable for gift or for self-purchase—on housewares, clothing, and other products where gift purchase is significant. Typical wording: "Do you think you would be more likely to buy this product for yourself, as a gift for someone else, or both?"

Self
Gift
Both

ANALYZING RESULTS

The buying-intent question is the key measure of concept interest. Standard ways of analyzing the buying-intent question are to look at either the "top box" ("definitely buy") score or the "top two boxes" ("definitely buy" plus "probably buy"). Both of these measures identify the proportion of potential buyers who have a strong interest in the product, and they usually produce nearly the same ranking of concepts.

At the same time, some companies have moved beyond this simple "top box" system to a procedure which weights the buying-intent result to produce a number that seems to approximate penetration potential for a product. A weighting system often used is shown in Table 1. The weights in this case assume that only about three-fourths (.75) of the people who say they'd "definitely buy" the product will actually buy, about one-fourth

Table 1. A common weighting system for buying-intent responses.

Buying-intent scale	Test responses		Weights		Weighted "score"
Definitely will buy	21%	X	.75	=	15.8%
Probably will buy	29	X	.25	=	7.3
Might or might not buy	30	X	.10	=	3.0
Probably will not buy	15	X	.03	=	.5
Definitely will not buy	5	X	.02	=	.1
Total:	100%				26.7%

(.25) of those who say they'd "probably buy" will really buy, and so forth. In this example, the estimated potential trial purchase level for the hypothetical test product is 26.7 percent—which is then discounted for expected awareness and distribution.

Another way to analyze concept test results is to plot the *buying-intent* and *uniqueness* scores for each concept. This is illustrated in Figure 20, which plots actual test results for several dozen new product ideas.

The quadrant of the grid in which the concept falls indicates its likelihood of success and the best approach to marketing it, as amplified in Figure 21.

Figure 20. Buying-intent and uniqueness scores for 95 new product ideas.

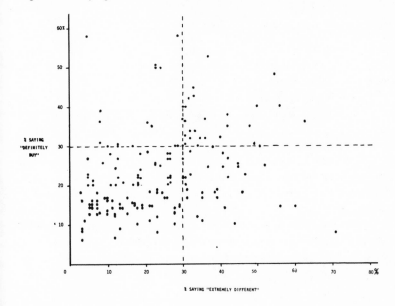

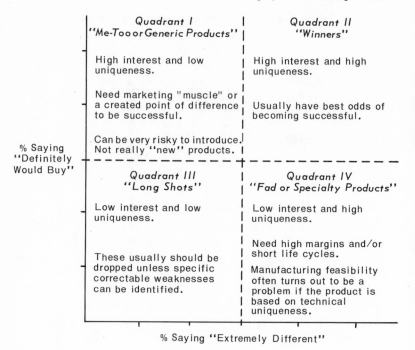

Figure 21. Characteristics of new product ideas.

DOES IT WORK?

It's difficult to find concept test results to show in a book. Clients' successes are their most closely guarded secrets, as are their failures— although for different reasons.

All the results of my company's projects are proprietory to the clients who pay for the projects, so a couple of years ago we decided to conduct our *own* concept tests to show how the technique works. We scouted around for several products that were in test market, then developed concept statements describing them. The product concepts were then tested in a market where they were *not* being sold. Here are results of the testing for two household products that show how sharply even early concept testing can differentiate new product ideas.

The two products tested were "Ironsides" trash bags from Kimberly-Clark and "Spill-Mate" paper towels from Crown Zellerbach. Figure 22 shows the concepts we developed to reflect the claims being made for the products in their test market advertising.

Results for the two products were dramatically different. On buying intent, the most critical measure, Ironsides generated a very healthy 33 percent "definitely buy" score, while Spill-Mate showed a mediocre 20 percent. The other measures helped explain the difference in buying interest:

	Ironsides	*Spill-Mate*
% saying product is "Extremely Different"	40%	7%
Does this product solve a problem not being solved by products now on the market? % saying "Yes"	59	26

In other words, consumers see little that is new and different about Spill-mate, while Ironsides is seen as different in a way that solves a problem better than current products.

DEVELOPING A CONCEPT-SCREENING PROCEDURE

Companies that have not done any concept screening often wonder how to get started. A good way to begin is to conduct a "development project" to validate the applicability of concept testing for the company's products and to begin developing guidelines for spotting "winners" and "losers."

This type of project involves testing, in concept form, products already marketed by the company or its competitors—both successful and unsuccessful products. Testing these products as concepts validates the ability of the test to predict—or "backcast"—proven successes and failures. This is a low-risk, economical way to demonstrate the accuracy and value of concept testing.

A CAUTION ABOUT CONCEPT TESTING

Sometimes concept testing is conducted in conjunction with product testing by showing consumers a product concept and offering those who indicate a positive buying intent—"definitely buy" or "probably buy"— samples to try at home.

One manufacturer, Clairol, became concerned that interviewers could be introducing a conscious or unconscious bias toward favorable concept reactions, since a positive reaction would make it easier for the interviewer to satisfy the placement quota for the in-home test. Therefore, Clairol conducted an experiment, testing an identical concept under two conditions: one

Figure 22. Concept boards used for testing the effectiveness of concept screening.

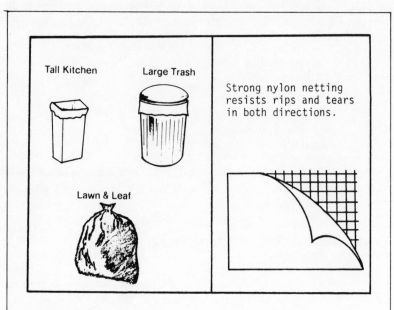

IRONSIDES trash bags.

THE TRASH BAG WITH GUTS!

The "guts" of every Ironsides trash bag is nylon.

Strong nylon netting is sealed right into these polyethylene bags, so they resist rips and tears in both directions. They even stand up to sharp and jagged objects, like no plain plastic bag can.

Available in three sizes for kitchen waste baskets, garbage cans, and lawn & leaf bags.

SPILL-MATE towels.

THE PAPER TOWEL THAT WORKS LIKE A SPONGE.

Spill-Mate paper towels are specially designed to be super

absorbent. They're constructed to be extra porous, so they

work like a sponge in cleaning up spills. . . fast!

Available in a variety of solid colors and decorator prints.

involving home-use test placement of the product, the other testing the concept only. The results of the experiment are shown in Figure 23.

From these and other similar results, Clairol concluded that even when attempts are made to reduce an overt interviewer bias, an unconscious pyschological bias seems to persist which distorts the data. The company found that 10 percentage points at least are pushed into the ''probably buy'' box and 5 to 8 percentage points are added to the ''definitely buy'' box by conducting product tests as part of concept tests.

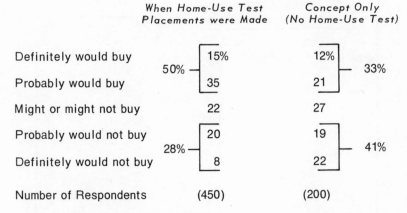

Figure 23. Results of an experiment comparing home-use test placement of a product with concept testing.

The only solution seems to be to separate the concept evaluation activity *completely* from the product placement activity. Use one set of interviewers to screen concepts and another to make product placements. Don't do the two together.

Unfortunately (or fortunately) this bias does not *always* occur. Similar research by others has not always shown the same biasing effect. Nevertheless, the possibility of this distortion is serious enough to make the separation of concept screening and product placement in the early stages of development a wise precaution.

SUMMARY

The most critical questions for evaluating interest in new product concepts relate to the following points:

Buying intent (the real key).
Uniqueness/difference of the product.
Expected frequency of use.
The consumer's opinion on whether or not the product solves a problem.

Other questions that can be included as diagnostic measures include:

Open-end questions: "Why do you say that?"
Questions on attractiveness of price/value.
Questions about products replaced.
Questions aimed at identifying confusing things about the concept.

Questions to determine whether the product is more likely to be bought as a gift or self-purchase.

Concept testing works. Its widespread use by the most sophisticated marketers of new products is proof of that. The huge payoff from identifying the one idea in a thousand that could be a runaway success has made new-product-concept testing one of the biggest segments of marketing research today.

24

Advertising Research

□□□

John Wanamaker, the famous retailer, is supposed to have complained, "I know half the dollars I spend on advertising are wasted—I just don't know which half." That was the problem many years ago, and it's still the problem today. Business people intuitively know that some advertising is more effective than others, so it ought to be possible to research advertising. But nobody can agree on how to do it.

HOW DOES ADVERTISING WORK?

Most of the problems with advertising research begin with a fundamental problem of advertising theory: nobody knows for sure how advertising works. And if no one is sure how advertising works, it's difficult to measure how effective an advertisement is. For years it was assumed that advertising worked according to the following steps:

1. Information
2. Attitudes
3. Action

In other words, advertising provides information, which creates positive attitudes toward a product, which eventually leads to purchase. For many products this does seem to be the pattern, so this theory (which often includes a larger number of more finely defined steps) is useful for thinking about researching advertising for some kinds of products. Let's ignore, for the moment, what constitutes "information" or precisely how attitudes get created or changed.

Then it was found that for some types of products there is another order for these steps:

1. Information
2. Action
3. Attitudes

One of the clearest examples of this type of advertising is the billboard along the desert highway that says, "Last gas station for 100 miles." In that case, information often leads to action. Research indicates that many products bought on impulse also follow this pattern. Attitudes don't necessarily change prior to purchase—they may change *after* purchase as the buyer justifies his actions to himself.

To make things even more confusing, it has been theorized that yet another pattern seems to hold for some purchase decisions:

1. Action
2. Attitudes
3. Information

This appears to be the pattern for many expensive or ego-involving purchases. An example is the man who buys an expensive red sports car, gets a great ego boost from driving it, then seeks information about its features and performance to rationalize his action. Many major appliance purchases also seem to fall into this category.

These three theories of how advertising works—and there are many more—illustrate how difficult it is to define the precise role of advertising. In some cases its job is to change attitudes. In other cases its objective is to precipitate immediate action. And in other situations it may be used to justify actions that already have taken place.

Since it's difficult to come up with a simple definition of exactly what advertising is supposed to be doing, it is equally difficult to define how to measure its effectiveness.

OBSTACLES TO ADVERTISING RESEARCH

But maybe this is making the whole thing too difficult. The real purpose of advertising is to generate sales. Right? So why not just measure the sales effect of advertising directly? That would be better anyway.

Unfortunately, using sales information as a direct measure of advertising effectiveness has several drawbacks:

1. *Advertising is only one element in the marketing mix.* It usually is impossible to isolate the effect of advertising from that of distribution, sampling, in-store promotions, shelf position, and all the other marketing variables that contribute to the success of a product.

2. *Competitive activities make sales measures difficult to interpret.* One competitor may increase its advertising or stop it all together. Another may introduce a new product in the category. Yet another may run a high-value coupon program. How can the effect of these actions be separated from the effect of your advertising?

3. *Even where advertising has a direct effect on sales, the result often does not appear immediately.* There usually is a lag between the time an ad runs and the purchase that may result from it—and there may be an even longer lag before the manufacturer feels the effect in its shipments.

4. *Advertising has cummulative effect.* For example, the sales result of a single ad for Kodak film is based, at least in part, on all the advertising that Kodak has run for its products over the years. So isolating the sales effect of a single ad, especially for a well-established brand, can be very difficult.

5. *Manufacturers' sales records can smooth out and hide sales responses.* Even if the sales effect of advertising were direct and immediate—which it usually is not—it would be difficult for most manufacturers to read relatively tiny, short-term bumps in retail sales. Most manufacturers do not sell directly to retailers. They may ship their products to regional chain store warehouses, which then distribute the products to individual stores. This "pipeline" can absorb small spurts in sales and make it difficult for the manufacturer to read anything except long-term sales results.

WHAT CAN BE MEASURED?

Since it is virtually impossible to measure the overall effect of a single ad or campaign on sales of a product, research usually focuses on measuring the extent to which an advertisement achieves a specific, well-defined goal that has been set for it.

If it is assumed that a decision to purchase is made in stages—although admittedly those stages may take place in different order—it's possible to measure the extent to which an ad or a campaign is successful in moving potential buyers through one stage or from one stage to the next. Examples of the actions or attitudes which advertising might be expected to generate include:

Product and/or brand awareness
Recognition of product benefits, features, or claims
Favorable attitudes
Predisposition to purchase
Motivation to purchase
Actual purchase

Reinforcement of satisfaction with purchase
Repeat buying

*Most advertising research techniques focus on measuring the effective-
ness of an ad in meeting one of these objectives.* Does it create awareness?
Does it really communicate the benefits of the products? Does it create a
predisposition to purchase? (Examples of specific techniques designed to
evaluate each of these dimensions are described later.)

TYPES OF ADVERTISING RESEARCH

The term "advertising research" is really misleading, since it connotes a
single type of research, when, in fact, many very different types of research fall under this heading.

Table 2 shows some types of advertising research techniques and the
types of decisions each technique is designed to help make. Many of these
techniques either do not involve survey research or incorporate
approaches—such as segmentation or positioning studies—which also have
applications outside advertising research.

In the following section describing specific techniques, attention will be
focused on copy research and commercial tests that are designed to help in
deciding "how to say it" and "how effective it was." These are the areas
of advertising testing where survey research is most often used.

Table 2. Types of advertising research.

To decide:	One must choose a:	Using techniques known as:
What to say	Theme, copy, platform strategy	Concept tests, positioning studies, category studies
To whom to say it	Target audience	Market segmentation studies, category studies
How to say it	Copy, commercial execution	Copy research, some commercial tests
How often to say it	Frequency of exposure	Studies of repetition, flighting
Where to say it	Media plan	Media research, audience studies
How much to spend	Budget level	Sales analysis, marketing models
How effective it was	Measure of results	Test markets, in-market ad tests, AAU studies, some commercial tests

Adapted from *Advertising Research: The State of the Art,* Charles Ramond, published by the
Association of National Advertisers, 1976.

SPECIFIC ADVERTISING TESTING TECHNIQUES

Techniques used to evaluate the effectiveness of advertising are too numerous to list. Here is an overview of some of the most widely used approaches to advertising research.

Qualitative research on copy. A first step in the early stages of development for many ads is qualitative research—either focus groups or one-on-one interviews—to get consumer feedback on the ad. The purpose here usually is to determine whether consumers find anything about these ads unclear or confusing and whether they "take away" from the ad the main point which the advertiser intends. Because it is qualitative research, it is necessarily imprecise; but it can be useful for discovering major problems with alternative approaches early, while there is still time to correct them.

Some advertisers and advertising agencies have developed small-scale quantitative techniques to provide this same type of "early feedback" information. Typically these techniques involve showing a test ad to consumers, then asking them to indicate on a series of scales or on a checklist their reactions to the ad. These reactions are tabulated and compared with profiles of other successful ads to indicate the extent to which the commercial is seen as believable, informative, humorous, and so on. This is another way of testing the copy in ads early in the development of a commercial.

On-air recall techniques. One of the best known of these techniques is "day-after recall." A test ad is shown on the air in three or four test cities. The next day, a sample of telephone interviews is conducted with respondents who claim to have watched the program on which the test commercial was telecast. These respondents are questioned, on an unaided and aided basis, about their recall of the ad. Those who remember seeing it are asked what they recall about the ad and what it said.

These results are then compared with a data bank of ads for other products in similar categories to provide a measure of the effectiveness of the test ad in generating recall. Burke is one of the best known companies offering this type of service.

Theater persuasion measures. Groups of consumers are invited to a theater setting, usually with the explanation that they are being shown pilot episodes of new television programs. Before the show, members of the audience are asked to indicate their preference among certain brands of products—including the test product category—usually under the pretense that a drawing will be held, with consumers awarded the products for which they have the strongest preference. Then some type of program film is shown with several commercials inserted in it. In this way it simulates the environment in which a commercial might actually be shown. After seeing the program and the commercials, the audience is again asked to express their relative interest in the products in the category. The measure of effectiveness used here is the change in purchase intention or preference for the test product between "before" and "after" an ad was shown.

Two of the best known companies offering this type of service are McCollum/Spielman and Research Systems Corporation (ARS).

In-store purchase measures. A sample of consumers is intercepted as they enter a food store and shown a series of ads, one of which is an ad for the test product. As a "thank you" they are given a book of coupons good for money off on several products, again including the test item. Another sample of consumers is given the same book of coupons, but is not shown the ads. The measure of advertising effectiveness is the difference in purchase rate between those consumers who saw the ad and those who did not. The best known company doing this type of testing is Tele-Research.

Portfolio testing of print ads. A portfolio is made up of six or eight ads, one of which is the test ad. Respondents are invited to look through the portfolio, taking as much time as they need. Then the interviewer takes back the portfolio and closes it. Next the interviewer asks the respondent to remember what products and brands he or she recalls seeing. If the test ad is remembered, the interviewer asks what the respondent can remember about it. If the respondent does not mention the test ad, the interviewer asks about it on an aided basis. If there is still no recall, the interviewer may open the folder to the test ad and ask the respondent about the ad. This technique attempts to get at recall, as well as communication effectiveness, of the advertisement.

PREPARING COMMERCIALS FOR TESTING

Production of a commercial is often the most expensive part of testing finished television advertising. Producing a finished TV commercial can easily cost $40,000 or more.

Research has been done which shows that rough execution of commercials, particularly photo boards and live action, do an adequate job of providing copy testing material. So it may not always be necessary to go to final form to produce ads for testing. This makes testing a larger number of ads at the early stages of development much more feasible.

TEST EARLY

It used to be said jokingly that the motto of Mayor Richard J. Daly, the late political boss of Chicago, was, "Vote early and vote often." Most advertisers would be glad to be half as successful with their advertising testing as Mayor Daly was at getting himself and his fellow Chicago Democrats elected. So maybe his advice is good: "Test early and test often."

Studies of how advertising research is used indicate it's most often used to make "go/no-go" decisions—often after considerable time and money have been spent producing finished ads for testing. To be most useful, however, research should be pushed forward in the process to help plan and guide the development of the advertising—not just to produce a score of "good" or "bad" at the end. Too often researchers serve as scorekeepers, when a more helpful role would be as players on the team that's working to develop effective advertising.

25

Package Testing

Maybe you can't tell a book by its cover, but you can tell a product by its package—at least many people think so. Decisions to buy a product, especially a new product, are often strongly influenced by whether the package attracts attention and makes the contents seem appealing.

A package is much more than just a container. It also plays the role of:

Attention-getting device
Point-of-purchase advertising
Reminder to current users
Source of information about directions, ingredients, and cautions
Announcement of special offers or deals
Builder of expectations about what's inside

All in all, then, the package is one of the most important marketing tools for a product. The package is the only piece of communication about the product which every buyer sees.

This means that having a better package can make a difference for a product, particularly a new product. Research can help select the best package for a product and assure that what the package communicates is consistent with the overall strategy for the product.

WHEN TO TEST

Most packaging research is done on new products. At that point it's still easy to explore alternatives, even to consider "far-out" package designs.

But once a package is on the market, major changes are unusual. There's always a fear that regular buyers won't be able to find a redesigned package, so changes are made only for good reason. Some of the major considerations that could justify considering changing an existing package are:

151

An improvement in the physical package (new package material, new closure, new shape, and so on).

"Improved," reformulated, or redesigned product.

Eroding market or other competitive activity.

Major product repositioning.

More contemporary graphics or more modern "look."

Test as early as possible, preferably before final packaging is developed. Even mock-ups are expensive to make, and if large numbers of four-color packages are required for testing, it simply becomes too costly for most companies to test.

For this reason, photographs and slides are useful for testing in the early stages of development. In a photograph, a mock-up often cannot be distinguished from a finished package. So using photographs of mock-ups (and often only one or two sides of the package need to be mocked up for a photograph) makes it practical to test packages early, before package production costs are incurred.

It is easiest to test alternatives for new products. That way the alternatives can be "horse-raced" against each other and the best alternative selected. It is difficult to test existing packages directly against alternative new packages. The familiarity of a package that has been on the market will usually make it easier for consumers in the test to recognize an existing package. In addition, the associations which have been built up in consumers' minds will make it difficult to separate the image of the brand from the connotations of the current package.

WHAT TO TEST

Make sure there is a measurable difference among the alternative packages being tested. Among the differences which usually are significant enough to be measurable in a test are:

Product name
Principal color
Illustrations or photos
Logo
Type of package (bottle vs. box)
Shape
Size
Main panel elements

But you can't and shouldn't test everything. Although there may be important changes—maybe even legally required ones—not every package revision is measurable. The effect on the package of temporary deals or premium offers rarely can be tested. Neither can revisions in secondary panel elements (preparation directions, ingredient listings, and cautions).

Since a package has to perform many roles, it stands to reason that a package cannot be adequately evaluated on just one dimension. That is the primary weakness of many single-measure package testing techniques.

There are three principal components of a package's effectiveness: visibility, image, and function.

Visibility

One of the most important jobs a package performs is to stand out and call attention to the product on the shelf, then tell consumers who notice it what's inside. The visibility element is made up of three components:

Display visibility.   Does the package stand out in an array of competitive products to consumers who are *not* specifically looking for it? In other words, does it demand to be noticed? Does it "jump off" the shelf?

"Findability."   How readily can the package be found on the shelf by people who *are* looking specifically for it? Can people who have seen the package in an ad find it easily? Do repeat buyers have trouble finding the product again?

Readability.   How quickly and easily are elements of the package perceived? Once consumers notice it, how easy is the package to read?

Each of these components must be measured to get a complete evaluation of the visibility of a package. The visibility measures are usually the most important in researching a new product. Among the methods used to research visibility are:

Tachistoscope.   The classic version of the "T-scope" uses a darkened box in which the package is placed. The box is illuminated for the respondent under controlled intensity and duration of lighting. While this method offers considerable control, the setting is somewhat unrealistic.

Eye cameras or pupilmeters.   These are devices for recording the pattern traced by the eyes as they look at a package or a display. It has the advantage of offering a very quantified measure of what respondents look at. The drawback is that analysis and interpretation can be difficult.

Find-time.   This type of test is usually conducted in an actual store or large simulated section display. Each respondent is told to find a specified product and pick it up as quickly as possible. The lapsed time required to find the product is measured from the point where the respondent enters a marked-off area near the display. This has the advantage of realism—it's done in an actual store or real section—but the problems of carefully controlling the mechanics of the test can make it difficult to find significant and consistent differences between alternative test packages.

35mm slides.   This approach uses timed exposures of actual shelf displays or individual packages. After each exposure, respondents are asked to report everything they saw or read. Because it uses photographs as stimuli, it can show the test package within a competitive category display. And mock-ups of packages are adequate for making slides. The timed slides offer a combination of the realism of "find-time" and the control of the tachistoscope.

Image

A package communicates much more than just the objective information printed on it. It can make the product look interesting or dull, appetizing or unappealing, different or run-of-the-mill. Good research should measure the connotations of a package, too. If only visibility were important, every package would be fluorescent orange.

Any method of showing the package can be used to measure image—actual packages, mock-ups, or slides. Among the issues which can be included to evaluate a package's image or connotations are these:

Probes.   These are open-end questions to determine what consumers like and don't like about the packages. They may uncover a weakness or "turn-off."

Profiles.   Rating scales can be used to obtain an overall picture of the image created for the product by each package.

Projective techniques.   Associations with types of consumers or product characteristics can indicate strengths and weaknesses of alternative designs. Especially on new products, if respondents have only the package to go on, the results can be a good measure of package connotations.

Perceptions.   Mapping techniques or other questions can be used to see how consumers see the brand fitting into the product category.

Preferences.   At the end of the interview, it's sometimes useful to ask consumers to express a direct preference among the alternatives. (A buying-intent question is another way of measuring this.) Although preference measures should not be allowed to override evaluations of visibility and readability, a strong preference result can increase confidence in selecting a new package alternative that is only marginally better on visibility and readability than others.

But use preference measures with caution. Consumers tend to prefer the familiar and the usual. In other words, they'll usually prefer the cereal package that looks like other cereal packages, the soap package that looks like other soap packages, and so forth. As a result, relying heavily on preference measures is likely to lead to choosing a "me-too" package even when a dramatic or innovative package alternative would be more successful.

Function

Of course the package must work. Often this doesn't need to be tested, since most packages are simply graphic variations of boxes, bottles, or bags that are already in widespread use. But if the package is a new design and there are questions about whether it might work, this dimension should be included in the research.

Among the functional elements which can be tested are ease of:

Reading and following directions and usage instructions
Grasping, holding, or gripping
Opening
Closing or resealing
Removing or emptying contents
Storing unused product

These measures can be especially critical for industrial or medical products, where package functionality is often more important than its visibility.

GUIDELINES ON TESTING

To be useful, package research should have three characteristics:

It should show products in a realistic setting of competitive products. Often a package that looks attractive and attention-getting by itself loses impact among competitive products on the shelf. This may be the case when many products in a category use similar colors in their packaging. The only way to determine this is by testing the product in its real-life competitive environment.

It should be comprehensive. Testing must provide a complete, objective evaluation of the strengths and weaknesses of a package. It should measure all the elements of a package's performance—at least all those about which there is any question or concern.

It should be controlled. Exposure to the packages and measurement of its visibility or image need to be carefully controlled. One way to do this is through the use of slides rather than actual displays, because exposure to the shelf display presented in a slide is more easily controlled. The other device for assuring maximum control is the use of some type of tachistoscope, which can be used to control light intensity and exposure duration.

Packages can also theoretically be tested under actual sales conditions, either in test markets or simulated sales tests. In practice, however, this rarely happens. There are substantial practical and cost problems involved with producing large quantities of product in two or more different packages. As a result, most companies do their package testing before proceeding to sales testing.

Although these testing techniques are used primarily for evaluating packages, they can be adapted to other research problems where visual impact and connotations need to be evaluated—such as point-of-purchase materials, special store display units, or billboard advertising.

26

Name Research

□□

"What shall we name the baby?" every parent-to-be asks. Jane? No, that's too ordinary. Humphrey? No, I never like Humphrey Bogart in the movies. Charlene? I had an Aunt Charlene who was a shrew, and I wouldn't want the baby to be like that.

Names are powerful because they convey so much information—not directly, necessarily, but through all the associations a name carries for each of us.

Companies, too, take a lot of care in naming their "babies." The name of a new product, for example, is one of the most important ways of communicating to potential customers what the product is like. Marketing research can play an important role in selecting names for products.

PRODUCT NAMES

Types of Names

Companies follow many different strategies in naming their products. The approaches include:

Company names.   Many companies attach their corporate names prominently to the products they market. Scott Paper, Pillsbury, Kraft, and Libby are examples. Other corporations—General Foods and Procter & Gamble are prominent examples—subordinate their company names to individual product brand names.

Line names.   Betty Crocker and Aunt Jemima are examples of line names assigned to a variety of specific products.

Descriptive names.   These names are meant to describe, in a literal yet appealing way, the physical product. Examples are Minute Rice, Rice Krispies, Light 'n Lively, Stir 'n Frost, and Buc-Wheats.

157

Imagery names.   These types of names, which are very common, do not literally describe the product, yet they are intended to indirectly suggest characteristics about the product. Examples include Log Cabin, Mrs. Butterworth, Mazola, A-1 Steak Sauce, Roman Meal Bread, Tasters Choice, and Pampers.

Manufactured meanings.   In recent years, as products have proliferated and the list of legally available product names has shrunk, a new type of brand name has begun to appear. These names usually have no literal meaning associated with the category, although they may have indirect meanings which the manufacturer hopes will reflect favorably on the product. Two categories, health and beauty aids and cigarettes, seem to be the most active users of this type of name. Examples include Aim, Scope, Fact, and True.

Dimensions of Product Name Research

Research on new product names typically involves five dimensions: connotations, suitability, pronunciation, memorability, and familiarity.

Connotations.   A key concept in most name research is the distinction between the "denotation" and the "connotation" of a name. The denotation is the literal, explicit meaning of a name. It usually is unnecessary to conduct research to determine this. The connotations of a name, on the other hand, are its associated implications, beyond the literal, explicit meaning of the name.

The difference between connotations and denotations often is dramatic. For example, the name Adolph literally means "noble hero." Yet how many people know that? It's a fair guess that the first association most people would make with the name Adolph is with Adolph Hitler—an association that is quite opposite to "noble hero."

Connotations are often stronger than denotations in giving meaning to names. As a result, understanding the connotations that potential names have for consumers is often the focus of name research.

One way to study the connotations of new names, which works particularly well with products, is to research the *types of people* consumers think would use a product with the name.

For example, consumers might be asked—either on a checklist or with some type of agree–disagree scale—which of the following types of people they would expect to be users of a product called such-and-such:

Banker
Factory worker
Scientist

Student
Poor credit risk
Artist
Teacher
Person like me

The list of types of people used in the research should include the kinds of people the brand wants to attract as well as those the brand is not intended to appeal to.

Connotations of product names can also be evaluated by measuring the *characteristics* associated with the name. For example, respondents might be asked what type of product they would expect each potential name to represent, if the product were available. The list of characteristics might include:

High quality
Low price
Unique and different
Flavorful
Smooth and creamy

With both approaches—studying types of users or characteristics associated with the names—the purpose is to draw a profile of the connotations associated with alternative new names. When these profiles are compared, it usually is possible to see the strengths and weaknesses of each name and identify the one that is most appropriate.

Suitability   After the general connotations of a name have been researched, it may be useful to measure whether consumers see the name as a "fit" with the company that is considering using it.

For example, consumers might be asked, toward the end of the interview: "Which of these products would you most expect to see marketed by a company like Johnson & Johnson?" For corporations with very strong company images—which would include companies that use their names as a prominent part of product brand names—this can be important information in selecting among alternative brand names.

Pronunciation.   Most product names aren't difficult to pronounce, so this issue rarely needs to be researched. But if the list of name candidates includes any highly unusual names—and coined names or very technological-sounding names often fall in this category—including a measure of the ease of pronunciation of the alternative is a good idea.

This is done toward the beginning of the interview, before the interviewer has uttered any of the names, by giving the respondent a list of the names and asking him or her to read them aloud. The interviewer then simply marks the pronunciation as correct or incorrect, according to the pronunciation indicated on the copy of the questionnaire. Remember to give the interviewer a phonetic spelling of any difficult names, even if pronunciation isn't being tested, so that the name will be pronounced correctly during the interview.

Memorability.   Being easy to remember is an important characteristic in a name, although it is difficult to measure accurately in an interview situation.

However, clues about which names may be unusually easy or difficult to remember can sometimes be developed in this way: At the end of the interview, after asking any demographic questions, the interviewer asks, "By the way, which of the names that we talked about during the interview do you happen to remember?" This can indicate any names which are particularly easy or difficult to remember.

Another way to measure memorability is to conduct a callback interview a couple of days later and ask which, if any, names the respondent remembers from the interview. This is much more expensive, of course, than simply asking the question at the end of the interview, but it gives a better indication of long-term memorability.

Familiarity.   A name generally shouldn't seem too familiar, or it may be difficult for a company to communicate that the product is new and different.

One way to measure this is to ask, early in the interview, whether respondents think they've heard of a product by this name before. To make this question more credible, it probably is good to mix the alternative new names with several actual brand names from the category.

If a name generates a significant degree of claimed recognition, it may suggest the brand name is confusingly similar to existing brands or so ordinary that it sounds as if it ought to exist already. Both situations are clearly undesirable, for a brand shouldn't sound too familiar before it reaches the market.

COMPANY NAMES

According to anthropologists, elderly Eskimos used to take new names, believing they would thereby get to start a new life. Many companies seem to have a similar belief in the revitalizing power of a new name.

Companies most often select new names to overcome a weakness or limitation in an existing one. For example, Standard Oil of New Jersey changed its name to Exxon several years ago when it felt the name Standard Oil wasn't adequate to describe the company's diversified businesses.

Two types of research can be done to help management evaluate whether a company name change should be considered:

☐ Studying a company's existing image will indicate the potentially valuable associations of a current name.

☐ Testing the types of products or markets associated with an existing name will show whether that name has the breadth to be associated with the variety of businesses in which the company now is or which it may enter.

Types of Company Names

Companies take many different kinds of names. Some of the types of names are literally descriptive of their products, while others bear no direct relationship to the business they are in.

Descriptive names.   These include many well-known companies, such as General Motors, General Electric, U.S. Steel, and Control Data.

Alphabetical names.   These initials may be developed as the name of a company, or they may simply represent a company adopting as its official name an alphabetical name already in widespread use. IBM, 3M, ITT, RCA, and LTV are examples.

Coined names.   These names may be adopted because they have no literal meaning, or they may represent combinations of old, longer company names into a single, shorter names. Many company name changes in recent years have been moves in this direction. Examples include Xerox, Exxon, Uniroyal, Alcoa, and Airco.

Location names.   Many companies originally took names reflecting their locations. Ashland Oil, Cincinnati Milicron, Texas Instruments, and Minnesota Mining & Manufacturing are a few examples.

Family names.   The founders of companies gave their names to such firms as Chrysler, Du Pont, Kaiser Industries, and Litton Industries.

Traditional names.   A common practice is to couple an industry or product category name with such words as Allied, United, General, American, Continental, or International.

Combination names.   Companies with more than one founder, or businesses born through the merging of two companies, have spawned such names as Allis-Chalmers, Gulf + Western, Borg-Warner, and Hewlett-Packard.

The same research dimensions apply to company names as to product names: connotations, suitability, pronunciation, and memorability. The same basic research approaches that work for products also work for company names.

In addition, for company names, the associations between alternative names and specific characteristics can be researched. For example, respondents can be asked which characteristics they would expect a company called such-and-such to have:

Industry leader
Large
Reliable
Old-fashioned
Undependable
Technological leader

ANALYZING NAME RESEARCH

It is important for those who will be making decisions on the basis of name research to think about how they will interpret the results *before* the results are available.

You should sit down with the questions asked in the research and develop a "profile" of the connotations you hope the new name will have—which desirable connotations you hope will be strong and which undesirable associations you hope the final name will *not* have.

Most of the individuals involved in name research have their favorite candidates. And if a discussion of decision rules is postponed until after the results are available, there is a natural tendency for each person to look for ways to justify the selection of his favorite candidate.

Discussing decision rules beforehand helps make the analysis more objective and increases the odds that the research will lead to a better name choice.

OTHER CONSIDERATIONS

Availability.   An astonishing number of names, even many not currently in use, have been registered and are unavailable for use. In addition, laws in foreign countries make certain types of names unprotectable by registration there, which may be an important consideration in selecting a product name for a multinational company.

For this reason, legal availability of all alternatives included in the research should be checked before the research is conducted. Otherwise, there is a risk of finding, at the conclusion of the research, that the "winner" isn't available.

Creativity.   This is the element which sometimes overrides all the logic behind name research. Occasionally a name that doesn't seem to fit a product can be successful precisely *because* it doesn't fit the product. An example is "Charlie" perfume introduced several years ago by Revlon. Before the product was introduced, the name "Charlie" probably had no connections that made it particularly suitable for a new perfume. But the name formed the basis for a marketing campaign that sold the product as something different and unconventional—and made it the world's top-selling fragrance for a time.

These occasional examples are sometimes used to point out why name research isn't necessary. But most examples of these types of names come from the cosmetics field, where the difficulty of achieving demonstrable product differentiation makes the use of unusual product names more common.

Also, most people forget that Charles Revson, the founder of Revlon, named "Charlie" after himself. Who could argue with the boss?

For most products in most categories, however, finding a name that has desirable connotations about the product is important. A name with strong positive associations can be a powerful marketing tool.

27

Image and Identity Research

□□

Reputation, reputation, reputation!
O! I have lost my reputation.

—*William Shakespeare,* Othello

The "image" of a company is sometimes mistakenly thought to be nothing more than puffery resulting from a public relations campaign. The sterotyped advertising man of books and movies is always telling the client that his company needs to "fix its image"—which usually requires only a quick dose of advertising.

We all enjoy being with other people whom we like, respect, and trust. Similarly, we generally like to buy the products of companies toward which we have positive feelings. But think of a company's image as its reputation or the overall impression that people have of it, and it's easier to see why image is important.

So image research is really a matter of measuring the overall impression that people have of a company or product. In this sense, image is a very real, very important thing.

IMAGE AND IDENTITY—WHAT ARE THEY?

While the two terms are often used interchangeably, they actually have different meanings. *Identity* refers to all the ways a company identifies itself to the outside world. This includes advertising, packaging, trucks, stationery—easily dozens of things for most companies. A company's *image,* on the other hand, is the result of this identity. It is the perception of the company by all its publics, created by the identity.

Identity is cause; image is effect.

WHEN TO DO RESEARCH

Image research can be precipitated by a number of things. Companies most often conduct image research when they are considering a name change or logo/symbol change. Determining what impression consumers have of the company is an important first step in deciding how to identify the company.

Image research can also be an important first step in planning corporate advertising efforts, since it helps identify areas of the company's reputation or operations that consumers may be unaware of or confused about. These often become the focus of corporate communication programs.

Finally, image research is often done as part of acquisition or merger evaluations. When one company purchases another, a large share of what it is buying is the reputation and "goodwill" of the new company. If the firm to be acquired is in a field with which the acquiring firm is unfamiliar, an image study may help determine the quality of the reputation—and, therefore, part of the value—of the firm being acquired.

STEPS IN IMAGE RESEARCH

The typical image study involves two basic steps: (1) determining what characteristics are important to consumers, and (2) measuring how the company or product is viewed on these characteristics. For example, it's important to know whether "availability and delivery" is more important than the "technical knowledge of sales representatives." Once this is determined, you need to know how company A is viewed on these characteristics compared with its competitors.

But another step is also important: *identifying the characteristics on which the companies being evaluated differ the most.* Overlooking this can limit the usefulness of the research. A classic example of this is the airline industry. Any air traveler would agree that safety is a critical element of the reputation of any airline—if it's absent. At the same time, however, most travelers probably believe that all airlines are about equal on safety. No one airline is really much "safer" than another. Airlines are seen to differ most on things such as schedule convenience or quality of meals. Consequently, these characteristics, rather than safety, are more logical subjects for advertising.

In summary, then, it's necessary to measure which characteristics are important, but it is also critical to measure which characteristics are "discriminators." It's these discriminating attributes that become critical in turning research results into action.

AN EXAMPLE

The easiest way to illustrate how image research works is to describe an example. The hypothetical company doing this image study is Acme Chemical Co.

Step 1

The first step is to determine how Acme and its competitors are viewed overall by the market. Let's suppose that Acme's key competitor is Universal Chemical Company. Respondents could first be asked to indicate their *overall opinion* of each company on a scale such as this one:

Entirely favorable	( )
Mostly favorable	( )
Mixed—about equally favorable and unfavorable	( )
Mostly unfavorable	( )
Entirely unfavorable	( )

This might be followed with a "Why do you feel that way?" question to determine, on an unaided basis, the most important top-of-mind impressions of each company.

This overall opinion scale serves two purposes. First, it gives a summary profile of each company. (What proportion of people feel positive, neutral, or negative about the companies?) Second, this scale can be the basis for later cross-tabulations and analysis. For example, it may be helpful to look at how the specific attitudes toward Acme of customers who have favorable opinions of the firm differ from those who have generally unfavorable opinions. This may help isolate the characteristics that are problems for Acme.

Step 2

The second step is to have respondents indicate their opinions of the importance of a list of company or product characteristics. This list is usually developed through exploratory research, such as group interviews. The results might be as in Table 3.

A word of caution: "product quality" almost always comes out on top on a list like this. But that can be deceptive, since quality *alone* is rarely the key factor in a market. To understand what people mean by "quality," it's usually helpful to know:

Are there other characteristics that go together with quality to form a "package"?

Do respondents really mean some "threshold" of quality, rather than

Table 3. Hypothetical ranking of company and product characteristics by customers.

Company or product characteristics	Percent rating characteristic as "extremely important"
1. Product quality	92%
2. Competitive prices	86
3. Prompt delivery	81
4. Salesman's knowledge	73
5. Technical service	70
6. Innovative research and development	65
7. Company size	40
8. Industry leadership	29
9. Effective management	23

absolute quality, is important? Obviously, no one wants a poor product, but neither do most people want the best product possible, regardless of price. People usually have a threshold of quality in mind, a minimum quality level that's acceptable. A product mustn't fall below this level, but neither should it necessarily be too far above it—or it risks being priced out of the market. Adding quality usually adds cost, too.

In short, then, don't accept an overly simplified, naive definition of "quality." Make sure you understand exactly what quality means in that market before you begin an image study, then build measures of the complete quality definition into the study.

After these importance ratings are obtained, respondents should be questioned about the characteristics on which they think companies in this industry differ most. Perhaps in Acme's market, buyers believe that suppliers differ most on prompt delivery and technical service. This would suggest that product quality and prices are important—and Acme must remain competitive in those areas—but aren't seen as characteristics that differentiate suppliers.

Step 3

The third step is to have respondents rate each of the companies on the list of more important characteristics. In our example, the results might look as in Figure 24.

In this example, it appears that one reason for Acme's better overall reputation, compared with Universal, is that it is more highly regarded on delivery and technical service—two of the characteristics that buyers earlier said were differentiating attributes among suppliers. On the other hand, Universal is seen as having more innovative R&D and being an industry leader, but these are much less important characteristics. In other words,

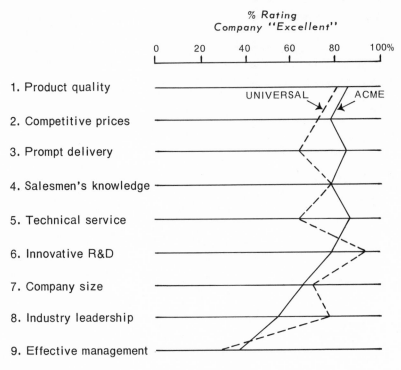

Figure 24. Hypothetical rating of two companies on characteristics deemed important.

Universal's strengths are in the less important areas, while Acme is strong in the areas that are most important to the market.

WHOM TO INTERVIEW

The two most important "publics" to include in any image research are customers and prospective customers. Customers are important, of course, because any company wants to understand why it is successful with the people who are buying from it. Prospective customers or competitors' customers are important because they are the people you hope to turn into future buyers.

In some cases stockholders and representatives of the financial community are important to study, too. Top management often believes, usually correctly, that a company's image can have a strong effect on its stock price.

Finally, don't forget to evaluate the image of a company among its employees and management. Any effort to change the image of a company must be consistent with the way people within the company think about it and want it to be seen. So understanding the attitudes and perceptions of employees, especially at the middle-management level and above, should usually be part of an image study.

28

Industrial and Medical Research

□□

Industrial and medical research are just like consumer research—only different. Most of the principles and techniques of consumer research can be applied to industrial and medical products. The difference is that the structure of these markets and the types of respondents to be interviewed make it necessary to revise and adapt the consumer research techniques. *But the basic approaches are the same.*

The term "industrial and medical products" is used here to refer to products bought by companies or institutions rather than by individual consumers. Examples of these products would be:

Building components
Computers
Hospital supplies
Heavy machinery
Office equipment
Corporate financial services
Institutional food service supplies

DIFFERENCES FROM CONSUMER RESEARCH

Industrial and medical research are different from consumer research in some important ways. These differences must be understood so that the appropriate adjustments can be made in consumer research techniques.

Market concentration.   Most industrial and medical markets are extremely concentrated—usually more than consumer product markets. In some cases, only a handful of companies make up the entire market. (The commercial aircraft market would be an extreme example.) A more typical

Table 4. Distribution of short-term general hospitals by size (number of beds), 1980.

Size Category	Hospitals		Total Beds	
	No.	%	No.	%
500 or more beds	306	5%	210,072	22%
400–499	235	4 ⌐15%	103,444	11 ⌐46%
300–399	376	6	127,514	13
200–299	712	12	172,010	18
100–199	1,377	23	193,657	20
Under 100	2,950	50	154,478	16
Total:	5,956	100%	961,175	100%

example is the hospital market, where 15 percent of the hospital units account for nearly half (46 percent) the potential market for many products (see Table 4).

At the other end of the scale, the hospitals with fewer than 100 beds account for half the hospitals in the United States, but only 16 percent of the total beds.

This problem of market concentration is dealt with through stratified sampling. Sampling is done according to the market volume represented by each size category, not the number of businesses or institutions in that category. In other words, in the hospital example, hospitals with 500 beds or more would represent 22 percent of the sample, not 5 percent. Since most industrial and medical markets are highly concentrated, stratified sampling is an important principle in designing research for these markets.

Universe identification.   It's often difficult to locate the companies in an industrial market so that they can be sampled. Sampling hospitals in the medical research field is an exception. These are easily identified. But in most industrial markets, there are no readily available lists or directories— it may even be difficult to estimate the number of potential customers in a market. For example, how many offices are there in the United States which are potential customers for some common office supply, such as cellophane tape? Probably hundreds of thousands. But it would be vary difficult to identify them all or sample them systematically.

This problem usually requires the use of multiple sampling sources. Lists of companies or institutions can be assembled from many sources to come as close as possible to a complete list for sampling. The kinds of sampling sources which are often used in the industrial research field include:

General directories, such as Moody's, Thomas Register, and Dun & Bradstreet
Trade associations

Government lists, such as state industrial directories and state business
  magazines
Telephone Yellow Pages
Mailing-list houses

Multiple purchase influences.   Unlike consumer products, where the
purchaser and the user are usually the same person (the homemaker),
industrial and medical products are often used by one person, but actually
purchased by someone else. In many cases, several people may be involved in some way in the purchase decision.

This often means doing multiple interviews to cover all the purchase
influences. It can mean doing different types of interviews with different
people in the purchase process. For example, the end user of an industrial
product may be the appropriate respondent for a product test, while the
purchasing agent might be the right person to interview in a new-product-
concept study.

Respondent accessibility.   Business executives, architects, and doctors
are difficult to reach, and they generally don't have a lot of time to talk
when you finally reach them. This doesn't mean they can't be interviewed,
but it does mean you have to work your schedule around theirs and be
briefer than with most consumer research.

Terminology.   Most industrial and medical markets have languages all
their own, which must be incorporated into questionnaires. You have to
use the technical terminology of the respondent to be taken seriously by the
person you are interviewing. This doesn't mean you can't be conversational. But you must deal with the subject of the interview in the respondent's own terms. For example, the person who operates the heart-lung
machine is called a ''perfusionist'' or ''pump tech,'' so that's the term you
should use.

The special terminology usually is not as mysterious, extensive, or difficult to learn as it first seems. A quick vocabulary ''cram session'' with
someone familiar with the market is often enough to get you by.

Intimidating interviewing environment.   Even the most assertive consumer interviewer is usually self-concious about going into an operating-
room suite or a company president's office to conduct an interview. This
generally means you need special interviewers to conduct industrial and
medical research. We've found that former nurses, trained in research
techniques, work best as interviewers in the hospital environment. Similarly, most interviewing services have trained, experienced ''executive
interviewers'' on their staffs.

These are mostly differences of degree, not kind. Industrial and medical
research can use most of the techniques used for consumer research, but the

differences must be recognized so that the research techniques can be adapted to overcome the problems.

SIMILARITIES WITH CONSUMER RESEARCH

Decisions are made by people. Although the customers in industrial and medical markets are technically companies and institutions, the purchasing decisions are still made by people. And people are not completely different on the job from the way they are at home. Their job may require them to be somewhat more rational and objective in their business decisions than their personal decisions, but even this is not always the case. It's really true that "people are people."

Interviewers and respondents. In industrial and medical research, you still have someone asking questions of someone else, so many of the proven techniques of consumer research interviewing can be applied to these fields. Also, the same principles of questionnaire design and scale construction apply.

Respondent motivation. Everybody likes to give his opinion, and this includes business executives, purchasing agents, and doctors—as well as homemakers. This form of flattery ("Your opinion is important to us") is basic to all types of marketing research. And it gets cooperation from most people, whether they are being interviewed as businessmen or individual consumers.

Sampling. As mentioned earlier in this chapter, sampling can be a problem in some markets. In other fields, such as the medical supply market, drawing a good sample is often easier than in consumer research. For example, a complete list of virtually every hospital in the United States, including bed size and a myriad other characteristics, is readily available. The same is true of product categories for which there are strong trade associations. Having this complete list is a sampler's "dream" that usually isn't available in the consumer research world.

So industrial medical research isn't as different from consumer research as is often thought. The basic components—respondent, questionnaire, and interviewer—are there, whether the topic is cake mix, machine tools, or surgical instruments.

RESEARCH TECHNIQUES

Group Interviews

It's easier than you'd think to get a businessman or doctor to attend a focus group. Getting industrial and medical respondents to participate in focus groups is a mystery to many researchers. Yet there is a simple secret: money. Obviously you can't "buy" a businessman or a doctor—you can't pay him enough to make it really worth his time. But you can easily insult him by asking him to give you an hour or two of his time for a token fee. You have to ante up.

The going rate for focus groups can be up to $100 an hour for doctors, which means $150 for the typical 90-minute focus group. For less specialized respondents, such as company purchasing agents, the fee might be one-half or one-third of this.

Beyond offering an adequate fee, appeal to the respondents' professional interest—most people like to keep up with new things that are happening in their field. Then try to keep the session businesslike but informal. (Forget trying to serve cocktails or a sitdown formal dinner. It's not worth the trouble.)

Another key to industrial and medical focus groups is scheduling—setting up sessions when it is easiest for your respondents to come. Many operating-room supervisors, for example, prefer a 4:30 P.M. session (right after they leave the hospital) to an evening group. Some businessmen may prefer a 6 P.M. group, with a box lunch or light snack, so they can be home by 7:30 or 8:00.

Telephone Research

Businessmen and doctors will usually answer the phone—even when there is an interviewer on the other end. In other words, telephone research works surprisingly well in the industrial and medical research field.

Telephone interviewing is replacing door-to-door contacts for many kinds of consumer research. Similarly, telephone interviewing is growing in popularity in industrial and medical studies. For example, most doctors prefer patients to phone with questions. The same is true with research. Where the telephone is suitable, most industrial and medical respondents seem to prefer the telephone to a personal interview.

We've done telephone studies ranging from five-minute interviews with office managers to 20-minute interviews with cardiovascular surgeons. And surprisingly, refusal rates often tend to be lower on industrial and medical studies than on consumer projects. With WATS line interviewing, telephone research offers an opportunity to get a larger, geographically more dispersed sample at a fraction of the cost of personal interviews. So in many cases in industrial and medical research, telephone interviewing not only is an acceptable alternative, it's actually *a better* alternative.

Personal Interviewing

When all else fails, interview the business executive or doctor at his office. Telephone is usually faster and cheaper, but sometimes—when you have a product to show or questions that involve lengthy rating scales—a personal interview is necessary. Personal interviews take time, since you have to set up an appointment. Be direct about what you want and why you're there—and be truthful about how much time it will take—and most people will grant an interview. Doctors usually expect to be paid for their time during an office interview, whereas this generally is not the case with businessmen.

Product Testing

Most consumer product companies wouldn't think of introducing a product which hadn't been successfully tested among potential users. Yet careful, well-designed product testing still seems to be the exception in industrial and medical markets.

Industrial and medical products *can* be tested. In hospitals or companies, this testing usually requires perseverance to get the testing cleared through all channels of the company or hospital. But it can be done.

Product tests with rotated order of use, paired comparisons, and most of the other techniques of consumer research can be carried out on most industrial and medical products. (Obviously this does not include drugs.) In the medical field, for example, we have successfully completed product tests on a variety of products, including many operating-room supplies, casting materials, tapes, sponges, and dental products.

Mail Research

A "forgotten" technique of consumer research—the mail survey—can sometimes still work in industrial or health-care studies. Doctors, for example, seem to read their mail. We've found that well-designed and pretested mail surveys sent with a token incentive can get up to a 70 percent response rate in the medical field (50 percent is our rule of thumb, and we regularly achieve it). This rate of return is unheard of in consumer research, where 10 percent would usually be good.

The key here is to use mail only on certain types of simple, straightforward, high-interest subjects. When time is taken to design the cover letter and questionnaire carefully, and a list of respondent names is available, mail can offer a good, low-cost alternative.

29

Simulated Sales Testing

□□

Cost is the principal appeal of simulated sales testing over real test marketing. And it's an important difference—the difference between $25,000 and $250,000 or more.

Regular test marketing works remarkably well. One study by the A. C. Nielsen Company showed that market tests which run eight months or longer are 75 percent correct in their predictions about products' success or failure. But full-scale test marketing has two important drawbacks:

Time. A market test takes a minimum of several months to conduct and can run a year or longer. During this time a competitor may introduce a product nearly identical to the one you are test marketing.

Money. Test marketing one product costs a minimum of about $250,000 and can run up to $1 million or more. Furthermore, since only one out of every three products in the test market actually goes national, the cost of testing a product is actually three times this cost.

In addition, full-scale market tests offer poor security. In most cases competitors quickly learn that a product is being test-marketed and are able to buy samples of it in stores. Also, controlling the marketing variables being tested can sometimes be difficult. A competitor may run a heavy wave of advertising during the test marketing, making it difficult to measure the effectiveness of advertising for the test product.

Simulated sales testing techniques were developed to overcome these problems. These techniques attempt to evaluate a new product in a way that reflects real-world behavior more accurately than concept testing, yet is faster and less costly then full-scale test marketing. This is the niche— between concept testing and test marketing—that simulated sales testing tries to fill.

Rarely is simulated sales testing used to completely bypass test marketing. Companies generally are not willing to risk a national rollout merely on the basis of a simulated sales test. Instead, this testing usually serves to weed out losing products and screen likely winners for full-scale test markets.

PROCEDURE

There are a number of research companies which offer different simulated sales testing techniques. These techniques vary in the underlying model or structure which is used to estimate sales potential, but all of them follow essentially the same general procedure for developing data.

Step 1: Exposure to advertising. Some form of advertising, either print or TV, is used to expose consumers to the concept of the product. An ad, rather than a concept description, is used to get as close as possible to the type of exposure consumers will get in the real world.

Step 2: Opportunity to buy. After seeing the ad, consumers are given an opportunity to purchase the test product, usually along with other products in the category. This is often accomplished through a small simulated store or store section—or sometimes in a real store.

Step 3: Use period. Consumers who buy the product take it home and use it as they normally would. In most cases, consumers are not told they will be called back later and re-interviewed. This is done to make the use period as realistic as possible and lessen the feeling among consumers that they are taking part in a test.

Step 4: Follow-up interviews. After a normal use period, consumers are contacted and questioned about their satisfaction with the product and their intention to repurchase it.

Step 5: Repurchase opportunity. Some techniques offer consumers an opportunity to actually repurchase the product. Again, this is an attempt to get a behavioral purchase measure rather than just a stated intention to repurchase.

The purpose of this procedure is to generate three consumer measures regarding the product:

1. *Trial rate*—the proportion of all consumers who try the product.
2. *Repeat rate*—the proportion of one-time buyers (or triers) who purchase the product at least a second time.
3. *Purchase frequency*—a measure of how often repeaters repurchase and how many units they purchase each time.

The end objective of simulated sales testing is to produce an estimate of sales potential, usually expressed either as a measure of market share (if the product is in a well-defined category) or as an absolute dollar or unit volume estimate.

STRENGTH AND WEAKNESSES

The primary strength of simulated sales testing as compared with concept testing is that it uses actual behavioral measures, so fewer assumptions about analogies to current consumer purchase behavior need to be made. Compared with full-scale test marketing, of course, simulated sales testing has the advantages of being quicker, less costly, more confidential, and better controlled. A typical simulated sales test costs at least $25,000, although the actual figure depends on the product category and exactly how the test is conducted.

At the same time, although simulated sales testing comes close to behavioral measures, it nevertheless is still not completely realistic. Advertising exposures, simulated shopping experiences, and repurchase intentions all fall a little short of the real world. Another weakness of simulated sales testing is that it cannot measure the long-term adoption dynamics in a market—how ongoing repeat and frequency rates for the products are going to develop. Nevertheless, many companies believe that simulated sales testing is accurate enough to serve as a screening device before full-scale test marketing.

SUPPLIERS

The most widely used simulated sales testing techniques and the companies which offer them are:

The *Laboratory Test Market (LTM)* from Yankelovich, Skelly & White, Inc.

The *COMP* Service of Elrick and Lavidge, Inc.

The *Assessor* Service of Management Decision Systems, Inc.

ESP (Estimating Sales Potential) from NPD Research Inc.

The *BASES* service from Burke Marketing Research.

Other models and procedures are offered by other research firms, but these are the best known.

30

Product Positioning Research

□□□

The concept of position is important in most sports. In football, defensive backs are careful to be aware of their position so they can defend the portion of the field for which they're responsible. Tennis players are told by teaching pros to watch their own position on the court and the position of their opponent. Basketball coaches discuss the importance of having strong players at each position.

In sports, the concept of position is a way to effectively compete and win. It's also important in marketing, where the "position" of a product is used as a way of describing how a product fits into a category relative to competition—and how it can exploit its location to compete more effectively.

WHAT IS A POSITION?

For the company, a position might be defined as the mental space a product occupies in consumers' minds. Put another way, a position is the product's "address" on the mental map consumers use to think about a category.

From the consumer's viewpoint, a position is a device people use to structure the world and simplify it. Most consumers have heard of literally thousands of products. Individuals are bombarded with hundreds of advertising messages every day. All of this is too much for the brain to handle. Some scientists believe the brain can focus on no more than seven items at a time. If true, that means the mind has to find a simplified structure to represent reality. It simply cannot retain all the information presented about every product. One way it seems to do this is to summarize its impression of products into a few key concepts, which become the product's "position."

179

In other words, a product has a position whether that's intended or not. Marketing and advertising people talk about "creating a position," as if there won't be a position unless they create one. Wrong. You can create a position—or try to—but even if you don't, the product will have one anyway. Consumers will form impressions and images about the product and create a position for it in their mental picture of the category. They don't need your permission to do it.

It's true that the position many products have is as "one of the bunch"—but this is simply an undifferentiated position. That's not the same as *no* position.

So when marketing people talk about "creating a position," they usually mean trying to influence where consumers position a product. A position is built by communicating to consumers—through advertising, brand name, and packaging—a consistent message about the product and where it fits into the market.

A classic example of positioning is the Avis campaign: "We're number two. We have to try harder." The 7-Up "Uncola" effort is another example. Another example is the well-established association of Marlboro cigarettes with rugged, outdoor men. Most well-known, successful brands have a clear position in their markets. That's one of the reasons they're successful.

WHAT GOES INTO A POSITION?

From the manufacturer's standpoint, there are two key elements of a product's position:

The things that *describe* the product.
The things that *differentiate* the product from competition.

Much of the wasted effort in thinking about positioning probably results from focusing simply on the descriptive issues, when it's the differentiating characteristics that are key.

The critical thing to finding a successful position is to identify characteristics that are both differentiating and important to consumers. A primary role of research in positioning work is to measure whether positioning characteristics are both differentiating and meaningful.

THE ROLE OF RESEARCH IN POSITIONING

Figure 25 shows a conceptual framework for thinking about the typical research steps on a new product. At the top of the pyramid, when a product is in the rough-concept stage, you're looking for "clues" about positioning. Where does it fit? What need does it fill? Where do the opportunities seem to be? And so on. As you move toward the bottom, you're looking

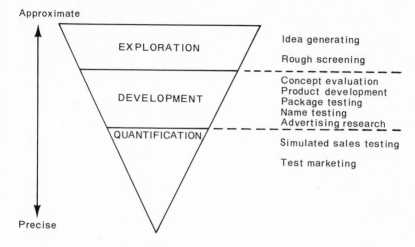

Figure 25. Conceptual framework for the research steps on a new product.

for product definition. Once you get to test market, the position you'll be using for a product must be finalized.

So the role of the research at the steps along the way can be seen as:

1. Early qualitative research: looking for positioning clues and opportunities.
2. Refining the product: identifying the position dimensions that are both differentiating and meaningful.
3. Final quantitative testing: making sure the position is effective.

The best opportunities for research to make a contribution to positioning are in the early stages, particularly in the exploration and development stages. By the time the product gets to test marketing or simulated sales testing, there's not much you can do to affect what happens.

This "model" of the research process—the approximate/precise dimension—also applies to restage or "repositioning" research on established products. In looking for new positions for existing products, you have to go back and start with the search for positioning opportunities, using very "approximate" research, then move toward refining those opportunities.

RESEARCH ISSUES

Here are the positioning issues that need to be addressed at the early stages of the development of a product—or in the first steps of a product's repositioning:

1. *Where are we now?* As mentioned before, every product has some sort of position, whether intended or not. So the first step is to find out what that is—either the established position of an ongoing product or the likely "natural" position of a new product. This includes specific issues such as:

□ What does the "space" look like? What are the most important dimensions in the category?
□ Where is our product in that space on each of the key dimensions?
□ What are the other products in that space? And where are they?
□ What are the gaps, unfilled positions, or "holes" in the category?
□ What are the primary attitude dimensions in the category?
□ Which dimensions are most important?
□ How do these attitudes differ by market segment?

2. *Where do we want to be?* Maybe right where we are, or maybe just slightly moved on one or two dimensions. Or maybe in a completely different position. Ideally, research can help find a key dimension which, if you could move on it, would produce a new position that was both differentiating and meaningful for the product.

How do you decide where you want to be? Some of the positioning opportunities for a product include:

□ Finding an *unmet consumer need* (or at least one that's not being adequately met now by competition).
□ Identifying a *product strength* that is both unique and important.
□ Determining how to *correct a product weakness* and thereby enhance a product's appeal. (The legitimate "new and improved" products reflect this type of positioning move.)
□ Changing *consumer usage patterns* to include different or additional uses for the product.
□ Identifying *market segments* which represent the best targets for a product.

3. *How do we get there from here?* This is where reality becomes a constraint. "Getting there" could come from one or both of two sources: (1) physical product differences and (2) communication.

Some positions are based strongly on physical product differences. Duncan Hines cake mix maintained leadership of that category for years by stressing that it was moister than other brands—a claim it could back up with its product. Years later, Pillsbury added pudding to its cake mix, changed the name to Pillsbury Plus, and rejuvenated its franchise by claiming even greater moistness than Duncan Hines. That's an example of positioning on the basis of product differences.

On the other hand, some positions are based almost solely on communication—finding a memorable and meaningful way to describe the product. Nothing really changed about Avis after it began describing itself as "number two." Calling 7-Up the "Uncola" did not involve any product changes. Creativity can be the key component of a position change.

The main point here is *not* to talk about a physical product difference that can't be backed up with performance. The product must be able to fulfill the expectations of it created by the position.

STRATEGY ISSUES IN POSITIONING

Selecting a strategy isn't simple, and some of the problems encountered are the same in almost any category. For example:

□ Is a large segment already being served by other brands better than a smaller segment that isn't being addressed by anyone? Should you hit-em-where-they-are or hit-em-where-they-ain't?

□ Should you focus on one product characteristic at a time or attack several simultaneously? Should you try specialization or offer something for everyone?

□ Is it more effective to emphasize product strengths or to try to overcome perceived weaknesses? The former could seem naive; the latter may come across as negative.

□ Can one product occupy several positions, perhaps in different market segments? Can you mean different things to different people?

□ What's the value of a creative "gimmick"? Some positions lend themselves more easily to clever names, packages, or advertising campaigns. What is this worth?

Research can provide information to help make all these decisions. Yet rarely will the information clearly indicate the decision or strategy that's best. In the end it's people—not computers or research techniques—who must select and develop a position. And in that process, experience and judgment—often disguised as hunches or intuition—usually play a crucial role. That's what makes positioning one of the most interesting facets of marketing.

RESEARCH TECHNIQUES

Positioning research is an approach, not a technique. Clues about the best positioning for a product or service can come out of many types of research. Qualitative research—using focus groups or one-on-one interviews—is a place to begin because it often stimulates ideas and generates hypotheses. A basic study of the usage of products in the same category and of attitudes toward them, conducted in person or by phone, usually gives an indication of the current positions of products.

Beyond this, multivariate techniques can be used to get a more quantified fix on current or possible positions. The most commonly used multivariate techniques for this purpose are:

Multidimensional scaling to provide a "map" of the market's perceptions of products' positions.

Cluster analysis to show either groups of products that are perceived as similar (if the products are clustered) or consumers who behave or feel similarly (if the clustering is applied to people rather than products).

Automatic interaction detector (AID) or some other segmentation technique to identify the factors that seem to create market segments, which also suggest positioning possibilities.

31

Group Interviews

A good listener is not only popular everywhere, but after a while he gets to know something.

—Wilson Mizner

Most of us, if we have a normal amount of curiosity, like to overhear conversations about things we're interested in. That's the basic purpose of a group interview: to listen to real people—customers or prospects—talk about a marketing issue that's important to us, and, in the process, to learn something.

A group interview is a unique opportunity to experience "the market" firsthand. Most marketing research studies reduce people to numbers and percents in a report, but in a group interview the people are alive and right there. For this reason, the group interview often provides a special opportunity to get a picture of person-by-person behavior and attitudes, rather than aggregate patterns that are the output of most large-scale studies.

Many of the concepts and techniques used in group interviews had their basis in clinical psychology. Group therapists discovered years ago that some people could talk more freely in a group and could benefit by listening to others. This approach, adapted to marketing problems, formed the basis for developing group interviewing techniques.

Today group interviews are one of the most widely used types of marketing research. There are many names used—focus groups, group discussions, qualitative research, and group depth interviews—but they all refer to the same approach, which will be called simply a "group interview."

WHAT IS A GROUP INTERVIEW?

There is no precise definition of a group interview, since the term describes a general approach, not a specific technique. Generally, however, a group interview involves six to ten people recruited to meet predefined characteristics (age, usage of a certain product, interest in a new product idea, and so on). The interview is usually held in a relaxed, informal atmosphere either conference-room or living-room style, to encourage conversation. The session typically lasts between one and two hours.

Group interviews are led by experienced moderators, who work from a topic discussion outline.

The sessions usually are arranged so that representatives from the client organization can observe the session, either through a one-way mirror or by closed-circuit TV. The interview usually is recorded, either on audio or video tape

Since the dynamics in an individual group can make any single session misleading, it usually is desirable to conduct more than one session per subject—two or three per topic is best. It is common to spread out the interviews geographically to get an indication of regional differences. Finally, it is best to have similar respondents in the same group. If young homemakers are mixed in a session with older women to talk about beauty products, for example, the differences among respondents in the group may make it difficult to see any trends or patterns. It would be better to have one session composed of young women and another group made up of older women.

Group interviews can be conducted with almost any types of consumers: women, men, children (minimum age is about six), and people in business or the professions (physicians, lawyers, or accountants).

USES OF GROUP INTERVIEWS

For many types of marketing problems, group interviews are a typical first step in research. They are a logical way to begin, because they are relatively inexpensive and flexible, so they can be adapted to a variety of problems and issues.

Although group interviews can be conducted on almost any subject, a large share of them is concentrated in two subject areas: new products and advertising.

Appropriate use of group interviews requires an understanding of the differences between group interviews and large-scale quantitative research. The differences can be summarized in this way:

Group interviews are . . .	*Quantitative research is . . .*
Descriptive	Diagnostic
Subjective	Objective
Exploratory	Definitive
Approximate	Precise

The specific uses of group interviews usually fall into the following categories:

1. *Suggesting hypotheses for further testing.* Groups are a common way to generate ideas to be tested in large-scale quantitative studies. These hypotheses may be about attitudes toward a product category, reasons for using a brand or type of product, or factors that are responsible for the structure of a market.

2. *Helping structure questionnaires.* A major use of group interviews is to hear how respondents talk about a category or the products in it. Knowing the words consumers use can help in phrasing questions in the language of respondents. It can also help suggest the range of answers that should be listed for a closed-end question.

3. *Looking at categories.* Group interviews can be a useful way to get a quick overview of or orientation to a new business or product category. This can be helpful for new-product teams looking at unfamiliar categories. It also can help companies explore markets in which they are considering acquisitions.

4. *Evaluating new product concepts.* Although group interviews are not appropriate for ranking new product concepts, they can be useful in indicating the major strengths and weaknesses of a new product idea. Often consumers are able to identify drawbacks to a new product idea that have been overlooked by the marketing people working on the new product. Groups can also be useful for checking whether the uses and benefits of a new product are clearly communicated in concept statements. This can be a valuable check before large-scale concept tests are conducted.

5. *Generating new ideas about older products.* Marketing teams can sometimes be stimulated to recognize new, alternative uses for established products by listening to consumers talk about ways they discovered to use a product.

6. *Suggesting new creative approaches.* Advertising agencies often use group interviews to provide input for creative teams. Listening to consumers talk about exactly how they use a product or the things they like about it—or even the problems they have with a product—can generate ideas for advertising.

7. *Interpreting quantitative research results.* Sometimes group interviews are used as a last step in research. If the results of a large-scale study raise questions about why respondents answered one question as they did, group interviews can be used to probe in detail for the reasons behind quantitative test results.

8. *Preventing disasters.* Sometimes groups are used simply as a "disaster check" for products, promotions, or advertising, to make sure some glaring problem or communications gap has not been overlooked.

WHY GROUP INTERVIEWS WORK

Group interviews are an effective way to develop information from respondents, because they allow a number of useful things to happen within the group:

Interaction. Consumers hear each other talk and are stimulated by the ideas and comments of others in the session. This usually generates a more lively conversation among the participants in a group than is practical in a one-on-one interview.

Synergy. Because of the group interaction, respondents are often able to be more creative, interesting, and thoughtful in their comments than they would be if interviewed individually. In this respect, a group can generate more ideas and information than would result if the participants were interviewed individually.

Commonality. It's important that group respondents share basic similarities in their attitudes and/or lifestyles. This creates a feeling of sharing and understanding, which helps stimulate discussion.

Security and freedom. On some types of sensitive subjects, the group can help respondents feel free to share unorthodox ideas and opinions. Hearing other respondents say they don't understand or don't like something about an ad, for example, may help respondents feel comfortable admitting that they share the same view.

Enjoyment. Most respondents enjoy taking part in a well-conducted group interview. It's usually fun and stimulating. As a result, participants want to make the session productive.

In addition to these factors which make group interviews productive, there are several reasons why groups are effective from the client or user standpoint:

Flexibility. With the clients or users viewing, it is relatively easy to revise the questions or the structure of the research, if needed, from one group to the next. If a question isn't working well, for example, it can be revised for the next session.

Speed. Results are virtually instantaneous, at least for those viewing the session. So where time pressures are heavy, group interviews can be a way to develop a preliminary understanding of a topic within a matter of days.

Firsthand experience. Hearing real, live people talk about a product or category provides very valuable firsthand experience for the viewers. Hearing how respondents actually talk about a product and the way they use it, for example, is important for a marketing team.

Stimulation. Group interviews are useful not only because of what happens in the group session but also because of the ideas that they can stimulate in the minds of the people who are watching the session. For this reason, it is valuable if the end users of the research can attend and view the session.

DANGERS AND DRAWBACKS

Although group interviews have many strengths, they are by no means foolproof. Group interviews can fail for a number of reasons:

A dominant individual. Probably the most common reason for a group interview to fail is one person dominating the interview. The moderator can try to encourage others to speak, but an outspoken person is often difficult to suppress.

Questioning, not discussion. Inexperienced moderators sometimes conduct a group interview by going around the group and asking a question of each individual, one at a time. This precludes the interaction that makes group interviews valuable.

Reliance on isolated verbatims. Sometimes viewers of groups pick up a chance comment by one of the respondents which supports their ideas or position on a question. In the course of most group interviews, almost any position can be supported by selecting isolated comments out of context. Basing conclusions on verbatim comments rather than the general tone of the group is a common misuse of group interviews.

Order effect. Reactions to ads or products can be affected by the order in which they are shown. This, of course, is the reason order is rotated in quantitative tests. If only one or two group interviews are conducted on a subject, however, completely rotating the order of exhibits or questions is impossible. This is another reason why holding more than one group interview on a subject is desirable. At the least, the possible biasing effect of the order in which questions were asked should be kept in mind during the analysis.

Group dynamics. Groups develop personalities, just as individuals do. The dynamics of a group can be either positive or negative. One group can, for some reason, be unusually positive about a new product concept, while the next group will turn sour on it. The moderator can attempt to limit this by balancing the direction of the group with his or her questions and comments, but group dynamics can sometimes be nearly impossible to control. This is another argument for doing multiple group interviews on a subject.

Inappropriate purpose. Clients can use groups for the wrong reasons— either as a definitive measure or as "quick and dirty" research to avoid a quantitative study. Counting noses in a group interview and projecting these numbers as a representative sample of the population would seem an obvious misuse, but it is done all too often.

DISCUSSION FLOW

The flow of a successful group interview is from general to specific. Things should usually begin with a general discussion of the product category, then later move toward a discussion of a specific product or perhaps even specific characteristics of a product. But the general topics should come first; comments will be biased if discussion of a specific product or brand precedes it.

PLANNING THE GROUP INTERVIEW

A "discussion guide" is usually prepared as a way of planning the group interview and allocating time among all the topics to be covered. The guide should be detailed enough to suggest all the issues to be covered, yet remain flexible enough to be adjusted as the group progresses. *It is a guide, not a questionnaire.* A good moderator will sound as if he or she is conversing with participants in the group, not working from a prepared outline.

Figure 26 is an actual group interview outline from a project on breakfast cereal. It's quite detailed. (Again, remember these are topics to be covered, not questions to be asked.) But it illustrates the flow of a typical group interview and demonstrates the wide range of areas that can be covered.

Figure 26. Sample group interview outline for a marketing research project.

DISCUSSION GUIDE
(Women)

I. Introduction

    A. Purpose of Group

    B. Ground Rules
       1. Relax.
       2. Own opinion.
       3. Don't be afraid to disagree.
       4. Mike/mirror.
       5. Introduce selves and family *briefly*.

II. Warm-up (Brief)
    A. Brief Review of Cereal Usage/Purchase Patterns
       1. Who in household eats cereal? How often?
       2. What do you normally buy? Favorites?

3. Who in household is eating which cereals? Types of cereal?
4. Considerations in choosing cereals. How do you decide which cereal to buy?

III. Reaction to the Concept of a Cereal with Half the Sugar

A. Explanation of Concept: a cereal with half the sugar content of most pre-sweets.

B. Reaction to Concept.
1. What is overall reaction to this idea? (Written.)
2. Perceived likes/advantages.   } vs. other
3. Perceived dislikes/disadvantages. } cereals

C. Interest in Concept.
1. How interested are you in a cereal like this? What about your children's interest?
2. Reasons for interest
3. Do you feel there is a need for a cereal that offers this?

D. Expectations
1. What do you expect a cereal such as this to be like?
   —Form/appearance? }
   —Taste?   } Why?
   —Texture?   }
2. Who is this cereal for?
   —Children?   }
   —Adults?   }
   —Family?   } Why?
   —Special diet?   }

Is any cereal currently available like this—i.e., a cereal offering half the sugar content of most pre-sweets? Which one(s)?

IV. Halfsies
A. Purchase
1. Why did you purchase Halfsies? Reasons. (Importance of reasons.)
2. Whose idea was it to purchase Halfsies? Why?
3. Did you buy Halfsies in place of another cereal? Which one(s)? Why?
4. In originally purchasing Halfsies, what were your expectations? Appearance? Taste? Texture? Your child's expectations?
5. Is Halfsies eaten "differently" from other cereals? In what ways (e.g., quantity, sugar, occasion)?
6. Do you plan to purchase Halfsies again? Why?

B. Awareness
1. How did you first learn about Halfsies?
2. Show adult commercial.
   —Have you seen it before?
   —Overall reactions to commercial? Likes? Dislikes?

    —Main message in commercial? What does it tell you?
    —Product expectations from commercial? Appearance? Taste? Texture?
    —Interest in product after seeing commercial.
3. Show children's commercial.
    —Have your seen it before?
    —Overall reactions?
    —Main message? What does it tell you?
    —Any different product expectations versus previous commercial?
    —Interest in product after seeing. Expected child's interest?

C. Package
  1. What do you recall the Halfsies package looks like?
  2. Show package.
  3. Reactions to package.
    —Overall reaction.
    —Likes?   } Child's reaction
    —Dislikes?   } (as appropriate)
    —Changes to improve
  4. Expectations for product on the basis of package.

D. Product
  1. Prior to bringing product out and trying it . . . recall product—e.g., appearance, taste, texture, etc.
  2. Show product in bowl.
    —Is this how you remember it?
    —How is it different?
  3. Reaction to product after tasting.
    —Overall reaction.
    —Likes?
    —Dislikes?
  4. Reaction to product's appearance.   }
  5. Reaction to product's taste.   } versus
  6. Reaction to product's texture.   } expectations
  7. Interest in product after trying. (Written.)
  8. What changes do you feel would improve the product?

E. Product Fulfillment
  1. On the basis of previous discussion on the *idea* of a cereal with half the sugar content . . . do you feel Halfsies is that cereal? In your opinion, does Halfsies offer what you want in a cereal with half the sugar content?

WAYS TO IMPROVE GROUP INTERVIEWS

Research projects—especially research done by ad agencies—probably involve focus groups more than any other single technique. Yet on no other type of research is there such a "formula" approach, almost regardless of the type of problem being studied. Strangely, most group moderators get excited about whether the table should be round or square—if they believe there should be a table at all—or whether a one-way mirror is better than closed-circuit TV. Who cares? What difference does it make whether you're watching through a mirror or on a TV screen if nothing is happening that's worth seeing?

Here are some ways to get out of the rut. They've been developed over several years through research on many products among all types of respondents, from physicians to six-year-old kids. Not all are suitable for every study, but one of them could probably add a dimension to your next qualitative research project.

1. Dual moderating. This approach is especially useful on highly technical subjects, where it's virtually impossible to give an outside moderator all the detailed background information he might need. We've had good results in these cases from using *two* moderators: our own moderator, plus a second moderator from the client. The client moderator often is an R&D expert or someone else familiar with the technical details of the product. Our moderator is responsible for the flow of the session and the basic probing, while the "expert" moderator follows up on technical issues that might otherwise be overlooked. This is particularly useful on projects studying new product applications for basic technologies. On less technical subjects, the client moderator can even be a product manager or account executive. But be careful: some clients come on like F. Lee Bailey if the respondents say anything negative.

2. Minigroups. Why is a group interview almost always made up of eight to ten respondents? Several studies of group dynamics have shown that people have difficulty interacting with more than six other people. And, at best, a 90-minute session allows only nine minutes of conversation from an average respondent.

We've found that fewer respondents produce better results on many types of subjects, especially where there is a lot of personal variation in opinion or behavior. Minigroups of four or five people are ideal for exploring new categories in depth. They're also helpful for interviewing professionals, such as doctors or nurses. And they're almost imperative for children.

3. Lifestyle groups. Marketers and advertisers believe in segmentation. Yet we often make no attempt to segment people in focus-group sessions. Consumers are *not* all the same. Having young, new-values consumers in the same groups with older, traditional consumers can be disastrous. Try screening respondents to represent different basic lifestyle types. You'll find that the contrast from group to group is often amazing. This is particularly useful in "needs" exploration for new products.

4. Respondent + client groups. Have you ever got excited observing a focus-group session, then been unable to remember a few days later what

had you so worked up? Group sessions are strong stimuli to clients, yet even "hot" ideas tend to cool off quickly.

Consider thinking of groups in pairs: a respondent session to provide input, then a formal review session among the client team. Use the review session to capture the ideas from the group and try to build them toward complete problem solutions.

5. **Helping respondent creativity.** This is the most underutilized area of focus-group research. The purpose of groups is to find out what's in people's heads—yet we rarely do much to help them tell us. Here are three ideas:

□ Encourage respondents to be wishful, unrealistic, playful and childlike. This is very effective in helping consumers break away from the constraints of reality and talk about real needs they have. The ideas that come out are often ones the client knows how to solve—although not always in the way the respondent would have expected.

□ Have respondents focus on feelings rather than just ideas. We ask questions like: How does cleaning the bathroom make you feel? How do you feel when you fix breakfast in the morning? How do you feel when the bank tells you you're overdrawn? We all live in a world where feelings are often the only real thing to us. Why not use this approach in conducting qualitative research?

□ Help the respondents in a group "keep score." A group interview is a task-oriented activity, even if the task is only to generate ideas. We often use large flip-sheet pads of paper to jot down the ideas that consumers mention in the groups. As the sheets fill up, we tape them to the walls of the room. Writing down the ideas lets every respondent know his or her idea has been heard and valued. And as the walls of the room become filled with sheets of ideas, the energy level of the group really accelerates when it might otherwise be lagging. (This idea runs counter to all the conventional wisdom of many qualitative-research gurus. But it works!)

6. **Groups "plus."** Think about having respondents do something before they come into a session. You might ask them to try a new product, go shop at a certain kind of store, or even just think about a question related to the subject of the group. This gives the group a common experience to talk about. It also helps respondents focus on the subject of the session, so you can move more quickly into the discussion.

Because groups are largely unstructured, they lend themselves to experimentation. If something doesn't work, you can quickly drop it and go on to something else. So the risk is low, and the payoff can be high.

Finally, it is important to point out that group interviews, although they are the most popular kind of qualitative research, are not the only kind. One-on-one depth interviews are another alternative that should be considered in some cases. Individual interviews can be useful for exploring subjects in which personal differences are so great that the interaction in a group interview may be more destructive than useful. One-on-one interviews would often be better, for example, for exploring political issues or some types of financial questions.

32

Research
in the Courtroom

□□

"The first thing we do, let's kill all the lawyers." Shakespeare said it, but many researchers have thought it while working on projects designed to be used as evidence in legal cases.

Actually, the association between marketing research and the legal profession is a recent one. Before the 1950s, the Hearsay Rule prevented marketing research results from being admitted as evidence. "Hearsay," in legal terminology, is the reported statement of someone who is not available to be sworn in under oath and cross-examined. To protect the rights of the parties in litigation, such evidence has historically been judged inadmissable. Since it obviously is impractical for every respondent in a survey to be available to testify, this precedent effectively excluded research from legal proceedings.

That has changed, however, as the courts have come to recognize that a sample of opinion is often the only accurate and practical means of measuring public attitudes. In addition, the government, primarily the Federal Trade Commission (FTC), has promoted the use of research in some types of legal proceedings by using research as a basis for filing complaints against advertisers.

Today research, if properly done, is well accepted as evidence in many types of legal proceedings, especially those involving advertising claims.

LEGAL APPLICATIONS OF RESEARCH

What types of projects might become evidence in legal cases? Everything. Even projects not designed with any legal application in mind may become involved in litigation. For example, if a product becomes the subject of a government complaint or a competitor's lawsuit, any research done on that product might be subpoenaed. Similarly, even qualitative research done in the course of developing advertising messages could be subpoenaed if it is later claimed that the advertising is false or misleading.

There are two types of legal proceedings in which marketing research might be used:

Judicial processes, where one company sues another over some issue.

Administrative procedures involving a government agency, most often the FTC. This type has grown rapidly with the increase in consumer protection and advertising regulation by government agencies. Today most of the research which is done for use in legal proceedings is involved with such administrative cases.

Here are specific examples of some of the kinds of cases in which research might be conducted by one of the parties for use as evidence.

Antitrust cases.   Research could be used to help define the relevant market for a product, which is often a key issue in antitrust proceedings. What do consumers consider the relevant market, or relative alternatives, for a riding lawn mower? a cola? a ballpoint pen?

Trademark infringement.   To what extent are consumers confused between brands with similar names? This is often the issue on which trademark infringement cases hinge.

Unfair competition.   Research is sometimes used in this type of case to help define a geographic trading area, for example.

Change of venue.   Although unusual, this type of case often gets publicity in the newspapers. In sensational murder cases, for example, the defendant may use a survey to support his claim that the trial should be moved to another city (a change of venue) because so many people are already convinced of his guilt that it would be impossible to select an impartial jury.

False or misleading advertising.   One company may challenge a competitor's ad, claiming that it is misleading or disparaging. This type of complaint may also be brought by the FTC. An advertisement may be determined to be misleading, even when every word is true, if the overall impression or effect created by the ad is misleading. This may be deliberate, but it need not be. Regardless of the intent, it is the result or effect of the ad that counts in determining whether it is misleading.

Substantiation of advertising claims.   This is a growing area of research, boosted by the FTC policy that advertisers must be able to substantiate, usually through research, every claim made in every advertisement. Advertising substantiation cases probably account for the largest volume of research involved in legal proceedings today.

For example, Swift's Peter Pan peanut butter made the claim: "In a survey, kids with a preference preferred Peter Pan's taste over Jif or

Skippy.'' The National Advertising Division (NAD) of the Council of Better Business Bureaus (another organization that monitors advertising) asked Peter Pan to substantiate this claim. Swift submitted results of blind product tests between Peter Pan and Skippy and between Peter Pan and Jif. Each panel of children, eight to fifteen years of age, included regular peanut butter users. The users of creamy peanut butter tested the creamy varieties, and users of crunchy peanut butter tested the crunchy varieties. The findings indicated that the children tested had a greater preference for the flavor of Peter Pan over Jif or Skippy at a 99 percent confidence level. After reviewing the data presented, NAD closed its file on the basis that the claim had been substantiated.

GENERAL GUIDELINES

Most legal processes are ''adversary proceedings,'' which means that each side tries to present its case as forcefully as possible, with an impartial party (or parties) reaching a verdict on the basis of that information. The implication of this for the researcher is that unfriendly attorneys may be examining your research files looking for ways to discredit the results. If they find something which suggests the research was not done properly, they will try to use it to have the research ruled inadmissible or at least to raise a question about the credibility of the research before the judge or the jury.

Therefore, research that may find its way into court has to be done with extra care. Here are some of the things to consider.

Study design.   Be particularly specific and precise in stating the objectives of the study and why it was conducted as it was.

Sample.   Include a detailed description of the sample and how it was selected, along with a statement of limitations of the sample, if that is necessary. Sampling is one of the most vulnerable areas of a study, since it is one of the easiest to raise questions about. Be sure to define the universe or population from which the sample was drawn.

Questionnaire.   Ask only the things related to the purpose of the research. Otherwise you may be collecting information which could later be used by the other side against you. (More on this later.)

Coding.   Be as narrow and specific as possible in developing codes and doing the coding. Try not to link together in a single code more than one idea or imply cause and effect.

Conclusions and implications.   Keep these direct, narrow, and data-based. Stick to the findings that are supported by the results. Be especially careful here to separate ideas and speculations from statements of findings. Better yet, avoid speculations altogether on this type of project.

SOME DO'S AND DON'TS

☐ Keep the research as simple and straightforward as possible. The people making the decision on the basis of the research will not be researchers or even marketers. Instead they will be judges, with legal backgrounds, or laymen, in the case of a jury trial. Either way, they most likely will not be familiar with research techniques or terminology. In advertising substantiation research, for example, be as straightforward and specific as possible in the way you measure opinions of the claim. Otherwise, you may end up with a chain of elegant, indirect logic which substantiates the claim, but which you cannot possibly explain to someone untrained in research.

☐ Get the lawyers involved early. Accepted definitions of what constitutes misleading advertising, for example, are constantly changing. The decisions finally reached will be legal ones rather than marketing decisions. While you must do good, sound research, you also must be certain that the results will be acceptable from a legal standpoint before you proceed. So talk with the lawyers early.

☐ Keep your objectivity in mind—the lawyers probably won't. Remember, the lawyers are trained to play an adversary role. That means that the lawyer you are working with is trying to prove something and probably will want to push as hard as he can to get the research to come out the way he wants it to. Protect your objectivity, particularly if you have any responsibility for analyzing or reporting the findings. Otherwise, you may later be asked to explain and defend a procedure which you never believed in.

☐ Maintain complete records and documentation. Good files are extremely important. You need a record of exactly what you did at each step of the way. You may be required to explain details of the sampling procedure, for example, and you will need complete records in your files to do this. It's possible that you will be asked to provide the names and addresses of every interviewer who worked on the study, along with a statement of their training and their experience at interviewing. You can't keep all this in your files, of course, but you need records complete enough to form a basis for creating very detailed information that you may be asked to supply.

☐ Remember that everything in your files can be subpoenaed as evidence by the other side. This is the flip side of complete records—you don't want them to be *too* complete. The FTC can and routinely does subpoena everything on an issue before it issues a complaint. In addition, in a judiciary proceeding, one side in a lawsuit can usually get access to everything in the research files of the other side. That includes every memo, letter, and report—even notes scribbled on scraps of paper, if they are in the files. So keep written documents to a minimum, and don't keep anything you would mind someone outside your company seeing.

□ Limit the number of people involved. This will make the project easier to control. It also will allow you to say, with more assurance, exactly what was done, by whom, and why. To maintain objectivity, as few people as possible should know the purpose of this type of research. Interviewers, of course, should never be told why it is being done.

□ Select interviewers carefully. Although respondents will probably never be called to testify, it's possible that some interviewers will be questioned. So the interviewers assigned to these types of projects should be the best available.

□ Beware of "fishing expeditions"—you may end up being the one caught. Every question asked in a survey becomes part of the record. So the extra question tacked on the end of the study could come back to haunt you. For example, suppose you decided to add this question to the end of some type of advertising research: "Is there anything about this ad you find unclear or confusing?" The answers could end up as evidence if a competitor were to claim that the ad being studied was false or misleading. Even a very small share of people saying the ad was misleading could be damaging to you. Extra questions run the risk of providing evidence for the other side, so be careful. Stick to the specific objectives of the study.

□ Keep in mind that decision rules are not the same as for commercial research. For example, advertising has been found to be misleading on the basis of as few as 5 percent of the consumers being confused or misled. In research done for a company's own decision making, a 5 percent level would rarely cause concern. But the rules are different—and often very unclear—in legal proceedings. That's another reason why the early involvement of a lawyer is helpful in designing these types of studies.

□ If you are called to testify, answer questions in concise statements. Never volunteer anything. If you don't know the answer to a question, say so. Don't speculate. Be careful of every answer you give so it cannot be used against you later.

□ Be careful. That is really the overriding guideline for doing this type of research. The rules of good research are basically the same; they're just enforced more strictly than when the research is done only for making a decision within the company. As a result, you have to pay special attention to the details of design, execution, and record keeping on projects that may be involved in legal proceedings.

Part V

Research Tools

□□□

33

Sampling Simplified

By a small sample we may judge the whole piece.

—*Cervantes*

We all believe in sampling, whether we realize it or not. Every cook determines whether the soup has enough salt by taking a spoonful (a sample) and forming an opinion—there's no need to eat the whole kettle to tell. No one needs to drink a whole glass of spoiled milk to tell it has gone bad—one swallow (a sample) is enough. Even the U.S. Census uses a sample to collect some types of information about the population.

Sampling is cheaper and faster than conducting a census of the entire market. And in most cases, of course, sampling is the only feasible research alternative—it simply isn't practical to even think about surveying the entire population. But if the sample is developed properly, it can provide more than enough accuracy for decision-making purposes.

Sampling in marketing research has two dimensions:

□ Selecting the units in the population to be included in the study.
□ Interpreting the results of the study in order to (1) estimate parameters of the population from sample data and (2) test hypotheses, usually about the differences between two samples or between a sample and an "expected" result.

There are entire books devoted to sampling, so it isn't necessary to describe every sampling concept in detail here. The purpose of this chapter is to serve as an introductory guide to the various types of samples and discuss the practical strengths and weaknesses of each kind.

DEFINITIONS

Sampling has its own terminology, and to make sense of discussions about sampling, it's important to understand these terms.

Population—all the units about which information is sought. For example, this could be all U.S. households, men between 18 and 55, companies which own computers, or short-term hospitals. The first step in drawing any type of sample should always be to carefully and precisely define the population to be studied.

Sample—a proportion of the population selected for a particular research study.

Sampling unit—one unit (a household, a teenager, a hospital, or whatever) of the population selected for inclusion in the study.

Sampling frame—a physical listing of all units in a population or a procedure for producing a result comparable to a complete listing.

BASIC SAMPLING METHODS

There are two broad categories of sampling methods: probability sampling and nonprobability sampling. Every sampling technique falls into one category or the other.

Probability samples are also called "random samples." Probability sampling methods involve essentially selecting respondents by chance, with no interviewer judgment or screening involved in the choice. Probability samples are theoretically soundest and most representative; they are also the most expensive. In fact, for many studies they are prohibitively expensive.

Nonprobability samples are all other kinds of samples—anything that is not completely random. Interviewing women in a shopping mall and calling men from telephone book listings are examples of nonprobability sampling.

Most research textbooks give primary attention to probability sampling. But this doesn't really reflect what goes on in the real world, where most studies use nonprobability samples because of budget constraints.

Both probability and nonprobability sampling have their appropriate uses. The trick is usually to: (1) identify the situations where only probability sampling will suffice and (2) determine the steps that can be taken to improve the "quality" of nonprobability samples where that's the only economically feasible alternative.

PROBABILITY SAMPLING

This is the most objective and scientific type of sampling. A requirement for probability sampling is that every unit in the population (in consumer studies these "units" would typically be either households or individual consumers) have an equal and known probability of being selected in the sample. There must be no interviewer judgment involved in the selection of respondents. There are several different forms of probability sampling:

Simple random sampling is the most basic type. It involves simply selecting respondents completely at random, much as names might be drawn out of a hat. Obviously, this requires a perfect sampling frame—that is, a complete listing of every unit in the universe.

Stratified random sampling involves first grouping the population into homogenous segments (or strata) and then sampling within each stratum. In probability samples of the United States, for example, it is common to stratify by region and/or degree of urbanization. Stratification prevents the disproportionate representation of some parts of the population that can result by chance with simple random sampling.

Cluster sampling involves sampling groups of respondents as a unit rather than as individual elements. For purposes of efficiency in door-to-door interviewing, for example, it is common to interview several house-holds (a "cluster") in a neighborhood that is selected to be part of the sample.

Systematic sampling includes every *n*th element from the population in the sample. This is a common procedure, which can be combined with both cluster and stratified sampling. For example, either clusters or individuals can be selected in this systematic way, or a systematic sampling can be done within a stratified sample.

The primary advantage of probability sampling is its accuracy. It is the best approach for developing a sample that is perfectly representative of the population. At the same time, probability sampling has several important drawbacks that keep it from being widely used:

□ To select a probability sample, it is necessary to have a list, or sampling frame, for the entire population. In the case of personal inter-views with households, this means having a list of all dwelling units in the United States. For some areas of the country, where new homes are being built and the population is rapidly growing, this can be a serious problem—particularly when the most recent census data become eight or nine years old. Regardless of the adequacy of the sampling frame, drawing a probability sample—especially for door-to-door interviewing—is a very detailed, time-consuming task.

□ Despite the best attempt at sampling, "nonresponse errors" can affect the accuracy of the results. Some respondents simply are not at home when the interviewer calls; others refuse to begin the interview; and still others may terminate the interview before completion. So a probability sample doesn't necessarily guarantee an accurate survey result.

□ Probability sampling is extremely costly to execute, especially for door-to-door studies. For this reason alone, its use is usually limited to studies where a high degree of accuracy is worth the additional cost. Also for cost reasons, national telephone studies are replacing door-to-door probability studies wherever the information can be collected by telephone.

SAMPLING ERROR AND NONSAMPLING ERROR

While good sampling methods can produce very accurate results, no sample is absolutely precise. For example, suppose a national probability sample shows that 40 percent of the households interviewed own a dog. It's unlikely that a census of every household in the United States would find that *exactly* 40 percent of all households own dogs. If the original sample were well drawn, well executed, and large enough, there's a good chance that the "true" ownership revealed by the census would be close to 40 percent, but it probably won't be *exactly* that figure.

These "errors"—or differences between the survey results and the comparable population figures—come from two sources: *sampling* and *nonsampling* factors. Sampling factors (or "sampling errors") usually get the most attention. Yet, other types of problems ("nonsampling errors") probably have greater impact on the results of projects. Both types of errors are important and must be controlled.

Sampling Error

In the dog ownership example, it would be possible to measure the "sampling error" in the study and attach a "confidence limit" to the survey figure in order to estimate the population figure—and in most research projects you're interested in using the survey results to estimate total population data.

Suppose the dog ownership study had used a probability sample of 1,000 households. In that case the 40 percent ownership figure would have a range of plus or minus 3 percent at the 95 percent confidence level. In other words, the chances are 95 out of 100 that the confidence range—37 percent to 43 percent (40 percent ± 3 percent)—includes the true percentage of dog ownership for the entire population.

That's what sampling error is: the range (expressed as "plus or minus X percent") that has to be attached to any survey result because it came from a sample. This range reflects the commonsense fact that no sample is likely to mirror exactly the characteristics of the total population.

Large samples have less sampling error (therefore tighter confidence ranges) than small samples. In our dog study example, the 95 percent confidence ranges at different sample sizes—assuming each study measured ownership at 40 percent—would be:

Sample Size	Confidence Range	
50	26–54%	(±14%)
100	30–50%	(±10%)
200	33–47%	(± 7%)
400	35–45%	(± 5%)
1,000	37–43%	(± 3%)
2,000	38–42%	(± 2%)
4,000	38–42%	(± 2%)

These ranges at different sample sizes illustrate two principles about sampling error:

1. The sample size must be quadrupled (50 to 200, 100 to 400, and so on) to cut the sampling error in half. This means tight confidence ranges are relatively expensive to achieve: you only get *half* of what you pay for.

2. The rate of improvement in sampling error slows down as sample size increases, and sampling error never disappears completely (unless you conduct a census or something very close to it). In the example, the confidence range with a sample size of 4,000 is actually 1.5 percent (half the range at 1,000). But it's difficult to imagine the circumstances where it would be worth the cost of 3,000 additional interviews (going from a sample of 1,000 to 4,000) to gain only 1.5 percent of "precision" in the results.

This trade-off of cost (in sample size) and precision (in confidence ranges) is the reason most marketing research studies use samples of between 200 and 1,000—and often toward the lower half of that range. This level of accuracy is adequate for most business decisions. Even television-ratings services and political polls—where more precision is desirable—rarely use samples larger than 1,200 people. It just isn't worth it.

A final word about sampling error: confidence ranges are applicable, strictly speaking, only to probability, or random, samples, which is a primary advantage of that type of sampling.

Technically speaking, it's not possible to make any statements about the sampling error in a nonprobability sample. From a practical standpoint, of course, researchers nevertheless make inferences about population data from nonprobability samples. If 600 respondents in a mall intercept study taste two products and prefer product A to product B by a two-to-one margin, most researchers will conclude that the population—or a probability sample—would prefer A, too. But those inferences cannot really be supported by statistical theory, even though the findings may be perfectly adequate for decision making.

Nonsampling Error

The importance and impact of "nonsampling error" are generally underestimated by researchers. Most textbooks devote at least a full chapter, often much more, to lengthy technical discussions of probability sampling theory, sampling error, and related statistics. Then all the other potential sources of error are dismissed with a short paragraph. In fact, the emphasis should often be exactly reversed!

Other sources of "error" are critical because there are so many of them. Despite their number, they're often controllable—but only if you appreciate their importance.

What is nonsampling error? As the name suggests, it's *everything else*—beside sampling error—that can introduce bias, inaccuracies, or uncertainty into the results of a study. Nonsampling error includes, but isn't limited to:

1. Inability to locate correct respondents (poor instructions, poor maps, nonexistent addresses, and so on).
2. Refusal by respondents to begin the interview.
3. Terminations by respondents during the interview because it is felt to be too long, too boring or tedious, or too threatening or personal.
4. Intentional lying by respondents.
5. Poor recall, biased guesses, inaccurate memory.
6. Misunderstanding of questions due to unclear wording.
7. Leading by the interviewer.
8. Nonverbal "clues" or biasing by the interviewer.
9. Recording errors by interviewers.
10. Coding errors.
11. Editing errors.

In other words, the accuracy of the best probability sampling methods can be negated by a problem in just one of these areas. Yet the impact of these potential nonsampling errors is largely ignored by most theory-based textbooks on sampling.

What's the solution to the nonsampling error problem? It's basically careful planning and close attention to the details of project execution. Don't stop at the theoretical level of sampling (although your sampling method must be conceptually sound), but carry through with:

Thorough interviewer training
Complete, clear instructions to interviewers
Precisely worded questionnaires
Pretesting
Easy-to-follow questionnaire formats
Careful coding and editing
Respect for the respondent's cooperation and goodwill

NONPROBABILITY SAMPLING

The second type of sampling is called *nonprobability sampling*. While this category includes everything *except* probability sampling, there are three basic types of nonprobability sampling methods:

1. *Convenience sampling* leaves the selection of respondents primarily up to the interviewer. For example, 100 women might be interviewed in a shopping center, with no quotas or qualifications for participation in the study.

2. *Judgment sampling* involves selecting certain respondents—perhaps category users or residents of certain communities or neighborhoods—for participation in a study. In many cases, significant costs can be saved by focusing a study on only a few subsegments of the population.

3. *Quota sampling* structures the sample to include specified numbers of respondents having characteristics that are known or believed to affect the subject of the research. For example, it's common to set quotas on interviews by age, income, or employment. Quotas are used in this way to help limit the possible bias in nonprobability sampling and make the end sample of respondents as similar as possible to the total population.

Obviously, most types of studies—product tests, shopping center interviews, group discussions, and most projects not done on a nationwide basis—have to use nonprobability sampling methods. So often there's not really a choice between doing probability sampling and nonprobability sampling. Nevertheless, steps can be taken to make nonprobability samples as representative as possible and minimize nonsampling error. These steps include:

☐ Conducting a study in as many cities as possible to lessen the potential effect of regionality.
☐ Spreading interviews within a city across different areas to provide broad representation of socioeconomic groups.
☐ Giving attention to question design, then pretesting the questionnaire, to make communication with the respondent as clear as possible.

☐ Writing detailed interviewer instructions covering the questionnaire and sampling procedures to cut interviewer errors.

TELEPHONE SAMPLING

As use of the telephone has grown for conducting many types of national studies, more sophisticated methods have been developed for drawing telephone samples.

Telephone Book Sampling

The most straightforward type of telephone sampling is telephone book sampling. This approach takes a systematic sampling of the numbers listed in telephone books covering the area being studied and selects every nth number for contact. This is a very simple and efficient way of sampling for telephone research.

The drawback is that even the most recent telephone book is not a complete listing of households that have telephones. Some new households have moved into the area since the book was printed; others have moved out of town; still others have chosen to have unlisted numbers. To overcome these problems, other methods of sampling for telephone studies have been developed, and these are described later in this chapter.

Despite the theoretical problems with telephone book sampling, however, the survey results using this method often produce remarkably accurate results. Many studies that have examined the differences between listed and unlisted samples have concluded that samples drawn from telephone directories produce virtually the same survey results as samples that include unpublished numbers.

For many types of studies, telephone book sampling is quite adequate, and its lower cost makes it attractive. But it is always theoretically better to use a sampling technique which includes households with unlisted numbers.

Random Digit Dialing

This is a sampling method developed to reach households with unlisted telephone numbers. It involves randomly generating telephone numbers so that unlisted numbers will be included by chance, along with listed ones. These numbers can be generated in a number of different ways to help minimize the likelihood of generating numbers that have not been assigned to households. For example, sometimes only the last four digits are randomized, using prefixes that are known to have been assigned. In other cases, all seven digits may be generated, but following a pattern determined to reflect the prefixes which are in use. A significant proportion of all households have unlisted numbers, either because they are too new to be listed or because they are unlisted by request. The proportion of unlisted numbers is greater than 20 percent of all households and is higher yet in large metropolitan areas, particularly in the Northeast or on the West Coast.

While the research results from random digit dialing may not be substantially different from those obtained by telephone book sampling, random digit dialing nevertheless comes closest to being a probability sample—it's the only telephone sampling method that allows you to reach virtually every household with a telephone. For this reason, it is the surest way to obtain a sample that is as representative as possible of the total population.

"Plus one" sampling is a method of telephone sampling that incorporates some of the characteristics of random digit dialing, but avoids some of the inefficiencies of that technique. "Plus one" sampling involves simply adding 1 to every listed telephone number. Thus 853-1414 becomes 853-1415 with this technique. Since telephone numbers are generally assigned in blocks, this technique maximizes the likelihood of generating a telephone number that has been assigned. Studies comparing "plus one" and random digit dialing confirm that "plus one" sampling is more efficient than random digit dialing. Its drawback is that it does not include numbers that are not adjacent to listed numbers. For this reason, not every household has an opportunity to be included. But it represents a compromise between telephone book and random digit dialing which includes some of the advantages of randomness while still being cost-efficient.

Telephone Interviewing versus Personal Interviewing

As telephone interviewing grows, the question is often asked: "Does telephone interviewing really produce results that are comparable to those obtained from personal interviewing?"

One study, done by Chilton Research Services, indicates that results from telephone interviewing are very comparable to—and in some cases better than—the results from personal interviewing. A study was done using two interviewing techniques—personal contacts and random-digit-dialing telephone interviews. A comparison of the demographic characteristics of the respondents showed that the samples were virtually identical in most respects. There was one difference: more interviews were obtained with individuals in elevator apartments on the telephone than through personal interviews. The reason for this difference is that it is often extremely difficult for personal interviewers to gain entrance to apartment buildings for face-to-face interviews.

This study produced another interesting result. It is commonly believed that telephone interviews are not as effective as personal interviews for obtaining information from scale questions. On this project, however, respondents were asked to indicate their interest in becoming involved in several selected activities on a six-point scale. (The wording was slightly different for the two approaches.) The results from the two approaches indicate that the telephone is very comparable to personal interviews in obtaining even subtle attitude information.

REAL-WORLD SAMPLING

With all the pros and cons of probability and nonprobability sampling, what method of sampling is used most frequently? Here are some rules of thumb:

Probability Sampling

□ Probability sampling methods most often are reserved for use on large, national category studies—particularly category awareness, attitude, and usage studies (AAUs)—in which precision is a major concern and the ability to compare data from wave to wave is an advantage.

□ Telephone interviewing is replacing personal interviewing on many types of studies—and this is certainly the trend in probability sampling. Telephone studies allow random respondent selection and facilitate multiple callback attempts—both important requirements of probability sampling.

□ Typical sample sizes are 500 to 1,000—perhaps up to 2,000 if subgroups are to be analyzed separately.

Nonprobability Sampling

□ The majority of real-world research projects employ some form of nonprobability sampling, most often either shopping mall intercept studies or prerecruited central-location tests.

□ Cost is the primary advantage of nonprobability sampling. If additional controls (such as quotas) are used, the results are usually entirely adequate for most day-to-day decision making.

□ Although sample sizes vary with the purpose and type of test, 200 to 500 respondents is a typical range for most product tests, attitude studies, and the like.

34

Basic Statistics—
All You'll Usually Need

□□□

Today's high temperature of 83 and low of 68 were above the normal high of 78 and low of 65. The current temperature is 73; the relative humidity is 54 percent; and the pollen count is 106.

Our lives sometimes seem controlled by statistics. From weather reports to stock market averages and blood pressure readings, we all deal routinely with a wide array of statistical measures.

Statistical analysis is useful to researchers because it's a tool to help summarize and interpret the large volume of numbers collected as part of even the smallest survey. The statistical principles used in marketing research borrow heavily from the behavioral and physical sciences. As a result, there are many entire books on statistics, probably more than on any other facet of research.

The purpose of this chapter is to give you an overview of the most important types of statistical measures used in marketing research. If you want more technical or detailed information, refer to one of many good statistics books available. These are basic statistics, but they're all you'll usually need.

USES OF STATISTICS

While there are literally hundreds of different statistical measures and tests that can be used by researchers, the most common ones all serve one of these three purposes:

Measuring central tendencies—Summarizing data in terms of a "typical" or "average" case.

Estimating population parameters—Drawing inferences from survey samples about the characteristics of the total population.

Determining significant differences—Are two subgroups within a sample different? Is this sample different from the population?

Measuring Central Tendencies

The purpose—or at least one of the purposes—of almost every research project is to describe the "typical" or "average" customer or prospect in the market. The three statistical tools most commonly used for doing this are the mean, the median, and the mode.

Arithmetic mean. This is usually called the "mean" or simply the "average." (The term "average" isn't technically correct or precise, but where it's used, it usually refers to the arithmetic mean. In any case, it's better to say "mean" than "average.") This is simply the sum of a series divided by the number of figures in the series.

The mean is appropriate to use when the results are symmetrical and normally distributed. But the mean can be very misleading as a summary statistic in other cases. For example, Table 5 shows the scores of three products on a product test using a scale question. All three products tested have the same mean. The mean of 3.0 on this scale is quite descriptive of the normal distribution of product 1, but it would be misleading if used to describe either product 2 or product 3. Most research results are normally distributed (that is, "bell-shaped" around a midpoint), but other distributions are common enough that you should always check, before using the mean, that it is in fact descriptive.

The mean has one other weakness to watch out for: it is affected by extreme observations. For example, if the incomes of two millionaires were averaged with the incomes of ten laborers, the average income for all twelve would be more than $200,000, which obviously is a misleading figure for the group's average income. Nevertheless, if you avoid using the

Table 5. Scores of three products on a scale question (spice level).

Spice Level		Product 1 "Normal"	Product 2 "Flat"	Product 3 "Bimodal"
Much too spicy	(5)	5%	20%	50%
Somewhat too spicy	(4)	10	20	0
Just about right	(3)	70	20	0
Somewhat too bland	(2)	10	20	0
Much too bland	(1)	5	20	50
Mean:		3.0	3.0	3.0

mean for abnormally distributed data or data including extreme observations, it's the most useful statistic for describing the "average."

Median. This is simply the *middle case* in a series. Half the observations fall above the median; half fall below. It has the advantage of being unaffected by extreme cases. So it is often used instead of the mean for describing "average income," "average sales," or any type of data which may include a few extreme cases that would distort the mean. To avoid confusion, always identify it as the "median"; don't call it the "average."

Mode. This is the most *frequent* observation. It's the "plurality," or the most commonly given response. If no one response occurs more frequently than any other, there is no mode (as for product 2 in the spicy/bland example above). If two different responses occur with the same frequency, then the distribution is bimodal (as for product 3 in the spicy/bland example). Because of these limitations, the mode is rarely used.

Estimating Population Parameters

Another thing researchers are often trying to do is make inferences about the population on the basis of results from a survey sample. In fact, that's what researchers are *always* trying to do. The fact that the 300 people in your test prefer product X to product Y by a two-to-one margin is important only in that it allows you to conclude—actually, infer—that the population as a whole also prefers product X. This is called "inferential statistics"—making a decision about the entire population on the basis of the characteristics of a subgroup or sample.

Survey results are often expressed as percentages—percent aware, percent preferring a product, or percent giving a certain response. To make an inference about the population, you must apply a *confidence limit* or *confidence range* to the percentage result you found in the study. For example, if your telephone study found 30 percent of the respondents aware of product A, it's unlikely that exactly 30 percent of the entire population is aware of product A—but the population figure should be close to 30 percent if your sample is large enough and well drawn. This difference between your sample results and the population is sometimes called the *sampling error*. The range attached to the survey result to estimate or infer the population figure is called the *confidence range*.

A chart of confidence ranges is shown as Table 6. It is read this way: in a sample of 400 interviews, if an observed percentage result is 50 percent, the chances are approximately 95 in 100 that a range of $\pm$ 5 percent (45 percent to 55 percent) includes the true percentage in the entire population.

Two points should be kept in mind when reading this chart:

1. For technical reasons, the confidence range around a result is larger

Table 6. Chart of 95 percent confidence range (two standard deviations).

Sample Size	*Percentage Result Obtained*						
	50%	40% or 60%	30% or 70%	20% or 80%	10% or 90%	5% or 95%	1% or 99%
25	±19.6	±19.2	±18.0	±15.7	±11.8	±8.5	±3.9
50	13.9	13.6	12.7	11.1	8.3	6.0	2.8
75	11.3	11.1	10.4	9.1	6.8	4.9	2.3
100	9.8	9.6	9.0	7.8	5.9	4.3	2.0
150	8.2	8.0	7.5	6.6	4.9	3.6	1.6
200	7.1	7.0	6.5	5.7	4.3	3.1	1.4
250	6.3	6.2	5.8	5.0	3.9	2.7	1.2
300	5.8	5.7	5.3	4.6	3.5	2.5	1.1
400	5.0	4.9	4.6	4.0	3.0	2.2	1.0
500	4.5	4.4	4.1	3.6	2.7	2.0	.9
600	4.1	4.0	3.8	3.3	2.5	1.8	.8
800	3.5	3.4	3.2	2.8	2.1	1.5	.7
1,000	3.2	3.1	2.9	2.6	1.9	1.4	.6
1,200	2.8	2.8	2.7	2.3	1.7	1.3	.6
1,500	2.5	2.5	2.4	2.1	1.6	1.1	.5
2,000	2.2	2.2	2.0	1.8	1.3	1.0	.4
2,500	2.0	2.0	1.8	1.6	1.2	.9	.4
3,000	1.8	1.8	1.7	1.5	1.1	.8	.4
4,000	1.6	1.5	1.4	1.3	1.0	.7	.3
5,000	1.4	1.4	1.2	1.1	.9	.6	.3

the closer the result is to 50 percent. So there's no single confidence range for a sample of 1,000, for example. It depends on whether the result (awareness, preference, or whatever) measured in the sample of 1,000 is closer to 50 percent or to 5 percent.

2. Strictly speaking, these statistics apply only to normally distributed data developed from probability samples. Unless a survey is drawn from a probability sample, technically it isn't possible to make inferences about the population. In practice, however, researchers commonly use these confidence ranges to provide guidelines for interpreting other types of survey results, too.

Determining Significant Differences

Often a research project is designed to compare results between two samples or subgroups. The most common comparisons are between:

Two or more subgroups within the same sample. Do people with incomes exceeding $25,000 have different opinions from those held by people with incomes lower than $25,000? Are men's evaluations of the product different from women's?

Samples drawn at different points in time. Has awareness of the product increased in the past year? Is market share higher than three years ago?

The first thing you do, of course, is take a simple, straightforward look at the results. If responses of men and women are the same, you don't need a statistical test to tell you any more. If market share is unchanged from three years ago, you've got your answer.

But if the results differ among any of your subgroups—as they almost always do—then you're faced with two basic questions: *Is the difference in results so small as to suggest it probably occurred by chance?* (That is, if you did the test again, is there a good chance that it will come out the other way?) *Or is the result large enough that it is probably the result of a "true" difference?* (That is, if you repeated the test again and again, is it very likely to come out the same way every time?) There are a number of statistical tests that help you answer these questions.

Before you can run a statistical test, you must have a *hypothesis*. This is simply a statement or relationship you would like to prove either true or false. In statistics, it's usually assumed that two populations or two subgroups are equal until proven otherwise. This is called a *null hypothesis*.

Starting with the null hypothesis, if the difference between two samples is small enough that it could easily have occurred by chance, then the null hypothesis cannot be rejected and you must conclude that the difference between the two samples "is not statistically significant at the 95 percent confidence level" (or whatever confidence level you choose). On the other hand, if the difference in survey results is so large that it would not be likely to occur by chance, you *reject the null hypothesis* and conclude the difference between the sample "is statistically significant at the 95 percent confidence level."

How big must a difference be to be "statistically significant"? That depends on two things:

The size of the two samples being compared. The bigger the samples, of course, the smaller the difference needed to be statistically significant.

The level of percentage being compared. Assuming it's a percentage that is being compared, the closer the percentage is to 50 percent, the larger is the difference required to be statistically significant.

Table 7 gives guidelines for determining the statistical significance of differences between survey results from two samples. The chart is read this way: in two separate samples of 500, if two observed percentages near the 50 percent level differ by 8 percent or more—46 percent vs. 54 percent, for example—the chances are 95 in 100 that it is a true difference and not due to chance alone.

Table 7. Chart of significant differences between two sample percentages (95 percent confidence level).

Sample Sizes Being Compared	Approximate Percentage Result Obtained				
	50%	40% or 60%	30% or 70%	20% or 80%	10% or 90%
2,000 and 2,000	4%	4%	4%	3%	2%
1,000	5	5	4	4	3
500	6	6	6	5	4
100	13	12	11	10	7
1,500 and 1,500	4	4	4	4	3
750	5	5	5	4	3
500	6	6	6	5	4
100	13	12	12	10	8
1,000 and 1,000	6	5	5	4	3
750	6	6	5	5	4
500	7	7	6	5	4
100	13	13	12	10	8
750 and 750	6	6	6	5	4
500	7	7	6	6	4
100	13	13	12	10	8
500 and 500	8	8	7	6	5
100	14	14	13	11	8
250 and 250	11	11	10	8	7
100	14	14	13	12	9
100 and 100	17	17	16	14	10

As with confidence ranges around a single percentage point, these differences apply, strictly speaking, only to results from probability samples. But in practice they're often used as indicators of the statistical significance of other types of survey results as well.

In addition to this measure of the difference between percentages in two samples, there are other, more specialized statistical tests, which are useful for evaluating some kinds of research results. Here are the most frequently conducted tests (look them up in any statistics book if they appear to apply to your problem):

Chi-square test.   This test can be used to compare survey results with theoretical or *expected* frequencies in the population. There are many versions of the chi-square test, which apply to a wide range of marketing research problems. The test can be used whenever the results, responses, or respondents can be arrayed in various categories.

Analysis of variance.   This test divides the variance found among test data into parts, assigning each part to some source or factor. You can then evaluate these variations and see if any are greater than would be expected by chance. This technique is often used to test the significance of differences among products in a product test. It is a very efficient and powerful way to analyze balanced test plans. One of the most common methods of analysis of variance (or "ANOVA") is called "Scheffe"; it is used in testing for differences in one-way scales, such as hedonic ratings.

Student's t-test.   Unlike analysis of variance, which compares ratings across products, this test compares ratings of each product to an optimum. It is especially useful in evaluating ratings or bipolar scales, where the midpoint is optimum and either end is undesirable.

There are far too many other statistical tests to even list here, but these are some of the most basic and most frequently used ones.

"Significant Differences"

Perhaps as important as, or more important than, knowing how to use statistical measures is knowing how *not* to use them and how to accurately represent what the statistics mean.

Be careful about saying something is "not significantly different" when what you really mean—and all you can truly say—is that two numbers are "*statistically* not significantly different." For example, market shares of 32 percent and 37 percent might not be statistically significantly different as measured in a test, but that difference could be very significant in the real world. Or suppose an opinion poll found a sample of people split 49 percent vs. 51 percent on an issue and concluded that the difference wasn't statistically significant. That 49 percent/51 percent split would make all the difference if it held up in an election or referendum.

So be precise and accurate in using the term "significant" and get in the habit of always modifying it with the word "statistically." All that researchers can usually talk about is *statistical significance*. What's really significant and what's not is often a much bigger, broader topic, usually far outside the scope of a simple research project.

Sample Size

Also keep this in mind about statistical differences: since the difference needed for statistical significance is related directly to sample size, another way of saying something isn't statistically significant is to say that the *sample size is too small!* Virtually any difference between two percentages would become statistically significant if the sample size were large enough.

Especially when survey sample sizes are small, it's often difficult to find differences that are large enough to be statistically significant. But be careful about saying they "aren't significant"—you're usually going further than the research results justify.

Both these last points boil down to keeping statistics in perspective. Use them to help analyze, qualify, and temper your results, but don't let statistical measures replace your common sense, experience, and judgment.

35

Experimental Design:
What If?

SCIENCE: The observation, identification, description, experimental investigation, and theoretical explanation of natural phenomena.
—American Heritage Dictionary

Substitute "marketing phenomena" for "natural phenomena" at the end of that definition, and the revised definition fits the goal of most marketing research projects.

And how is all this accomplished? In science, it's done through experiments; the same is true for marketing research. The dictionary definition of a scientific "experiment" is: "A test made to demonstrate a known truth, to examine the validity of a hypothesis, or to determine the efficacy of something previously untried." That's a pretty good definition of a marketing research project, too. Physicists and behavioral scientists (including marketing researchers) share the objective of understanding and predicting cause and effect.

In marketing research, this type of effort is called *experimentation,* which simply means the manipulation of one or more variables to show the effect of each variable.

EXPERIMENTATION CONSTRAINTS

Unfortunately, physical scientists have an easier time setting up and conducting their experiments than marketing researchers do. Chemicals and test tubes are easier to control than consumers and advertising campaigns. Among the differences between physical science and marketing research that create obstacles to perfect experiments are:

221

Imprecise measuring devices. Scientists can measure and weigh their "subjects." Marketing researchers, on the other hand, often have to obtain data by asking their "subjects" (people in the study) about attitudes, purchases, and preferences. Even the best-designed and most carefully administered questionnaire collects information that is far less precise than the physical scientist's. So the basic data of research experiments are often less precise than you'd like.

Influence of measurement on results. Weighing a test tube doesn't affect or change the test tube. But asking a person if he's ever heard of Honey Nut Cheerios does affect the person—for one thing, he's now heard of Honey Nut Cheerios, if he hadn't already done so. This potential interaction between cause, effect, and measurement makes designing good marketing experiments very difficult.

Time and cost limitations. Physical scientists often take years, generations, or even centuries to make conclusive discoveries. Yet most marketing problems require solutions—or at least decisions—in days, weeks, or at the most months. So there's rarely time or money to conduct a leisurely, detailed marketing experiment. There's usually a need to come up with an answer fast, then to go on to something else.

Complexity and control of variables. Sales—the hoped-for end result of all marketing efforts—are the result of many different factors, including product, package, price, and distribution. Each of those factors, in turn, is affected by many other issues. Understanding, even identifying, all the possible causes is virtually impossible, let alone being able to precisely control them in a marketing experiment.

For these and other reasons, pure scientific experimentation, though the "ideal" for any marketing experiment, is rarely, if ever, achieved. Nevertheless, the physical sciences provide a standard for marketing research experiments. And you should always try to borrow from the physical sciences and incorporate the attributes of those experiments into your marketing research whenever you can.

MOVING TOWARD PREDICTION

Research projects can be arrayed in a hierarchy based on the extent to which they provide *predictive* findings. The hierarchy has three stages:

1. *Descriptive research*—simply states what exists or describes something that happened in the past. Does not attempt to infer cause and effect. Can be as simple as focus groups or as complicated as a segmentation study. Most basic market studies or category studies fall into this category.

2. *Evaluative research*—adds value judgments to descriptive data to create a "compared to" dimension. Tells whether something is better than

norms or controls. Adds an element of implied cause and effect. Many product tests or advertising copy tests are of this type.

3. *Predictive research*—gives absolute, not just relative, meaning to research results. Puts cause and effect into the future tense. Says, "If you do this, such-and-such will happen." Well-conducted market tests or simulated sales tests are examples of this type of research.

It's the predictive level that research is always striving for. But the current state of the art in marketing research makes that difficult to achieve. Often you have to be content with moving something from the descriptive category into the evaluative category, and that's usually valuable. But if you can make a project's results at all predictive, then you've really done something.

WHAT IF?

Research "experiments" provide one way to move projects along the hierarchy and make them evaluative and sometimes even predictive. Most research experimentation is designed to answer a question beginning with the words "what if?":

☐ What if you double the advertising? . . . or cut it in half or drop it altogether?
☐ What if you make the product sweeter? . . . or bluer or harder or smaller?
☐ What if you change the package? . . . or the name?

Or better yet, what if you double the advertising *and* make the product sweeter *and* change the package?

Remember the definition of marketing "experimentation"? It was the manipulation of one or more variables to show the effect of each variable. The purpose of experimentation in research is to help you answer these kinds of "what if" questions.

Marketing experimentation is a technical and complex subject, which can't possibly be reviewed completely here. But awareness of two concepts will make you a better real-world researcher. The concepts are *control groups* and *rotation*.

Control Groups

The use of "control groups" is central to the design of many kinds of research experiments. A control group is simply a sample of respondents that is matched in every way possible to the test group—except that they are *not* exposed to one or more of the marketing variables. The control group provides a base measurement (of awareness, attitudes, purchase, or whatever) for comparison with the test group. This comparison permits a measurement of the real or true effect of the additional variable to which the test group is exposed.

Why is a control group necessary? *Because almost nothing starts at zero.* Medical researchers have long recognized the importance of including a control group in any study of the effectiveness of drugs. A certain proportion of control group patients—often a surprisingly high percentage—will show improvement after being given a placebo. So the effectiveness of the drug being studied is only the improvement beyond that produced by the control group's placebo.

A control group often serves a placebo-type purpose in marketing research investigations, too. For example, three telephone awareness studies measured the following aided awareness levels for two food products and a banking service:

	Aided Awareness
Betty Crocker Sweet Roll Mix	62%
Pillsbury Refrigerated Gingerbread	27
Custom Banking	30

Those are reasonably respectable awareness levels (especially for the sweet roll mix), except for one thing: *none of the three existed at the time of the telephone study.* This is called "yea saying," which means respondents agree to something (such as their awareness of these products) because it sounds familiar or plausible. "Yea saying" has been shown to exist in many other types of research, although not at a constant or predictable level.

So it's always advisable to use a control group—or, in the case of awareness measures, a pre-introduction "base wave"—to provide a base level of measurement against which the test group can be compared. Otherwise your experiment is likely to be worthless. Remember: *almost nothing starts at zero.* There are many complex and sophisticated research designs that incorporate control groups, but they all serve this same fundamental purpose of establishing a base level for comparison.

Rotation

This is the second general principle that contributes to the design of good experiments. The concept can be illustrated with the simple case of a three-product test. Assuming each person in the test was going to try all three products, one way would be to have all the people try product A first, then B, then C. But obviously, there are many factors—including the order of use and the effect of one product on evaluations of another—that would make that a poor idea. It would be better to divide up the respondents in the test so that an equal number test the products in each of the six possible orders:

ABC
ACB
BCA
BAC
CAB
CBA

This concept of "rotation" or "balance" is central to designing good research, for two reasons. First, it balances out any possible biases to ensure that they affect each of the products equally, thereby allowing comparison of the results across all products. Second, it allows an analysis of the order biases and product interactions that makes it possible to adjust the results further if these factors have not affected each product in the same way.

Whenever possible, all positions and combinations of products and variables should be rotated completely to eliminate or control sources of bias. Where this complete rotation isn't possible or feasible, two other alternatives exist:

Incomplete blocks or incomplete rotations. Test plans can be developed which balance the potential position and interaction biases for each product, even though a complete rotation of every product by each respondent isn't possible. This is necessary, for example, where a large number of products are being tested. These are called "balanced incomplete blocks," or BIBs, and are described more fully in Chapter 21, "Product Testing."

Randomization. As a last resort, randomization is the friend of the marketing researcher. When products or respondents can't be intentionally rotated, the next best alternative is to use a random process for selecting products or respondents. While randomization doesn't assure a perfect rotation, it removes any overt bias and usually produces a balanced result. And where other rotations aren't feasible, randomization is often the only alternative.

GUIDELINES FOR EXPERIMENTATION

Entire books are devoted to the subject of experimentation and experimental design, but here are some of the principles that will help assure the good design of any research project:

Use control groups to establish a base measurement for the test.

Use rotation—or randomization—to control bias from order or product interaction.

Consider multistage testing. Often it's possible to eliminate some alternatives with just small samples, then focus the bulk of the budget on measuring the differences between the better alternatives.

Have respondents do as many tasks as possible in a study. This eliminates, or at least minimizes, the influence of person-to-person differences on the results. This doesn't mean abusing respondents. That results in meaningless results. But get them to do as much as possible. It increases the statistical power of your results.

Create realistic test conditions. The real world often makes a poor experimental setting, so artificial "tests" have to be set up. But build in as much realism as possible. Study the product as close as possible to the time it's purchased or the place where it's used. That's one way to help make your results more reliable.

Try to get behavioral measures. What people *do* is always a better predictor than what they *say* they'll do. So it's better to try to move respondents in a test toward actually doing something. For example, a simulated shelf display may make a better stimulus than a list of brands. And a real store is better than a simulated display. And trying to get respondents to actually buy something—even if it's with only some of their own money and in a simulated store display—is a step closer to the real world than just asking them what they'd do.

36

Lifestyle and Psychographic Research

□□

Opinion is ultimately determined by the feelings, and not by the intellect.
—Herbert Spencer

We know instinctively that people aren't all the same. Some kinds of people just seem more likely to drive a certain make of car or smoke a particular brand of cigarettes.

Using demographic characteristics (age, income, family size, and so on) is one way of segmenting a population to explain product usage. Sometimes it works, but often it doesn't—at least not as well as you'd like. Not all the old people behave similarly, and neither do the rich people or the single people. In these cases you often sense that there's an "internal" dimension to people that would refine the "external" (or demographic) dimensions and segment a population into useful groups—if you could just get your hands on the right internal characteristics.

The internal dimension is addressed by *psychographics* or *lifestyle* research. As the name implies, it attempts to use psychology in the same way researchers have long used demography to identify market segments. Specifically, psychographics seek to explain why people behave and believe as they do by applying principles from the behavioral and social sciences.

While the terms "lifestyle" and "psychographics" are often used interchangeably, psychographics technically refer to general personality traits and values, whereas lifestyle measurements tend more toward specific activities, interests, and habits. Obviously, the two areas overlap considerably, and most projects incorporate both types of measures. So the distinction between the two has become blurred in everyday usage.

On a more commonsense level, psychographics attempt to sort people into piles so that the piles differ from each other but each pile is homogeneous—at least that's the goal.

227

USES OF PSYCHOGRAPHICS

This type of analysis is usually done to understand—and then by inference to "predict"—the characteristics that most strongly affect (1) brand usage (Why do some people drive Fords while others drive Chevrolets?) and (2) heaviness of usage (What are the attitudes that account for some people being heavy consumers of wine but light or nonusers of beer and hard liquor?). A psychographic study usually must explain one or both of these variables, or it risks resulting in interesting, nice-to-know results without any practical application.

This approach is useful for helping to draw a profile of a "typical user"—or multiple profiles of the typical user in each of several segments—which most often has application to advertising problems, such as developing strategy and campaigns, writing copy, and positioning or repositioning products. In essence, it helps advertising and marketing people picture the customer they're writing for or selling to. And it helps separate fads and media-created trends from reality.

Lifestyle analysis is most likely to provide new insight for

Discretionary purchases, such as leisure-time or luxury products, where the consumer has an interest in expressing his or her individuality or personal taste.

Major purchases, such as cars, clothes, or furniture, which the buyer may see as carrying prestige or status.

Often, psychographic variables have a surprising influence on the purchase of industrial products.

On the other hand, the lifestyle dimension is less likely to add much to the understanding of mass-market products, where habit or convenience may be the primary purchase factors. Morton Salt, for example, is purchased across all lifestyle groups.

HOW TO COLLECT PSYCHOGRAPHIC DATA

The first step in any psychographic or lifestyle study should be to develop clear, carefully worded hypotheses. This is usually done through qualitative research. The alternative is to try to collect information on every possible psychographic dimension, then hope some clear-cut pattern will emerge from the analysis. This is always wasteful and usually unsuccessful.

After a set of hypotheses is developed, these must be translated into a series of agree/disagree statements. These statements usually cover several subject areas:

Product attitudes related to the importance of such things as price, fashion, utility, or convenience.

"I usually buy the least expensive brand of dishwashing soap."

"I often try the latest hairdo styles when they change."

"I consider the dog a member of my family."

Activities particularly hobbies, work, or personal traits.

"I do a lot of work on my car."

"Television is a primary source of entertainment for me."

"I do not get enough sleep."

Interests such as family, community, or fashion.

"I enjoy trying new recipes."

"I like going to concerts."

"My children are the most important thing in my life."

Opinions about social issues, politics, economics, or the future.

"It's the fault of business that our lakes and streams are dying."

"I expect my economic situation to be better in five years than it is now."

"Inflation is our most important national problem."

Demographics Don't forget to include these in your analysis. They may add a valuable dimension to the psychographic measures of attitudes, activities, interests, and opinions.

Finally, be sure to collect detailed data on brand and volume usage, since this is what you'll be trying to explain with the psychographic information.

Once this information is collected in the field, a cluster or segmentation analysis is conducted to identify lifestyle or psychographic groups. Then a name is usually given to each of the groups to describe its members ("Retreater," "Achiever," or "Spaghetti Lover," for example). Finally, it's often useful to read over some actual questionnaires or do some group interviews among lifestyle groups to give some flesh-and-blood reality to the research results.

EXAMPLES

Two of the organizations most active in lifestyle and psychographic research are Yankelovich, Skelly & White and SRI International (formerly Stamford Research Institute). Both of them have conducted major, ongoing studies to develop lifestyle segments across the whole U.S. population. Although studies done on specific product categories would usually produce different groups, their segments provide a good illustration of real-world lifestyle research.

Yankelovich Monitor. This service tracks trends in the population among various "values segments," originally identified as *old-values segments* and *new-values segments*. The old-values segments comprise two groups:

1. "Traditionalist"—middle-aged people who have accepted the traditional values of hard work and material success.

2. "Retreaters"—older, poorer people who have given up on achieving success.

New-values segments consist of three types of people:

3. "New Conformists"—younger people who have largely substituted self-fulfillment for traditional, work-oriented values.
4. "Forerunners"—young, upscale people who place a high value on intellectual and creative achievement.
5. "Autonomous"—upscale consumers who have achieved success and turned their attention to self-improvement and fulfillment.

The Yankelovich Monitor then provides client companies with information about how these values affect consumption and trends for a large number of products and services.

SRI Values and Lifestyles (VALS).   SRI has identified nine lifestyle segments within three broad values categories:

1. "Need-Driven"—low-income people whose consumption is driven by need, not preference. Within this category are two subgroups:
   "Survivors"
   "Sustainers"
2. "Outer-Directed"—the largest segment; consumes largely for appearance and to impress others. Subsegments are:
   "Belongers"
   "Emulators"
   "Achievers"
3. "Inner-Directed"—purchase to please themselves rather than others. Four subsegments are:
   "I-am-me"
   "Experimental"
   "Societally Conscious"
   "Integrated"

TIPS ON PSYCHOGRAPHIC RESEARCH

Lifestyle and psychographic research has limitations. The results are rarely as clear-cut and dramatic as you'd like. So it's wisest to use the approach, at least at first, as part of another study. It's risky to let a large, major project rely solely on the outcome of psychographic segments.

While most researchers would agree intuitively that psychographic dimensions affect most products to some degree, the application of lifestyle research faces two problems on any study.

1. *Measuring attitudes, interests, and opinions accurately.* Whenever

you're doing lifestyle research, you're trying to measure very subtle emotions with very approximate tools. So develop your statements as carefully and precisely as you can, but nevertheless recognize it's going to be difficult to classify everyone into nice, neat boxes.

2. *Finding differences between segments that justify action.* Most successful products and services are so broadly used that volume isn't restricted to one segment. Even a segment with a high index of usage may, because of its small size, account for only a small share of product or category volume.

So while psychographics aren't the cure-all, they can be a useful tool on some studies in some product categories. Here are some tips for helping to get your results out of the nice-to-know and into the real-world action category:

Pay attention to sampling. Otherwise your data may come from a subsample to begin with, which can distort the results.

Avoid "don't know" or midpoints or scales. Some respondents will use these instead of thinking hard to answer a question, and those sorts of responses are of little value.

Use real-world language. Make your statements sound as if they were written by real people, not by a psychologist or researcher.

Include a balance of attitudes, interests, opinions, and activities. Don't bet everything on just one or two of these areas.

Include demographics. Don't overlook their potential contribution.

Try to keep statements product-specific. That way you're most likely to get understandable segments. Try to avoid obscure relationships that give no advertising, marketing, or product direction.

Use a balance of positive and negative statements. You can't necessarily infer agreement with a positive statement from disagreement with a negative one, or vice versa.

Don't include too many statements on the same topic. This redundancy wears out respondents and often just confuses the analysis.

Be careful about trying to measure illegal or socially unacceptable activities. People may be reluctant to tell a strange interviewer they use marijuana or hate their kids.

Use one-dimensional statements. How does someone who likes to jog but hates swimming respond to "I love to jog and swim"?

Don't presume facts that may not be true. For example, a statement such as "My children are important to me" assumes the respondent has children. Those who don't may be confused or irritated, and your analysis will be muddied.

Finally, be realistic in your expectations of lifestyle research. Think about yourself. How would you classify or segment your own personality or behavior? Would you be in the same psychographic segment in all aspects of your life—at work, at home, and in your leisure time? Probably not. Yet, if you have trouble classifying yourself—the one person you know better than anyone on earth—what chance do you have of neatly segmenting a thousand strangers who answered fifty questions for you?

We're all very complex people. Psychographics can often be a useful research tool, but it can't change that fact and make us seem simpler and easier to understand than we really are.

37

When to Use Multivariate Analytical Techniques

□□□

Statistics are no substitute for judgment.

—Henry Clay

Despite dramatic improvements in the techniques and equipment available to marketers, research often remains more an art than a science. There really is no substitute for creativity, insight, and judgment.

Nevertheless, there is an array of computer-based analytical procedures that can be valuable aids to judgment. A good researcher should be familiar with their applications and know when to use them.

ANALYZING VARIABLES

When several variables are analyzed together, the procedure is called multivariate analysis.

The first analytical step in most research projects is—or should be—a straightforward cross-tabulation of the results (see Chapter 19). This is a form of multivariate analysis, albeit a simple form, that often identifies the most significant variables and almost always eliminates a few as obviously not significant. But beyond compiling these cross-tabs, it's often desirable to look for more complex relationships that may not be apparent from the data tables.

The multivariate techniques most often used for analyzing marketing research results are:

Multiple regression analysis
Automatic interaction detector (AID)
Discriminant analysis
Factor analysis

Cluster analysis
Multidimensional scaling (perceptual MAPPing)
Conjoint analysis

The first three techniques—multiple regression, AID, and discriminant analysis—measure *dependence* between variables. These methods deal with two types of variables, and it's important to understand the distinction between them:

Dependent or criterion variables. These are the variables you are trying to predict or explain. A typical example is volume of product usage or brand usage.

Independent or predictor variables. These are the variables which explain or predict differences in the dependent variables. Demographic characteristics or attitude data are typical independent variables.

The other four techniques—factor and cluster analysis, multidimensional scaling, and conjoint analysis—are designed to measure *interdependence* among all the variables. Under these methods there are no dependent and independent variables. Each of the techniques is described in more detail below.

Multiple Regression Analysis

This approach develops a "prediction equation" relating a dependent (or criterion) variable and a set of independent (or predictor) variables. This is one of the most straightforward, most basic multivariate techniques. It is most useful for predicting a single metric (or interval) criterion variable, such as volume of usage, income, or price.

The procedure provides an equation which defines a line that gives the best fit to the data. The equation for this line can then be used as the "prediction equation." For example, suppose a frozen-pizza manufacturer wanted to predict annual household frozen-pizza consumption, using income and family size. The prediction equation might be:

No. of pizza = 5.1 + 6.5 (no. in household) + 1.1 (household income)

The numbers 5.1, 6.5, and 1.1 are values that are derived from the analysis.

Since this equation is developed by a procedure known as "least squares" and defines a straight line, it is not appropriate for situations where the relationship between the dependent and independent variables is not linear. Also, the predictor equation applies only within the range of data used to develop the equation and should not be extrapolated beyond those limits.

Automatic Interaction Detector (AID)

Like multiple regression, AID is a method for analyzing the relationship between a dependent variable and several independent variables. But whereas multiple regression analysis produces a single predictor equation describing the relationship, AID generates a series of two-way splits—choosing, at each split, the independent variable that accounts for the greatest variation in the dependent variable. Results take the form of a "tree" or branching diagram that splits the sample into successively smaller subsamples.

For example, a manufacturer of frozen dinners wanted to explore the relationship between the number of frozen dinners bought in the past month and several demographic characteristics. The result might look as in Figure 27. The results show that female education and household income are the most important characteristics in defining a heavy user, while light users of frozen dinners tend most often to be women with larger families who have not completed as much formal education.

Discriminant Analysis

This procedure determines the predictor variables that are most closely related to identifying sample subgroups (users/nonusers, heavy/light users, buyers of different brands). In other words, it identifies the variables that are the best "discriminators" among members of the subgroups whose behavior you want to predict. The technique can be used with two-group

Figure 27. Hypothetical automatic interaction detector (AID) analysis of frozen dinner market.

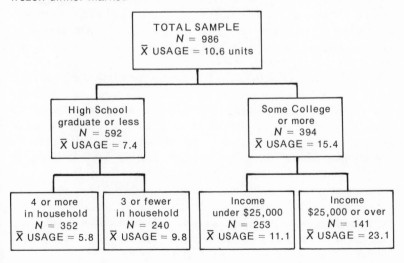

variables (such as users/nonusers) or for multiple group analysis (such as users of different brands).

A manufacturer of frozen waffles wanted to identify the demographic characteristics of users of the category, compared with nonusers. A sample of households was interviewed about their usage of frozen waffles, and demographic characteristics of the households were measured. An analysis of the data, using a discriminant analysis program, produced the following discriminant function, an equation for predicting group membership (user or nonuser) of a consumer:

$$D = .41 \text{ (no. of children)} + .32 \text{ (female's age)} + .20 \text{ (household income)}$$

The factors .41, .32, and .20 were derived by the analysis done on the computer. A discriminant score is computed for each respondent on the basis of the three discriminant variables. Then membership in the user or nonuser group is "predicted" by determining whether an individual's discriminant score is closer to the mean for the user or nonuser group.

Finally, the accuracy of the discriminant function (in backcasting the sample results) is determined by computing the proportion of respondents whose group is accurately predicted.

Factor Analysis

This is a general term for techniques that analyze interrelationships among variables and attempt to reduce them to a smaller set of underlying variables, or "factors."

In marketing research, it's common to measure a large number of product attributes or ideal characteristics and of consumer behaviors or attitudes. Yet it's reasonable to believe that in most cases all these variables are facets of a smaller number of underlying variables. The purpose of factor analysis is to ascertain the basic dimensions—factors—which underlie the larger number of variables.

For example, a manufacturer of health-care products wanted to have nurses evaluate the importance of a skin lotion for patients, using a list of nine product attributes. A factor analysis of these ratings would produce a series of "factor loadings," ranging from +1 to −1, that show the degree of positive or negative association of each attribute with underlying factors. The resulting table of factor loading might look like Table 8. (Only the factor loadings of .5 or more have been included in the table.)

Factor analysis is a purely mathematical procedure. The computer produces values for the relationships or factors, but it doesn't identify or name them. Looking at the attributes with high loadings on Factor 1, you might conclude it should be named "convenience." Perhaps you'd call Factor 2 "efficacy" or "effectiveness" and Factor 3 "price."

Table 8. Factor loadings in a hypothetical study testing nine product attributes.

Product Attribute	Factor1	Factor 2	Factor 3
Easy-to-use container	.81		
Perfumed scent		.71	
Expensive			−.83
Easy to apply	.62		
Absorbs quickly		.53	
Good all over body	.53		
Not sticky		.51	
Soothes rough skin		.83	
Well-known manufacturer			−.69

The next step often is to reduce respondents' ratings to "factor scores," which represent summary ratings for each underlying factor, then work with this reduced set of data for further analysis. Generally, the greater the number and variety of attributes measured, the more useful this procedure can be for reducing the data for analysis.

Cluster Analysis

This approach attempts to define the natural groups of objects (people or products) within a total population that are similar. Cluster analysis creates subsamples containing units that are more like each other than they are like the members of any other subsample. In other words, it identifies clusters of essentially (or ideally) homogeneous units.

A dog food manufacturer wanted to see where a new product concept fit into the dog food market—was it perceived as a dry product, a canned product, a semimoist product, or something else? Dog owners were shown a concept description of the new product, then asked to evaluate its similarity to seven other products already on the market. A hierarchical analysis produced the clusters in Figure 28.

The results show that the new product is seen as most similar to dry products, yet different from the products currently in the dry cluster, which is the position the manufacturer had targeted for the product.

In this example, products were clustered; but it's also possible to cluster *people* into homogeneous segments. This is an analytical method often used as part of market segmentation projects and lifestyle or psychographic studies (see Chapter 36).

Multidimensional Scaling (Perceptual MAPPing)

"MAPPing" (Mathematical Analysis of Perception and Preference) is another name for this technique, and it's a good one, because the objective

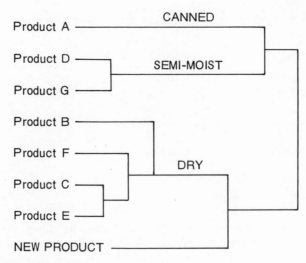

Figure 28. Cluster analysis for a new product concept.

is to represent consumers' product perceptions and preferences as points in a space. The results usually take the form of a map or graph.

The following example will illustrate the results. A candy manufacturer wanted to develop an understanding of the market for eight leading candy bars. Consumers judged the perceived similarity of each pair of products and also gave preference ratings for each of the candy bars. Finally, other information on the reasons for similarity ratings was used to identify the dimensions of the perceptual map. The result is shown in Figure 29.

The results show the positioning of each brand in consumers' minds, which allows manufacturers to determine if they have the position they want. It also identifies the most important product attributes. And finally, the resulting map shows opportunities for new or improved products—"holes" in the market.

Conjoint Analysis

This technique separates respondents' overall judgments about complex alternatives, such as product characteristics, into their components. The result is a series of "utility values" for analyzing and reconstructing the original overall judgments.

An example is razor blades. A manufacturer wanted to determine the importance to men of four characteristics: number of shaves, price, brand name, and blade material.

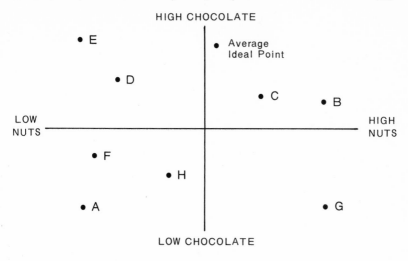

Figure 29. Perceptual map for eight candy products.

Since there were 54 combinations of variables (3 numbers of shaves, 3 prices, 3 brands, and 2 blade materials), an experimental design was used to cut down the number of alternatives a respondent had to evaluate. The respondents were presented with sets of attribute combinations and asked to rank them from most to least preferred.

Two types of results are produced by conjoint analysis:

1. For each attribute, a set of utility values which show the relative appeal of each alternative of that variable. For example, in the case of the razor blades, the utilities might be:

Number of Shaves

10	.2
25	.7
50	.9

Brand Names

Schick	.8
Gillette	.6
Bic	.3

2. A measure of the importance of each attribute in relation to the others, obtained by comparing the relative size of the utility ranges for each attribute.

This technique is particularly useful for giving direction to product development, either for improving existing products or for developing new product entries.

TYPES OF VARIABLES

There are three types of variables that can be used in marketing research as input for multivariate techniques: nominal, ordinal, and metric.

Nominal.   People and products are often classified into categories such as male/female, users/nonusers, working/nonworking, or brand name. These are nominal variables. For tabulating purposes, numbers are often assigned to these categories, but the numbers do not have any real meaning. ("Users" could be 1 and "nonusers" 2, or vice versa—it wouldn't make any difference.) Nominal scales assign "names," but mean nothing more.

Ordinal.   These scales give an order, as well as names, to the points. Examples are income categories and ranking data. On these scales there is a clear order—highest to lowest, most to least, or most preferred to least preferred. The distance between all points on the scale is not necessarily equal, but there is a clear order.

Metric.   These are also called "interval" or "ratio" scales because there is a measurable interval from one scale point to the next. Volume of usage and household size are examples, as are scales which are developed to have equal intervals between adjacent points.

Each multivariate technique is suitable only for certain kinds of variables. Before you use a technique, learn which variables are appropriate to it and don't try to force another type of variable to fit that method.

TIPS ON USING MULTIVARIATE TECHNIQUES

Don't be like the drunk who uses the lamp post for support rather than illumination. Don't let multivariate analysis become a crutch for sloppy field work or a replacement for thinking. Remember these guidelines:

Fit the technique to the problem, not the problem to the technique. Be careful of falling in love with one method and trying to force-fit it to every study. Don't become technique-oriented.

Remember that the results are only as good as the data. Multivariate techniques won't fix bad data. So always be careful in writing the questions and conducting the field work.

Think before, not just after conducting the test. Don't dump everything you can think of into the computer in the hope it will sort it all out and make sense of it for you. Develop hypotheses first. Then pretest your questions. You can be almost certain you'll find you need to revise some wording.

Consider sequential research. You always learn as you go along—about things you wish you'd added and other things you find you could have left out. One or two pilot phases will improve the quality of your final big study. Multivariate analysis is expensive, so proceed in a planned, careful way.

Find ways to clearly communicate results. Most line marketing people and general managers aren't familiar with these techniques, so there's a risk of losing them in data and jargon. Look for ways to communicate the techniques and their results in easy-to-understand form.

Keep multivariate analysis as the means, not the end. "Running a cluster analysis" isn't much help if it doesn't contribute to the overall objective of the study. Start with the problem, not the technique.

Multivariate analytical techniques can be extremely valuable tools. Their most useful role usually is in supplementing straightforward analysis and judgment by bringing complex variables together in a single analysis. It's risky to bet a whole study on a single technique (say, "doing a segmentation study"). A better approach is to experiment with these techniques as parts of studies done for other purposes, then go ahead with a larger study after the value and applicability of the technique have been proven.

Part VI

Working with Research Companies

□□

38

Ten Tips on Being a
Savvy Research Client

□□□

Contrary to what you might think, the best research client is a smart client. In fact, the smarter the better. The more clients know about my business, the easier they are for me to work with. The best client of all, in terms of a smooth working relationship, is often one who has actually worked on the research supplier side.

I've worked in the marketing research business for 15 years. My experience includes several jobs on the client side. I've also done about everything you can do on the supplier side, from interviewing to managing my own research company. (In addition, I even worked a year as a management consultant for one of the "Big 8" accounting firms, but I don't count that, since I didn't do anything the whole time I was there.)

If a client who *hadn't* worked on the supplier side asked me what he should do to get the most from his research—and his research suppliers— here are some tips I'd give him. (By the way, I'd bet most of these points also apply—in slightly modified form—to the advertising agency business.)

1. *Get your research supplier involved early.* The earlier the better. That's the way you'll get the most for your money. If the research firm is involved up front, it can help develop the research program. Otherwise it will be reduced to just executing your ideas. That's O.K., of course. It may even be all that you want. But you'll have lost a good chance to get some new, fresh thinking on your problem that could have come if the research firm had been involved at the start.

2. *Give them all the background.* Surprises and secrets between clients and research firms are invariably destructive. Openness starts at the very beginning of a project. For example:

Reprinted with permission from *Advertising Age,* November 24, 1980, page 42. Published by Crain Communications Inc.

☐ If cost and timing constraints exist, discuss them up front. Don't be afraid to talk about price at the outset.

☐ Are there decision rules for taking action? If there are, tell your research supplier.

☐ It's not nice to let people wander unaware into a mine field. The same is true of research issues surrounded by company politics or inter-departmental power struggles. Giving some minimal warning to your research company is the decent thing to do.

Of course, most background involves straightforward things such as the history of the product and the objectives for the study. Tell your supplier everything you can think of. Even small details help give a flavor of the project and indicate what needs to be done.

3. *Challenge your research firm to give you ideas—and to save you money.* After you fill in the background, ask your supplier to give you some alternatives for the research that could be done to answer your questions. If you're sincerely open to suggestions and ideas, the odds are that you'll get some new perspectives.

Finally, after the research design is set—but *before* things get started—ask your supplier what you could do to save money. Is there a way to cut some fat out of the project? You'll probably be told there is, *if* you're willing to trade off information. Of course, you may not want to give anything up, but wouldn't it be nice to have the choice? Well, then, ask. You'll be surprised how often the research company can tell you how to save a buck. And you may feel that some of the "nice-to-know" information is expendable when you see a price tag on it.

4. *Avoid last-minute changes.* This is a major cause of both aggravation and extra cost. Obviously, there are genuine last-minute emergencies, but otherwise changes have to be cut off at some point. Self-discipline in this respect will save you money, keep the goodwill of your research firm, and decrease the likelihood of foul-ups.

5. *Once things get underway, leave the research firm alone to do its job.* There's a fine line between "client communication" and "hand-holding." But if you recognize that there is a line (and that it is costly and inefficient if you cross it too often), you should be O.K.

6. *Everybody needs feedback.* We all like to get paid, and clients should know that compliments on a job well done are a very inexpensive way to make sure you get a good job from your research firm next time, too. Perhaps surprisingly, kudos from clients are rare enough that they have great impact. The scarcity makes them valuable. At the same time, if you don't like the job you're getting from your research firm, tell them about that, too. Chances are they already sense things aren't going well with you. Talking about it may help identify and fix the problem.

7. *Don't accept jargon*. Research, like most businesses, has its own jargon. And that can be simple gobbledygook if you don't know the code. Don't hesitate to ask, "What does that mean in real English?" Straightforward language helps everyone keep his thoughts straight, too, so your questions will probably have the side benefit of making everyone examine his thinking.

8. *Tell them what happens*. After a research firm conducts a study on a product, it develops a sense of ownership in it. Clients can use that to advantage. Tell them what happens. They'll love you for it, and they'll work harder for you next time. It's another way you can "pay" your research supplier in currency that costs you nothing.

9. *Research is a team sport*. The legal profession is built around the adversary relationship, and some clients seem to regard research firms as adversaries. They think they'll get better work if they lean on their suppliers. They're wrong. The best clients treat their research companies as parts of their team. That doesn't mean you don't still expect the supplier to do its job, but the "team" attitude really makes a difference. It'll pay dividends to you. Nobody wants to feel like a lackey.

10. *Don't put your eggs in too many baskets*. Clients that work with dozens of different research firms usually lose the chance to get the full attention and commitment of any of those firms. Find a few research companies with which you can work, and which you can trust. Then stick with them. You will be more important to them, and they'll be able to learn your business and know your products. That way you'll get better work from them—and with less learning time needed on each project, you should get it done cheaper and faster, too.

Good clients are demanding, but their demands are reasonable and focus on issues that really make a difference. Otherwise it becomes nit-picking, and that doesn't help anyone.

Clients usually get what they expect—and deserve. The things I've described in this chapter should help you develop the kind of relationship with your research suppliers that will get the best work for you.

39

Who's Who in Marketing Research

□□

How many marketing research suppliers are there in the United States? Nobody knows for sure, but the number is certainly in the hundreds, perhaps the thousands.

Most of the companies have names like "John Doe & Associates" and consist of John Doe (and often *no* associates) operating out of his home or a small office. John is most often a researcher who used to work for a large manufacturer or research supplier and decided to try to make it in his own business. In a couple of years, "John Doe & Associates" will probably disappear, as John goes back to work for another manufacturer or research company.

Regardless of the size of the company, all research services fall into one of three categories: syndicated services, standardized techniques, or custom research. A few companies offer more than one type of service, but the majority of firms fit into one category.

SYNDICATED SERVICES

These companies provide information from common pools of data to different clients. Audits, purchase mail panels, and audience share measurements are the major types of syndicated services. For example, the same audit data on volume movement and brand shares in the cake mix category are available to Pillsbury, General Mills (Betty Crocker), and Procter & Gamble (Duncan Hines). The Gallup and Harris Polls are also syndicated services; they're available for purchase by any newspaper.

The companies that provide syndicated services tend to be among the largest in the research business. The major suppliers of syndicated research are:

- A.C. Nielsen Co.—Retail Index audit tracks volume and market share for food and drug products; also well known for its TV audience measures.
- SAMI (Selling Areas Marketing Inc.)—Subsidiary of Time Inc.; provides category volume and market share data through computerized records of withdrawals from grocery chain warehouses.
- IMS International—Audit data for the pharmaceutical/medical industry.
- Arbitron Co.—Measurement of TV and radio audiences.
- Louis Harris & Associates—The Harris Poll; also, custom studies.
- The Gallup Organization, Inc.—The Gallup Poll; also, custom studies.
- NPD Research, Inc.—Consumer purchase panel (original name was National Purchase Diary); also offers ESP simulated sales test.
- Starch INRA Hooper—Audience measurements, advertising readership, and custom studies.
- Marketing Research Corporation of America (MRCA)—Mail purchase panels.

STANDARDIZED TECHNIQUES

These are standardized studies conducted for different clients—but always in the same way. Many advertising testing techniques and simulated sales tests are examples. Results of one study are comparable to norms, or a data bank, from other comparable studies, but each project's results are proprietary to the individual client.

Advertising tests. There are many firms specializing in advertising research. The major ones are:

- ASI—Theater technique. Also has a subsample with dials on which respondents can register their like/dislike for segments of the ads as they are shown.
- Burke—Ads are shown on TV; measures of recall are made 24 hours later by telephone.
- McCollum/Spielman—Theater technique.
- Research Systems Corp. (ARS)—Theater setting, before-after brand preference measure.
- Tele-Research—Ads are shown to consumers in a mobile trailer outside food stores, and shoppers are given coupons good on the purchase of test items.

Simulated sales tests. These techniques are described more fully in Chapter 29, "Simulated Sales Testing". The five major products in this area are:

Laboratory Test Market—Yankelovich, Skelly & White, Inc.
COMP—Elrick and Lavidge, Inc.
Assessor—Management Decision Systems, Inc.
ESP (Estimating Sales Potential)—NPD Research Inc.
BASES—Burke Marketing Research

CUSTOM RESEARCH

Most research companies (including my own firm, Custom Research Inc.) provide this type of service: *one-of-a-kind projects*. Custom-designed projects probably account for the largest *number* of all studies done, although not the biggest share of all research *dollars* spent.

The following list represents some of the largest firms in the custom research business (although some also offer standardized techniques).

AHF Marketing Research Inc.
Audits and Surveys, Inc.
Brand, Gruber and Company
Spencer Bruno Research Associates
R.H. Bruskin Associates
Burke Marketing Research, Inc.
Chilton Research Services
Commercial Analysts Company
Consumer Response Corporation
Crossley Surveys, Inc.
Custom Research Inc. (CRI)
Data Development Corporation
The Data Group Incorporated
Decisions Center, Inc.
Drossler Research Corporation
Ehrhart-Babic Associates, Inc.
Elrick and Lavidge, Inc./Equifax
Field Research Corporation
The Gallup Organization, Inc.
Gallup and Robinson, Inc.

Louis Harris & Associates, Inc.
Management Decision Systems, Inc.
Market Facts, Inc.
Marketing and Research Counselors (MARC)
Marketing Information Service
Market Opinion Research Company
Opinion Research Company
Oxtoby-Smith, Inc.
Palshaw Measurement, Inc.
Research 100
Research Information Center Inc. (RICI)
Response Analysis Corporation
U.S. Testing Company, Inc.
Walker Research, Inc.
Westat, Inc.
Yankelovich, Skelly & White, Inc.

Another way to look at the research business is by the major types of standardized and syndicated data and the suppliers that offer each type of service.

Volume and market share measures. These are two major sources of category volume and brand share tracking data:

A. C. Nielsen—Gathers data through audits of a large sample of grocery, drugs, and discount stores.

SAMI (Selling Areas Marketing Inc.)—Monitors withdrawals from food store chain warehouses to individual food stores.

Custom audits. Several firms specialize in conducting audits of product categories, usually to measure new-product movement in test market:

Audits and Surveys, Inc.
Burgoyne, Inc.
Ehrhart-Babic Associates, Inc.
Market Audits
Store Audits Incorporated

Controlled store tests. Firms in this category conduct market tests by both handling distribution of the product to the stores and auditing movement of the shelves:

Ad-Tel (also ties in cable TV and consumer purchase devices to measure the effect of advertising)
Burgoyne, Inc.
Ehrhart-Babic Associates, Inc.
Market Facts, Inc.
Market Audits

Purchase diary panels. Consumers are recruited to keep diaries of all their purchases in a number of product categories. The two major firms in this category are:

NPD Research Inc.
MRCA. (Every five years, MRCA also has a subsample of its panel keep a record of all the food dishes served in a two-week period— including all the ingredients that go into homemade dishes. This service is called the "Menu Census.")

Mail panels. Large samples of homes agree to return custom mail questionnaires mailed periodically by these research companies:

HTI (Home Testing Institute)
NFO (National Family Opinion)
Market Facts, Inc.

A final note: The research field is volatile. Companies are constantly introducing new services and discontinuing others. So it's impossible to keep my list of suppliers and the services they provide completely up to date.

40

How to Work with a Research Company

□□□

Like a marriage, the relationship between a research company and its clients is complex. And just as each marriage has its own arrangements that allow the couple to get along together, every client–supplier situation is a little different from the next.

That makes rules for the relationship difficult to establish. What works in one situation won't necessarily work for the next. Nevertheless, guidelines are helpful in that they show how other people handle similar situations. For that reason, the Council of American Survey Research Organizations (CASRO) established a Code of Business Practices to serve as a guideline for common practices in the research business.

The Code is included here as reference for typical methods of handling some of the most common details of the client–supplier relationship.

Council of American Survey Research Organizations
Code of Business Practices
December 1980

GLOSSARY

This section is intended to clarify the meanings of terms used in describing certain business practices. When these terms are used in this Code, their meanings are as stated here.

Parties To An Agreement

1. *Research company*   A member of CASRO, and thus a company that has satisfied Section IV of the CASRO By-Laws.

2. *Contractor*   A research company that has made an agreement for its services, between itself and a client.

3. *Client (or sponsor)*	An organization that has contracted for the services of a research company.
4. *Prospective client*	A company, organization or appropriate unit of same that a research company has reason to think will enter into an acceptable contract for research or related services.
5. *Competing companies*	Two or more research companies, or two or more prospective clients, whose products or services are such that when a customer buys from one of them, the need to buy from others is correspondingly reduced.

Instruments To An Agreement

6. *Custom study*	A study that typically is designed and carried out to satisfy the objectives of one client. Unless otherwise noted, all practices described in this Code apply only to custom studies. Custom studies may have commercial and/or non-commercial clients.
7. *Proposal*	A written document describing a research plan, which normally includes a statement of problem, study objectives, research method, sample design, study specifications, etc., as well as estimates of cost and time for completion. A proposal usually requires that the research company include its own recommendations about how the work should be carried out. Such recommendations for procedure may be appropriate for one or more of these reasons: (1) all specifications are not provided; (2) there are ambiguities about the specifications that require resolution; and (3) the proposal request asks for recommendations for design and procedure.
8. *Cost estimate*	A research company response to a type of proposal request: that is, when a prospective client provides a set of specifications which are complete, and which a research company can use to work out its bid price for a contract.

Products Of An Agreement

9. *Questionnaires*	These are forms that are used for data collection, nearly always in a procedure that includes one respondent at a time. Questionnaires may be interviewer-administered (face-to-face or by telephone), or may be self-administered by respondents.
10. *Report*	The agreed upon product(s) of a contract. Reports may be oral or written, formally or informally

presented. Reports may be sets of tables, or a data tape, as well as a narrative or text.

Sometimes a report may be a set of completed questionnaires. In this instance, questionnaires are an end product of a contract, instead of a means to another type of product such as tables or text.

This glossary is not exhaustive. There are other terms with specialized meanings in the Code, which are not in this glossary. The glossary includes only those terms that especially seem to need clarification.

SECTION I:
PRACTICES RELATED TO PRECONTRACT NEGOTIATIONS

A. It is a principle of the professional research firm to avoid conflicts of interest and to treat all information acquired from a client as confidential. It is *not* a conflict of interest to work for or attempt to work for competing clients when:

1. Both grant explicit permission.
2. The nature of the service is syndicated or shared cost.
3. The work or project involves a standard methodology offered to anyone.
4. The nature of the work that the contractor would do for Company B is completely different from what the contractor is or has been doing for its client, Company A. By "completely different" is meant that nothing that the contractor has learned about Company A from its relationship with Company A could benefit Company B or the services rendered to Company B.

B. Conditions Governing *Submission* of Proposals

1. Proposals prepared in response to a client request even though entirely at the expense of a research company.

   Practice These should be submitted to the requesting client only. If that client does not authorize the work, then the proposal may be submitted to other prospective clients unless so doing would reveal confidential information.

2. Proposals for which a prospective client pays either part or all of the cost incurred by the research company in preparing the proposal.

   Practice If a prospective client does not want to go ahead with the work, a research company may submit the proposal to another prospective client only if it has received permission to do so from the original client.

C. Gifts to Clients

Bribery of any kind is out of the question and is so outrageous an offense as to require no statement of practice in this Code. By contrast, the providing of gifts and entertainment (such as paying the bill in a restaurant) on an occasional basis is an acceptable practice, as is the offering of promotional gift items of nominal value.

The controlling guidelines are reasonableness and appropriateness to a client-contractor relationship.

D. Practices Related to the *Content* of Proposals and Cost Estimates

The intent of this section is to ensure that both parties to the contract have the same expectations about procedures and, to some extent, how these procedures would be implemented.

Applicability of procedures. Some items in this section are appropriate for some types of work and not others. For example, a proposal for a developmental study that would obtain information only via group interviews would include only some of the practices described below.

The practices are mainly geared to quantitative studies in which data are from a number of separately administered questionnaires.

The guideline is that if a procedure is part of doing the work, statements in this section about that procedure should be observed.

1. Method of communicating proposals and cost estimates.
   Practice It is good business practice to submit either proposals or cost estimates in writing. If communicated verbally, they should be confirmed in writing, especially if the project is authorized.
2. Conditions of offering services.
   Practice Proposals and cost estimates should specify how long a period of time after submission each of the following will be honored by the research company if the prospective client accepts the proposal or cost estimate and authorizes the work:
   a. Statements about the amounts to be billed to the client.
   b. The schedule for accomplishing the work.
3. Related to sharing of responsibilities with client.
   Practice Proposals and cost estimates should include a description of tasks that are expected of the client as part of the research procedure (for example, lists of customer names and the manner in which the lists will be provided).
4. The specifications for a project ideally should include:
   a. Questionnaire size criteria such as number of questions, types of questions, length of interview, etc.
   b. Universe and sample design description.
   c. Estimated incidence(s) of eligible respondents. In instances where actual observed incidence varies from assumptions in the proposal in a direction that would increase/decrease contractor costs so substantially as to make renegotiation of the contract appropriate, the contractor should notify the client as soon as possible of such fact. A contractor should not seek to renegotiate a contract unless the possibility of such renegotiation, under stated circumstances, is disclosed in the proposal or cost estimate.
   d. Number of callbacks to be made.
   e. Statement as to whether written and/or personal interviewer briefings are to be used on the project.

    f. Minimum percent of completed (and not otherwise monitored) interviews that will be validated.

    g. Minimum percent of coding to be checked.

    h. Minimum percent of keypunching that will be verified.

    i. Type of editing/cleaning utilized, i.e., clean to questionnaires vs. machine cleaning.

    j. Number of banners (and banner points) to be used in tabulating.

    k. Approximate number of tabulations (or number of pages of tabulations).

    l. Storage—see Section II, B.2.

  5. Related to report.

    Practice The end product of the contract will be specified in terms of what it is and—if a written report or tables—the number of copies to be supplied.

E. Ownership Rights Related to Proposals

Absent a contrary agreement between the prospective contractor and prospective client:

1. Proposals prepared at the expense of a prospective contractor.

    Practice a. Such proposals are the property of the company that prepared them, and may not be used by a prospective client in any way to its benefit, without the permission of the prospective contractor.

              b. Any part of proposal content, including questions or a questionnaire (which is constructed by the prospective contractor), are the property of the research company that prepared them.

2. Proposals prepared wholly or in substantial part at the expense of a prospective client.

    Practice Such proposals are the property of the company that has requested and paid for them, and are considered to be "reports" as the term "report" is used in this Code.

SECTION II:
OWNERSHIP OF AND RIGHTS TO RESEARCH PRODUCTS, INSTRUMENTS, AND RESOURCE MATERIALS

A. Client Supplied Data

Scope. In view of the confidential relationship that frequently exists between a client and a contractor, the contractor may obtain, during the course of preparing a proposal or conducting a research project, private and confidential information concerning the client, its organization, personnel, business activities, policies, public relations or advertising practices, plans or products. Customer lists, subscription lists and dealer lists are included within the meaning of this section. This information may be obtained in writing or orally.

 1. Dissemination.

Practice   The research company should not reveal such information to anyone outside of its own organization for any purposes whatsoever without the express written consent of the client.

The research company should limit the internal distribution of such confidential client information to those employees who require the information in order to fulfill their duties and should inform employees of the practices to be followed with respect to client-supplied information.

 2. Storage.

Practice   In carrying out this policy, the research company should exercise reasonable care in the handling of any client-supplied information and maintain the information in an appropriate storage place until its return to the client or its destruction, whichever is desired by the client.

 3. Employees.

Practice   It is considered good business practice for a research company to obtain non-disclosure statements from employees.

B. Questionnaires

 1. Ownership.

Practice   Completed questionnaires on custom research projects are the property of the contractor unless otherwise specified in the client/contractor agreement. Under any circumstance, respondent identification is subject to the conditions specified in the CASRO Code of Standards. If completed questionnaires are provided to a subcontractor (for data conversion or analysis, for example), the contractor retains responsibility for proper storage and disposition of questionnaires.

 2. Storage.

Practice a. The contractor is responsible for establishing a specific period of time during which questionnaires (original data forms) will be stored and for communicating this policy to the client.

b. Normal storage procedures for completed questionnaires should provide reasonable protection from external hazards, such as fire and water damage, from inadvertent misplacement or loss, and from deliberate misappropriation.

c. Completed questionnaires may be stored with names, addresses and identifying information attached unless the specific needs of a project require a different procedure. Survey data containing such identifying information should be kept in a locked container or locked room when not being used in routine survey activities. Reasonable caution should be exercised in limiting access to such survey data to only those who are working on the specific project and who have been instructed in any special confidentiality procedures for that project.

d. Procedures for special projects where the data have been determined to be particularly sensitive may include the storage of completed questionnaires in locked containers or rooms during survey activities, the removal of identifying information from the questionnaires, and the coding of completed questionnaires with a number that can be linked to a special file containing identifying information.

3. Disposal.

Practice a. The client should be notified in writing of any plan to destroy completed questionnaires at least 30 days prior to planned destruction.

b. That notification should specify the date destroyed if the client does not respond with other instructions by that date.

c. The client may request continued storage beyond the specified date. If compliance with the request involves a charge to the client, the contractor should so notify the client upon receiving the request.

d. If by mutual agreement the questionnaires are to be delivered to the client, the contractor must first remove all individual respondent identification. Responsibility for shipping costs should be agreed upon, if possible, in advance of shipping.

e. Destruction of completed questionnaires should be by the normal process of the research organization for disposition of waste paper. Procedures such as shredding and/or burning certified by a company officer are to be considered special procedures.

4. Rights to questionnaires for syndicated or multi-client studies. Questionnaires for these types of studies ordinarily are the property of the contractor.

Practice If there is nothing about rights to questionnaires in the agreements between a contractor and its clients, then the contractor should observe the same practices regarding storage as for custom study questionnaires (see B.2.).

At the end of the stated storage period, however, the contractor may destroy or retain the questionnaires without asking permission of anyone else.

C. Tabulating Cards and/or Computer Tapes/Discs

Scope. The provisions of this section apply to all materials (e.g., codebooks) that are necessary to utilize these cards/tapes. Specifically excluded, however, are any privately owned programs and/or systems by which the data are processed.

1. Ownership.

Practice Tabulating cards and/or computer tapes/discs specifically produced for a research project are the property of the contractor unless otherwise specified in the client/contractor agreement. The contrac-

tor is responsible for storing such materials for a stated period of
time after completion of the research project and for communicating
this policy to the client.

2. Storage.
   Practice a. These materials should be stored in such a way that any
              additional analyses requested by the client can be made.
           b. Unless otherwise specified, the client ordinarily would be liable
              for charges in connection with producing duplicate cards/tapes
              for his use while having the research organization continue to
              store such material.

3. Disposal.
   Practice a. The client should be notified of any plan to destroy cards/tapes/
              discs at least 30 days prior to destruction.
           b. That notification should specify the date on which cards/tapes/
              discs will be destroyed if the client does not respond with other
              instructions by that date.
           c. The client may request continued storage beyond the specified
              date. If compliance with the request involves a charge to the
              client, the contractor should so notify the client upon receiving
              the request.
           d. If by mutual agreement the cards/tapes/discs are to be delivered
              to the client, the contractor must first remove all individual
              respondent identification. Responsibility for shipping costs
              should be agreed upon, if possible, in advance of shipping.

4. Rights to tab cards and/or computer tapes/discs for syndicated or multi-client
   studies.

   Tab cards and data tapes/discs for these types of studies ordinarily are the
   property of the contractor.
   Practice If there is nothing about rights to tab cards or data tapes/discs in the
           agreements between a contractor and its clients, then the contractor
           should observe the same practices regarding storage as for tab cards
           and tapes/discs generated for custom studies.
           At the end of the stated storage period, the contractor may destroy or
           retain the tab cards or data tapes without asking permission of
           anyone else.

D. Reports

   Practice Reports are the property of the client.
           However, the research company should include, as a part of the
           agreement between them, reference to the relevant sections of the
           CASRO Code of Standards on public release of information.
           The use of reports and/or analyses produced in connection with
           syndicated or multi-client research projects shall be governed by the
           conditions within the specific contract for the service.

SECTION III:
PRACTICES RELATED TO
FINANCIAL MANAGEMENT

A. Contractor Billings to Client

    1. Condition included in proposal or cost estimate.
       Practice Payment procedures and terms should be established as part of a proposal or cost estimate.

    2. Billing practices.
       Practice Invoices should include payment terms.

B. Contractor Payments to Subcontractors and Other Suppliers

    Practice Contractors should endeavor to pay undisputed bills from subcontractors (e.g., field services, data processing companies) in accordance with agreed upon terms. It is understood that the subcontractor is responsible for tendering written invoices in the appropriate amount of detail.

C. Client Indemnification of Contractor

    Practice It may be appropriate in some circumstances to include an indemnification clause in the agreement between research company and client. Such a clause might be included, for example, in studies that include demonstration or use by respondents of products supplied by the client. Since the efficacy of an indemnification clause may be affected by varying state laws, the precise wording of the clause ordinarily should be reviewed by company counsel to ensure that it satisfies the objectives of the contracting parties. The following indemnification clause is offered for illustrative purposes only:

    "The client shall indemnify and hold harmless the research organization and its agents and employees, against all claims against any of them for personal injury or wrongful death or property damage caused by distribution and/or use of any product supplied by the client or his agents for the purpose of this research project and from all costs and expenses in suits which may be brought against the research organization, its officers, agents and employees on account of such personal injury or wrongful death or property damage."

SECTION IV:
OTHER PRACTICES RELATED TO
THE BIDDING PROCESS

NOTE: CASRO recognizes that the following section does not pertain directly to the actions of CASRO members. Clearly CASRO members cannot dictate the actions of others. *However,* it is strongly felt that encouraging these practices will contribute to the professionalism of marketing research and hence its effectiveness as a management tool. Thus, this Section IV is included.

This section applies only to proposals whose cost of preparation is borne partly or entirely by the research company. Proposals whose cost is borne entirely by a prospective client are considered to be contracts and not proposals.

When soliciting proposals for a research project or survey, the prospective client should inform prospective contractors, whenever possible, of (1) the specific tasks the successful contractor will be expected to undertake and (2) the criteria to be used in selecting a contractor.

Practice 1. Research firms that are asked to submit cost estimates should be given a complete set of specifications (written if possible) covering the following items where applicable or known:

    a. Tasks to be performed by the client and by the contractor.

    b. Description of questionnaire (or questionnaires) by (1) number of questions by type of question—i.e., open-ended, single response closed-end, multiple response closed-end, etc.; or (2) duration of interview in minutes plus number of open-ended questions.

    c. Estimated incidence(s) (%) and description of incidence groups.

    d. Sample design and universe.

    e. Household selection/respondent selection.

    f. Percent of keypunching that will be verified.

    g. Type of edit/clean utilized, i.e., clean to questionnaire vs. machine clean.

    h. Number of banners and banner points for tabulation.

    i. Number of cross-tabs.

    j. Total copies of reports and/or tabs.

    k. Special hand-tabs required.

2. If more than one research firm is asked to submit a proposal, the prospective client should indicate how the successful proposal will be determined. Factors that might be used to determine the contractor selected could include:

    a. Understanding of how the results of the research will be used.

    b. Recognition of the types of information that will be useful.

    c. Ability to provide the necessary information—personnel, facilities, equipment, etc.

    d. Relevant experience of the research firm.

    e. Background/experience of individuals to be assigned to the work.

    f. Recognition of the limitations of the research.

    g. Cost of services.

41

Ethics in Research

Knowledge without integrity is dangerous and dreadful.

—Samuel Johnson

All marketing research is based on an assumption of public trust and cooperation. We assume people will agree to be interviewed and will give honest responses to questions.

But what's the source of people's trust and willingness to cooperate? It's *their* assumption that researchers will not abuse them—that it's in their interest to cooperate and be interviewed.

That's why ethical business practices are so important in the research business: we have to constantly protect the foundation of trust on which our whole profession is built.

GENERAL GUIDELINES

It's impossible to draw up a list of ethical practices that covers every possible situation. So it helps to have some general guidelines for decisions.

Act with integrity. "Integrity" is a good word, because it connotes more than just a minimal adherence to legal and ethical standards. We all like to deal with people who we feel have integrity, so that's a good standard for our own behavior, too.

How much vs. how little. It's sometimes tempting to ask, "How *little* do I have to do to avoid clear violations of ethical standards?" Probably a better question is, "How *much* can I do to assure that all my actions will be above reproach?"

262

"Do unto others . . ."   That's a very old rule, but still a good one. Would you feel O.K. (as a respondent or as a client) being on the receiving end of the action you're considering? If not, chances are your behavior isn't completely ethical.

What if they knew?   If everyone involved knew exactly what you were doing and why, would it make a difference? Obviously, some things, such as explaining the purpose of projects to respondents, have to be disguised somewhat to retain objectivity. But that's a separate issue. It probably wouldn't make a difference in their willingness to cooperate. But could your actions stand the scrutiny of others for fairness? If not, think again.

The long run.   None of us is in business for just today or tomorrow. We intend to be around next month, next year, and long afterward. Yet most questionable business practices have very short-run benefits that almost invariably can't justify the long-run risk of losing goodwill and trust.

RESPONDENTS AND THE PUBLIC

Most ethical issues in the research business relate to dealing with respondents. There are very clear, generally accepted practices for handling these issues.

Anonymity.   It's reasonable for survey respondents to assume that their answers are anonymous and won't be associated with them individually. It's a reasonable assumption, even when they aren't specifically told that's the case. And since the guarantee (implied or stated) of anonymity is an important component of cooperation, that anonymity must be protected. *This means that names of individual respondents generally should not go beyond the questionnaires.* Identifying respondents risks their being contacted for sales purposes or other reasons that would violate the respondents' anonymity.

One caution: anonymity may be difficult to protect on some government-sponsored studies because of provisions of the Freedom of Information Act. On these projects, then, it may be necessary to tell respondents that their responses may *not* be entirely anonymous.

Privacy.   This is almost more a matter of courtesy and politeness than of ethics. Nevertheless, it's important to remember that we risk invading respondents' privacy if we don't first ask permission to conduct an interview and give a sincere "thanks, anyway" if they refuse to cooperate.

Respondents in a group interview should usually be told that the session is being observed by closed-circuit TV or through a one-way mirror. That's good practice, even though most people would probably recognize that comments made to seven other group participants and a moderator aren't completely private. The situation can usually be explained by the moderator in this way: "There are some people who are interested in hearing what you have to say, but we decided it would be better for them not to crowd into this room with us, so they're behind this mirror." This seems to satisfy respondents—in fact, they seem to quickly forget that anybody is even watching.

Disguised sales efforts. One of the most common abuses of research is the telephone caller who introduces himself as a survey-taker but later turns out to be a salesman for aluminum storm doors, magazines, or whatever. You have an obligation as a professional researcher to object to this practice and try to stop it whenever you learn about it.

But beyond that you should make sure you never contribute to research abuse by misrepresenting *any* type of sales effort—even if it only involves developing sales "leads" through a survey.

"Sales waves" of some research techniques, such as simulated sales tests, can fall into a gray area and require special attention. This includes things such as calling people back after a product test and asking if they'd like to buy some of the product they just tried in the test. The distinction here is that the purpose is really to do research (get a behavioral measure of buying intent) and not to make a profit (in fact, the prototype samples sold in such tests usually cost many times the price respondents are charged). The danger, however, is in giving respondents the impression they have been deceived into a sales situation. So some introduction should be used to clarify the situation, such as: "As you know, the product you tested is new and not available in stores. As part of the research study, however, we're making it available to people who want to buy it. Would you care to purchase any?"

Industrial espionage. This is much less common than novelists and TV script writers would have us believe. But it does exist. Using research as a guise for obtaining confidential information is clearly unethical. For example, contacting XYZ Company and asking about its sales (or number of employees, or product line mix) as part of a fictitious survey that actually is a fact-gathering effort for a competitor is clearly unethical.

CLIENTS AND SUPPLIERS

Research companies often need to have access to their client's confidential information to conduct a project. Indeed, the very fact that a research project is being done on a new product is itself often confidential. So special care must be taken to protect the confidentiality of this information.

Conflict of interest. These days, as corporations become more diversified, it's nearly impossible for research firms to avoid working for clients that compete in some line of business. So it usually isn't practical for suppliers to eliminate every possible conflict of interest by the companies they work for.

The key is this: *Can a supplier be fair to, and give his best efforts for, both companies he works for?* As a rule, it's impossible for a research company to work for two clients on a directly competitive issue. The company can't give its best effort to one without compromising its relationship with the other. Since it's impossible for any client to directly monitor this situation, it becomes the research company's responsibility to decline work that would create such a conflict.

Sponsorship.   The name of the client sponsoring a study should not be divulged to respondents without the client's consent. This is the other side of respondent anonymity: respondents can be sure the sponsor doesn't know who they are; likewise, sponsors know respondents won't be aware of the sponsor's identity.

Some industrial-survey respondents, because of concerns about industrial espionage, won't take part in a survey without knowing the identity of the sponsor. In these cases, the study sponsor should be asked if the respondent's cooperation is worth revealing the client's identity.

Professionalism.   There is often a way the sponsor of a study hopes the results will come out (the new product is better than the current; the product beats competition; and so on). For the researcher, there is a real risk of misinterpreting these hopes as pressure to affect the outcome of the study. But a researcher always has a professional obligation to provide unbiased design, honest fieldwork, and objective analysis. After all, what's the point of trying to believe the new product is better if it really isn't? The marketplace doesn't lie, so the truth will eventually come out anyway.

COMPETING RESEARCH COMPANIES

Research is an idea business. Researchers have little to sell but their thoughts, usually in the form of designs for research studies. And these designs are rarely protectable in any formal, legal way (such as copyrights).

As a result, pirating other researchers' ideas is primarily an ethical issue. Where the study design is a unique, original one, it's unethical to steal another research company's idea or give a proposal on a unique project design to another research firm.

APPENDIX

Several industry groups in the marketing research field have developed codes of ethics or business practice guides. These include:

American Marketing Associations (AMA)
American Association for Public Opinion Research (AAPOR)
Market Research Association (MRA)
Council of American Survey Research Organizations (CASRO)

The CASRO "Code of Standards" is included here for reference, because it covers the ethical responsibilities to all the parties connected with research: respondents, clients, the public, and interviewers.

Council of American Survey Research Organizations (CASRO)

Introduction

This Code of Standards sets forth the agreed upon rules of ethical conduct for survey research organizations. Acceptance of this Code is mandatory for all CASRO members.

The Code has been organized into sections describing the responsibilities of a survey research organization toward respondents, clients and outside contractors and in reporting study results.

This Code is not intended to be, nor should it be, an immutable document. Circumstances may arise which are not covered by this Code or which may call for modification of some aspect of this Code. The Standards Committee and the Board of Directors of CASRO will evaluate these circumstances as they arise and, if appropriate, revise the Code. The Code, therefore, is a living document which seeks to be responsive to the changing world of survey research.

I. Responsibilities to Respondents
  A. Confidentiality
    1. Survey research or ganizations have the responsibility to protect the identities of respondents and to insure that individuals and their responses cannot be related.
    2. This principle of confidentiality is qualified by the following exceptions:
      a. Respondent names, addresses and/or telephone numbers, obtained in the course of an interview, may be used during or immediately following completion of a study by those research professionals responsible for supervising the survey for purposes of:
        (1) validating the fact the interview was conducted by the interviewer;
        (2) substantiating or amplifying the nature of one or more specific responses; and/or
        (3) determining an additional fact of analytical importance to the study.
      In these cases respondents must be given a sound reason for the

re-inquiry. In all cases a refusal by respondent to continue must be respected.

b. Respondent names, addresses and/or telephone numbers for a study may be maintained in a confidential file by a company and accessed for later use under these conditions only: (1) when study design requires measured recourse to original respondents as in the use of panels or other types of longitudinal studies; and/or (2) when to meet the study purpose it is desirable to match survey data about individual respondents with data about the same individuals from a different source.

3. The principle of confidentiality includes the following specific applications:

a. Restricting the company's own personnel from the use, or discussion, of respondent-identifiable data beyond legitimate internal research purposes.

b. Accepting the responsibility for seeing that subcontractors (interviewers, interviewing services, validation, coding and tabulation organizations), as well as contractually hired consultants, are aware of and agree to adhere to the principle of respondent confidentiality.

c. Denying requested access to respondent-identifiable opinion or fact (in questionnaires or other survey documents) on the part of the client, sponsor or any other organization. Care should be exercised, when there is a legitimate reason to produce questionnaires (with respondent names deleted) for findings, documentation or the like, that there are no other means throughout the body of the questionnaire that permit identification of the respondent. Two exceptions to the above requirement are permitted:

(1) Client validation of interviews is permitted if this does not result in harassment of respondents through multiple validation contacts and if the survey research organization is convinced that the client is capable of conducting the validation in a fully professional manner. The maintenance of respondent confidentiality, however, should be agreed upon by the client in writing.

(2) Where different survey research organizations are conducting different phases of a multi-stage study (i.e., a trend study), requiring re-contact of respondents, it is desirable to have respondent identification pass directly from one research organization to another, but it is permissible for the client to be an intervening agency. The maintenance of respondent confidentiality should be agreed upon in writing by all parties involved.

Guiding these exceptions is the understanding that all use of respondent-identifiable information outside the original survey research organization is permissible only if the survey research organization gives permission and obtains in writing a statement of the purpose and a description of how the information is to be used and written assurances that the principle of confidentiality will be maintained.

      d. Rejecting the use of secretly identified mail questionnaires to connect respondent answers with particular individuals.

      e. Studies for legal purposes and subpoenas for survey information often require submission of respondent identified information. Where possible, survey research or ganizations should request that respondents names be kept in strict confidence by the court or government agency.

B. Privacy and the Avoidance of Harassment

  1. Survey research organizations have a responsibility to strike a proper balance between the needs for research in contemporary American life and the privacy of individuals who become the respondents in the research. To achieve this balance:

      a. Respondents will be protected from unnecessary and unwanted intrusions and/or any form of personal harassment.

      b. The voluntary character of the interviewer-respondent contact should be stated explicitly where respondent might have reason to believe that cooperation is not voluntary.

  2. This principle of privacy includes the following specific applications:

      a. Survey research organizations must respect the right of individuals to refuse to be interviewed or to terminate an interview in progress. Techniques which infringe on these rights should not be employed, but survey research organizations may make reasonable efforts to obtain an interview including: (1) explaining the purpose of the research project; (2) providing a gift or monetary incentive adequate to elicit cooperation; and (3) re-contacting an individual at a different time if the individual is unwilling or unable to participate during the initial contact.

      b. Research organizations are responsible for arranging interviewing times that are convenient for respondents.

      c. Lengthy interviews are a burden. Research organizations are responsible for weighing the research need against the length of the interview and respondents must not be enticed into an interview situation by a misrepresentation of the length of interview.

      d. Research organizations are responsible for developing techniques to minimize the discomfort or apprehension of respondents and interviewers when dealing with sensitive subject matter.

      e. Electronic equipment (taping, recording, photographing) and one-way viewing rooms may be used only with the full knowledge of respondents.

II. Responsibilities to Clients

A. Relationships between a survey research organization and clients for whom the surveys are conducted should be of such a nature that they foster confidence and mutual respect. They must be characterized by honesty and confidentiality.

B. The following specific approaches describe in more detail the responsibilities of research organizations in this relationship:

1. A survey research organization must assist its client in the design of effective and efficient studies that are to be carried out by the research company. If the survey research organization questions whether a study design will provide the information necessary to serve the client's purposes, it must make its reservations known.
2. A research organization must conduct the study in the manner agreed upon. However, if it becomes apparent in the course of the study that changes in the plans should be made, the research organization must make its views known to the client promptly.
3. A research organization has an obligation to allow its clients to verify that work performed meets all contracted specifications and to examine all operations of the research organization that are relevant to the proper execution of the project in the manner set forth. While allowing clients to examine questionnaires or other records, the survey research organization must continue to protect the confidentiality and privacy of survey respondents.
4. When more than one client contributes to the cost of a project specially commissioned with the research organization, each client concerned shall be informed that there are other participants (but not necessarily of their identity).
5. Research organizations will hold confidential all information which they obtain about a client's general business operations, and about matters connected with research projects which they conduct for a client.
6. For research findings obtained by the agency which are the property of the client, the research organization may make no public release or revelation of findings without express prior approval from the client.

III. Responsibilities in Reporting to Clients and the Public
   A. When reports are being prepared for client confidential or public release purposes, it is the obligation of the research organization to present survey results clearly and in an objective and truthful way. It is the obligation of the research organization to insure that the findings they release are an accurate portrayal of the survey data, and careful checks on the accuracy of all figures are mandatory.
   B. A research organization's report to a client or the public should contain, or the research organization should be ready to supply on short notice, the following information about the survey:
      1. The name of the organization for which the study was conducted and the name of the organization conducting it.
      2. The purpose of the study, including the specific objectives.
      3. The dates on or between which the field work was done.
      4. A definition of the universe which the survey is intended to represent and a description of the population frame(s) that was actually sampled.
      5. A description of the sample design, including the method of selecting sample elements, method of interview, cluster size, number of callbacks, respondent eligibility or screening criteria, and other pertinent information.

6. Description of results of sample implementation, including (a) the total number of sample elements contacted, (b) the number not reached, (c) the number of refusals, (d) the number of terminations, (e) the number of non-eligibles, (f) the number of completed interviews.

7. The basis for any specific "completion rate" percentages should be fully documented and described.

8. The exact wording of the questions used, including interviewer directions and visual exhibits.

9. A description of any weighting or estimating procedures used.

10. A description of any special scoring, data adjustment or indexing procedures used. (Where the research organization uses proprietary techniques, these should be described in general and the research organization should be prepared to provide technical information on demand from qualified and technically competent persons who have agreed to honor the confidentiality of such information.)

11. Estimates of the sampling error and of data shown when appropriate, but when shown they should include reference to other possible sources of error so that a misleading impression of accuracy or precision is not conveyed.

12. Statistical tables clearly labeled and identified as to questionnaire source, including the number of raw cases forming the base for each cross-tabulation.

13. Copies of interviewer instructions, validation results, code books, and other important working papers.

C. As a *minimum,* any general public release of survey findings should include the following information:

1. The sponsorship of the study.

2. A description of the purposes.

3. The sample description and size.

4. The dates of field work.

5. The names of the research agency conducting the study.

6. The exact wording of the questions.

7. Any other information that a layperson would need to make a reasonable assessment of the reported findings.

D. A survey research organization will seek agreements from clients so that citations of survey findings will be presented to the research organization for review and clearance as to accuracy and proper interpretation prior to public release. A research organization will advise clients that if the survey findings publicly disclosed are incorrect, distorted, or incomplete, in the research organization's opinion, the research organization reserves the right to make its own release of any or all survey findings necessary to make clarification.

IV. Responsibility to Outside Contractors and Interviewers

Research organizations will not ask any outside contractor or interviewer to engage in any activity which is not acceptable as defined in other sections of this Code of Standards.

Part VII

Just for Fun

□□

42
A Funny Thing Happened on the Way to the Interview

□□

Everything is funny as long as it is happening to someone else.
—*Will Rogers*

Even though this book is about "real-world marketing research," it nevertheless describes the way things are *supposed* to happen. Things do go wrong—or at least turn out different from what you expect. Fortunately these deviations are more often humorous than disastrous. But a book on how research really gets done would be incomplete without a few stories about the crazy things that go on out there.

DOOR TO DOOR

If you knock on enough people's doors, you're bound to encounter a few kooks. Most interviewers can tell of trying to maintain their composure while talking to a man who just answered the door naked. Yes, it really happens.

Slightly more creative was the fellow who came to the door in a clear plastic cape designed to protect his clothes while he had a permanent—except that he had no clothes on under the cape.

Another interviewer, going door to door in a rural area, was invited into the living room of a farmhouse by the small child who answered the door. The interviewer was supposed to interview farmers about animal feed, and this farmer—standing behind the sofa—seemed very nervous as he started answering the questions. It wasn't until page three of the questionnaire, when the farmer moved a little, that the interviewer realized all he was wearing was his Jockey shorts. Moral of the story: don't get too relaxed, even in the supposed privacy of your living room. Your repose may be interrupted by a determined interviewer.

273

TURNING THE TABLES

Occasionally respondents get more involved in the research than they expected. One time we were conducting a pizza taste test in a church basement. Things were hectic as pizzas were being baked, cut, and served; tables were being cleaned; questionnaires were being handed out, checked, and collected. It was a real madhouse.

About two o'clock the kitchen crew finally got a short break. During the lull, one of the kitchen helpers asked the supervisor, ''How much longer do I have to do this? I don't mean to complain, but I didn't realize it would take this long.'' It turned out that this poor soul was a *respondent* who had arrived early for the test in the morning. Someone assumed she was a new interviewer assigned to the project and promptly gave her an apron, hairnet, and pizza cutter. She had worked for five hours before speaking up. (The happy ending is that she liked the job so well she later applied to the interviewing service for a full-time job.)

A similar thing happened at a group interview. A well-dressed young woman showed up late and was assumed to be a client coming to watch the session. She was shown into the darkened viewing room on the other side of the one-way mirror and took a seat in the back row. At the end, after the respondents left, she innocently asked, ''What do you want me to do now?'' You guessed it: she was a respondent and had no idea what she was doing in the client room.

WOULD YOU REPEAT THE QUESTION?

Sometimes a slight misunderstanding about a question produces unexpected answers.

For example, one telephone study included the question, ''How long have you been a resident?'' One truthful person replied, ''Only once, for drunken driving. But that was in 1973, and I've been straight ever since.''

A telephone interviewer, calling numbers selected from the directory, called the S. Jones household early one Saturday morning. ''Is this Mrs. Jones?'' he asked. ''Well, not yet,'' came the reply. ''But he's promised to marry me as soon as his divorce goes through.''

An interviewer approached a lady walking through a shopping center and said, ''We're conducting a study on hair-care products.'' The potential respondent hurried past and shouted back over her shoulder, ''I can't. I'm on a diet.'' (You figure that one out.)

Of course, typos are sometimes another source of amusement. A set of interviewer instructions was supposed to say, ''Obtain a large, busy mall to conduct this study.'' Instead, the interviewers were told to find a ''large, busy male.'' Maybe that would have worked better.

A telephone survey with executives about security systems turned up a questionnaire on which the respondent told about how he carefully locked up his whorehouse every night. We thought we'd found an unusually frank massage parlor owner or something, until checking showed he had really said "warehouse." The interviewer's error in recording the answers had added some excitement to an otherwise uneventful study.

Random digit dialing is a sampling system that generates essentially random telephone numbers. With this system, at least theoretically, you'd finally call everybody. Using this approach, we've found ourselves asking to speak with "the lady of the house" at a call-girl service. Also at a convent. Sorry, their responses have not been preserved.

THE WHOLE TRUTH

Sometimes people give you answers that are almost disarming for their directness and honesty.

A study among physicians about a category of prescription drugs asked why doctors didn't prescribe a certain drug. One reply: "It's too hard to spell." Suspicions confirmed.

Researchers in Miami asked a sample of people there the seemingly simple question: "How do you get to work every day?" The truthful response of 13 percent was, "I don't know." We've all had days like that.

A call to a dentist's office reached a harassed receptionist who told the interviewer, "I'm too busy to talk to you now. Would you mind speaking to the doctor?"

A product study on two disposable washcloths done in a hospital showed that Respondent #206 was a male when he used the first washcloth and a female when she used the second. Probably a joke or an error. Or was it?

A telephone call to Texas was answered after several rings by a man. The interviewer politely asked if the respondent had a few minutes to talk. He replied, "Why sure, little lady. I was just makin' love to my wife here, but I'll be very happy to answer any questions y'all have first." That's cooperation!

ASK A SILLY QUESTION

If you ask enough people any question, you'll finally get some off-the-wall answers.

For example, we once asked a question about TV viewing. It was phrased in terms of whether people usually watched one hour or more of TV during certain periods of the day. Most of the periods were at least two hours long. But one period, the 11 P.M. to 11:30 P.M. local news slot, was only one-half hour long. Yet 9 percent of the people in this mail survey claimed they watched at least an hour of TV during this half-hour period. Those are heavy viewers!

Even though the U.S. Census is the biggest, best controlled research project in the world, it suffers from these same problems. For example, the 1970 Census in New York uncovered 20 residents of Staten Island who claimed they *walk* to work in Manhattan.

Just one more. Our company is headquartered in Minneapolis. A survey of Minnesota homemakers about laundry products showed that a startling 95 percent said they did their wash in Tide during the winter months. Why? A follow-up study showed that most said they felt it was too cold here in the winter to do their wash "out tide." No, that didn't really happen, but it's the only marketing research story I know. Maybe truth *is* stranger—and funnier—than fiction.

43

Research Doodles

□□□

Just for fun, here are some familiar marketing research terms expressed in unfamiliar form. How many can you identify? If you get stuck, the answers are at the bottom of the next page.

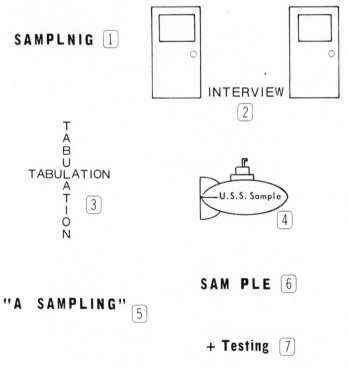

SAMPLNIG [1]

INTERVIEW [2]

T
A
B
U
TABULATION
A
T [3]
I
O
N

U.S.S. Sample [4]

SAM PLE [6]

"A SAMPLING" [5]

+ Testing [7]

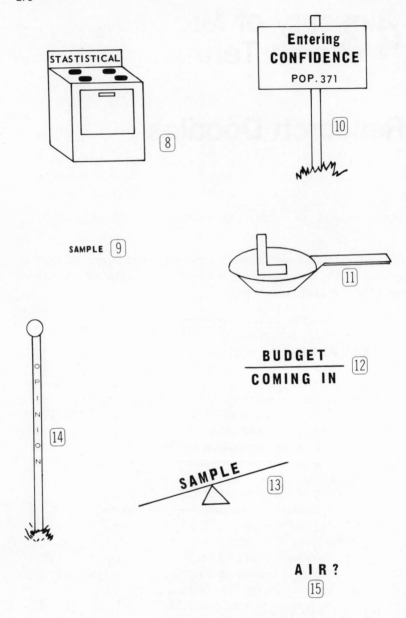

STASTISTICAL ⑧

Entering
CONFIDENCE
POP. 371 ⑩

SAMPLE ⑨

⑪

BUDGET
COMING IN ⑫

⑭

SAMPLE ⑬

A I R ?
⑮

ANSWERS: (1) sampling error, (2) door-to-door interview, (3) cross-tabulation, (4) subsample, (5) quota sampling, (6) split sample, (7) ad testing, (8) statistical range, (9) a small sample, (10) confidence limit, (11) a panel, (12) coming in under budget, (13) unbalanced sample, (14) opinion poll, (15) questionnaire.

Glossary of Marketing Research Terms

Like every business, marketing research has its own terminology and jargon. Here are some of the most frequently used terms that have unique or particular meanings within the research field.

AAU   See awareness, attitude, and usage study.

AID   (Automatic Interaction Detector)—A method of multivariate analysis often used in market segmentation studies.

analysis of variance (ANOVA)   A method of analysis for determining the level of statistical significance of differences between two sets of data.

audit   A method for measuring sales in a store by counting beginning inventory, adding new shipments, and subtracting ending inventory.

Automatic Interaction Detector (AID)   A method of multivariate analysis often used in market segmentation studies.

awareness   The proportion of people who have ever seen or heard of a product or brand name.

awareness, attitude, and usage (AAU) study   A type of tracking study that monitors changes in consumer awareness, attitudes, and usage levels for a brand or product category.

Balanced Incomplete Block (BIB)   An experimental design procedure for rotating a large number of products or items in a test.

banner   The series of column headings, or cross-tab breaks, which runs horizontally across the top of a computer table.

base   The number on which the percentages in a table are calculated.

BIB   See Balanced Incomplete Block.

bipolar scale   A scale with opposite end points and a "just right" midpoint. Examples: spicy/bland, moist/dry, large/small.

buying intent   A scale used to measure respondents' likelihood of purchasing a product.

callback   A second attempt to interview a respondent, either because the person could not be reached on the first try or to complete an after-use interview in a product test.

cathode-ray tube (CRT)   A TV-like terminal with a keyboard, used for getting data to or from a computer. Often used in research to display questions and enter responses into the computer for tabulating.

central-location study   A survey conducted at a conveniently located site to which respondents come to be interviewed. Sometimes used to mean any location where respondents are interviewed, such as shopping malls.

chi-square test (χ^2)   A test of statistical significance.

clarifying   A follow-up technique for getting complete responses to open-end questions by asking respondents to explain vague or general terms in their answers. (Also see *probing*.)

closed-end question   Any question with a limited number of prelisted answers.

cluster analysis   A multivariate technique for identifying homogeneous groupings of products or people.

coding   The process of translating responses to questions into numerical form for data processing.

concept description   A brief description of a new product or service.

confidence range   The range around a survey result for which there is a high statistical probability that it contains the true population parameter.

conjoint analysis   A multivariate technique for separating consumers' judgments into their components.

convenience sample   A sampling procedure that leaves the selection of respondents totally to the interviewers, with no quotas or qualifications imposed.

criterion variables   The variables being predicted or explained in a study. Examples: volume of category or brand usage. Also called *dependent variables*.

CRT   See cathode-ray tube.

day-after recall   An advertising testing technique that measures the proportion of people recalling seeing a TV commercial within 24 hours of its airing.

demographics   Personal or household characteristics, such as age, sex, income, or educational level.

dependent variables   See *criterion variables*.

disappointment score   The proportion of respondents in a product test who indicate, after trying the product, that they would not buy it.

discriminant analysis   A multivariate technique for analyzing the predictive value of a set of independent variables.

discussion question   See *open-end question.*

distribution check   A study measuring the number of stores carrying specified products, along with the number of facings, special displays, and prices of the products.

editing   The process of checking questionnaires for completeness and accuracy.

exhibit   Anything shown to respondents during an interview. Examples: a print advertisement, a card listing income categories.

factor analysis   A multivariate technique for analyzing interrelationships among variables.

frequency   A measure of how often repeat buyers repurchase and how many units they purchase each time.

group interview   A qualitative research technique involving a discussion among eight to ten respondents, led by a moderator. Also called focus groups, group discussions, panels, and group depth inverviews.

hedonic scale   A scale for measuring general, overall opinion of a product.

incidence   Any figure referring to the percentage of people in a category. Examples: incidence of users, incidence of people qualifying for a study.

independent variables   See *predictor variables.*

intercept study   An interviewing method whereby people are stopped in stores or shopping malls for an interview.

interval scale   See *ratio scale.*

judgment sample   A sample containing certain types of respondents, who are selected on the basis of the judgment that their attitudes or behavior will be representative of the population.

lifestyle research   Research that attempts to explain behavior by analyzing people's attitudes, interests, activities, and opinions. Often associated with psychographic research.

mall intercept   See *intercept study.*

MAPP   Mathematical Analysis of Product Perception. See *perceptual mapping.*

marginals   A computer-generated frequency count of the number of people giving each answer to all the questions in a questionnaire. Also called an 80-column dump.

marketing concept   The business philosophy that a company's effort should be adapted to the needs and wants of it customers.

metric scale   See *ratio scale.*

monadic   A test in which a respondent evaluates only one product.

multidimensional scaling   See *perceptual mapping.*

multivariate analysis   Any analysis which analyzes several variables together.

nominal scale   A scale which classifies people into groups that have no inherent numerical order or value. Examples: male/female, user/nonuser.

nonprobability sample   Any type of sample that is not a probability, or random, sample.

nonsampling error   All the sources of bias or inaccuracy in a study besides sampling error. Examples: leading by the interviewer, recording errors.

objectives   The information to be developed from a study to serve the project's purpose.

open-end question   A question that has no prelisted answers. Example: "Why do you say that?" Also called *discussion question* or *subjective question*.

ordinal scale   A scale which classifies people into groups that have an inherent order. Examples: preference data and rankings.

paired comparison   A test in which a respondent evaluates two products.

panel   "Purchase panels" are composed of people who record and report their purchases in specified product categories. "Mail panels" are made up of people who have agreed to participate in mail surveys. Group interviews are sometimes called "panels."

perceptual mapping   A multivariate technique designed to represent consumers' product perceptions and preferences as points on a map or graph. Also called *multidimensional scaling* or *MAPPing*.

placement interview   An interview in which a respondent is recruited and given the product to use in a product test.

population   See *universe*.

positioning   Location of a brand or product in consumers' minds relative to competitive products.

predictor variables   The variables that explain or predict the differences in dependent variables. Examples: demographics, attitudes. Also called *independent variables*.

prerecruited central-location test   A survey conducted at a conveniently located site to which respondents—who have been previously contacted and qualified—come to be interviewed.

probability sample   A sample in which every unit has an equal and known probability of being selected. Also sometimes called a *random sample*.

probing   A follow-up technique for getting complete responses to open-end questions by asking, "What else?" until the respondent has nothing more to add. Also see *clarifying*.

product placement study   A type of test in which respondents try a product under normal usage conditions. Example: in-home test of a food product. Also called a *product test*.

psychographics   Research that attempts to explain behavior by analyzing people's personality traits and values. Often associated with *lifestyle research*.

purpose   The reason a research project is being conducted; usually focuses on the decisions for which information from the study will be used.

qualitative   Exploratory research involving small samples. Example: group interviews.

quantitative   Research done with large samples to provide definitive, quantified results.

quota sample   A sampling procedure that includes specified numbers of respondents having characteristics known or believed to affect the subject being researched.

random digit dialing   A telephone sampling procedure that generates random combinations of telephone numbers in order to include unlisted numbers in a survey sample.

random sample   See *probability sample*.

ratio scale   A scale with measurable intervals between scale points. Also called *interval scale* or *metric scale*.

regression analysis   A multivariate technique that relates a dependent variable to one or more independent variables.

repeat rate   The proportion of first-time triers of a product who purchase the product at least a second time.

repeat-pairs technique   A product testing procedure in which respondents express a preference between two products, then repeat the task with an identical pair of products.

sample   A proportion of the population selected for a research study.

sampling error   The range, usually expressed as ± X percent, attached to a survey result to estimate the likely population parameter.

sampling frame   A physical listing of all units in a population used to draw a sample, or a procedure for producing a result comparable to such a physical listing.

scale   A closed-end question for measuring attitudes.

sequential testing   A testing procedure in which a respondent tries one product, evaluates it, then tries and evaluates a second product. (This is also sometimes called a sequential monadic test, which is technically a misnomer, since use of the second product is by definition not monadic.)

simulated sales test   A procedure designed to estimate a product's sales potential by simulating trial and use conditions of the marketplace.

stratified sampling   A procedure which groups the population into homogeneous segments (or strata) and then samples from each of the stratum.

stub   The responses to the question being tabulated, which run vertically down the left side of a computer table.

subjective question   See *open-end question*.

systematic sampling   A procedure that selects every *n*th unit for inclusion in the sample.

tachistoscope (T-scope)   A device for controlling the intensity and duration of light exposure. Sometimes used in package testing.

T-scope   See *tachistoscope*.

topline   Preliminary results from a project, usually showing responses of the total sample to a few key questions.

tracking   Studies repeated over time to monitor changes in a brand or product category.

trial rate   Measures the proportion of people who buy a product at least once.

unipolar   An ordinal scale with one positive end and one negative end.

universe   The set of all the units from which a sample is drawn. Also called the *population*.

validation   A procedure for recontacting respondents to confirm that interviews were conducted correctly.

Index

Date Due